EUROPEAN UNION
ECONOMIC DIPLOMACY

'The EU's external activities have grown enormously in the last decade: the Euro, the Lisbon Treaty, new leadership in EU Foreign Affairs, have all raised its global profile. The immense value of Woolcock's book is to trace this evolution systematically, starting from external trade which required an international presence – through wider relationships with non-EU countries and overseas development policies – to the vast policy panorama that exists today.'

Roderick Abbott, ECIPE (European Centre for International Political Economy), Brussels, Belgium

Global Finance Series

Edited by
John Kirton, University of Toronto, Canada,
Michele Fratianni, Indiana University, USA and
Paolo Savona, University of Rome Guglielmo Marconi, Italy

The intensifying globalization of the twenty-first century has brought a myriad of new managerial and political challenges for governing international finance. The return of synchronous global slowdown, mounting developed country debt, and new economy volatility have overturned established economic certainties. Proliferating financial crises, transnational terrorism, currency consolidation, and increasing demands that international finance should better serve public goods such as social and environmental security, have all arisen to compound the problem.

The new public and private international institutions that are emerging to govern global finance have only just begun to comprehend and respond to this new world. Embracing international financial flows and foreign direct investment, in both the private and public sector dimensions, this series focuses on the challenges and opportunities faced by firms, national governments, and international institutions, and their roles in creating a new system of global finance.

Also in the series

The New Economic Diplomacy
Decision-Making and Negotiation in International Economic Relations
Edited by Nicholas Bayne and Stephen Woolcock
ISBN: 978-1-4094-2541-0

Financial Crisis Management and the Pursuit of Power
American Pre-eminence and the Credit Crunch
Mine Aysen Doyran
ISBN: 978-1-4094-0095-0

Global Financial Crisis
Edited by Paolo Savona, John J. Kirton, and Chiara Oldani
ISBN 978-1-4094-0271-8

Full series listing at the back of the book

European Union
Economic Diplomacy
The Role of the EU in External Economic Relations

STEPHEN WOOLCOCK
London School of Economics, UK

ASHGATE

Published by
Ashgate Publishing Limited
Wey Court East
Union Road
Farnham
Surrey, GU9 7PT
England

Ashgate Publishing Company
Suite 420
101 Cherry Street
Burlington
VT 05401-4405
USA

www.ashgate.com

British Library Cataloguing in Publication Data
Woolcock, Stephen.
  European Union economic diplomacy: the role of the EU in external economic relations. –
  (Global finance series)
  1. European Union. 2. European Union countries – Foreign economic relations.
  3. International economic relations. I. Title II. Series
  337.1'42-dc22

Library of Congress Cataloging-in-Publication Data
Woolcock, Stephen.
  European Union economic diplomacy: the role of the EU in external economic relations /
    by Stephen Woolcock.
    p. cm.
  Includes bibliographical references and index.
  ISBN 978-0-7546-7930-1 (hbk.: alk. paper) — ISBN 978-0-7546-9835-7 (ebook: alk. paper)
  1. European Union countries—Foreign economic relations. 2. European Union countries—
Commercial policy. 3. European Union countries—Economic policy. I. Title.
  HF1531.W59 2011
  337.1'42--dc23

2011036630

ISBN: 9780754679301 (hbk)
ISBN: 9780754679318 (pbk)
ISBN: 9780754698357 (ebk)

Printed and bound in Great Britain by the
MPG Books Group, UK

Contents

List of Figures

List of Acronyms

ACP	African Caribbean and Pacific States
AIFD	Alternative Investment Funds Directive
ALDE	Alliance of Liberals and Democrats for Europe
BCBS	Basel Committee on Banking Supervision
BfF	Bundesanstalt fuer Finanzdienstleistungen
CAP	Common Agricultural Policy
CCP	Common Commercial Policy
CDM	Clean Development Mechanism
CET	Common External Tariff
CFPS	Common Foreign and Security Policy
CITES	Convention on International Trade in Endangered Species
COP	Committee of the Parties
CRNM	Caribbean Regional Negotiating Machinery
CSP	Country Strategy Programme
CTS	Carbon Trading Scheme
DAC	Development Assistance Committee
DCI	Development Cooperation Instrument
DDA	Doha Development Agenda
DG	Directorate General
EBA	Everything But Arms
EC	European Community
ECB	European Central Bank
ECOFIN	Economic and Financial Affairs Council
EDF	European Development Fund
EEAS	European External Action Service
EEC	European Economic Communities
EFC	Economic and Finance Committee
EIB	European Investment Bank

EMS	European Monetary System
EP	European Parliament
EPA	Economic Partnership Agreement
EPP	European Peoples Party
ESFS	European System of Financial Stability
ESRC	European Systemic Risk Council
EU	European Union
FCCC	Framework Convention on Climate Change
FDI	Foreign Direct Investment
FSA	Financial Services Authority
FSAP	Financial Services Action Plan
FSB	Financial Stability Board
FTA	Free Trade Agreement
GATS	General Agreement on Trade in Services
GATT	General Agreement on Tariffs and Trade
GNP	Gross National Product
GSP	General System of Preferences
HRCFSP	High Representative for Common Foreign and Security Policy
IAIS	International Association of Insurance Supervisors
IASB	International Accounting Standards Board
IMF	International Monetary Fund
IOSCO	International Organization of Securities Commissions
INTA	International Trade Committee
IPA	Instrument for Pre-Accession
LDC	Least Developed Country
NGO	Non-Governmental Organisation
NIC	Newly Industrializing Country
NIEO	New International Economic Order
NIP	National Indicative Programme
ODA	Official Development Assistance
OECD	Organisation for Economic Cooperation and Development

OLP	Ordinary Legislative Procedure
PCD	Policy Coordination for Development
QMV	Qualified Majority Voting
REIO	Regional Economic Integration Organisation
RIP	Regional Indicative Programme
SBCD	Second Banking Coordination Directive
SCA	Sub Committee for Agriculture
SEA	Single European Act
SEM	Single European Market
SFM	Single Financial Market
TEC	Treaty Establishing the European Community
TEU	Treaty on European Union
TFEU	Treaty on the Functioning of the European Union
TPC	Trade Policy Committee
TRIMs	Trade Related Investment Measures
TRIPs	Trade Related Intellectual Property Rights
UN	United Nations
UNCTAD	United Nations Committee on Trade and Development
US	United States (of America)
VER	Voluntary Export Restraint
WGIEI	Working Group on International Environmental Issues

Chapter 1
The European Union in Economic Diplomacy

Introduction

The aim of this volume is to contribute to a better understanding of European Union (EU) economic diplomacy, or decision-making and negotiation in the external economic policies of the EU. It addresses a number of questions. The first is the straightforward, but seldom simple question of how EU economic diplomacy functions. In other words it looks at the internal decision-making processes that determine the EU's policy preferences and how the EU handles negotiations at the international level. The second question the volume addresses is what role the EU plays in economic diplomacy? When does the EU appear as a distinct actor with common goals pursuing coherent negotiating objectives, and when is the EU's role more one forum or level in a wider process in which EU member states lead? The book seeks in particular to identify the factors that determine the role the EU plays. The third and most challenging question addressed is what shapes the effectiveness of EU economic diplomacy?

Before discussing how the book approaches these questions it is necessary to set the scene in terms of the general place the EU assumes in economic diplomacy today. The EU's place in international economic negotiations has emerged progressively over many decades. This was the case for international trade in which the EU's role has evolved from a limited but active role with the creation of a customs union, through a more important but defensive role in the 1970s, to a more outward-looking and proactive role in the 1980s and 1990s. In the field of international environmental policy the EU has also established a place for itself in the key international negotiations on topics such as climate change. This came later than trade with the EU's place really only being established in the 1980s. In the field of development policy the EU, counting member state and EU level official development assistance (ODA), remains the largest provider of development aid. In other policy areas central to international economic relations, such as finance, the EU's place appears to be less well established.

Looking at the EU in international economic negotiations from a broad systemic perspective, the EU has emerged from what was the dominant transatlantic or developed country 'club' that shaped international economic relations from the establishment of the Bretton Woods system in the 1940s until perhaps the 1990s. The role of the European Economic Community (EEC) and then the European Community (EC) was initially that of a follower behind the leadership of the United

States (US) for much of the period.[1] The EC was then part of the Organisation for Economic Cooperation and Development (OECD) Club Model during the 1980s and 1990s. In line with the evolution that saw a greater role for the EC in some policy areas than others, the EC assumed an important role in trade from a fairly early date, with the EU participating in the quad (USA, EC, Canada and Japan) that influenced trade policy during the 1980s and 1990s. As Chapter 3 of this volume shows, even though the EC could be said to have been an actor in trade from a relatively early date in the post-war period and was a member of the quad, the EC's position on trade was very much shaped in response to US leadership. It was not until the 1990s that the EU emerged as an actor with leadership aspirations in international trade. In some cases international policy has been shaped by more inclusive organisations such as environment policy in the UN. Here, as Chapter 5 will show, the EU has also moved from the shadow of US leadership. In others negotiation and policy-making remains strongly influenced by a dominance of transatlantic links, such as was the case in international financial market regulation, at least until the financial crisis of 2008 and the greater use of the G20.

The dominance of the OECD club in shaping international economic diplomacy has been steadily eroded since the 1990s by the growth of the major emerging markets and challenges by developing countries seeking a greater say. The EU's place in international economic diplomacy must therefore be seen in terms of these broad structural shifts in relative economic power within the international economic order. Will the EU be able to provide leadership in international negotiations? If it cannot do this alone, will it hold to established links to the US and other like-minded OECD countries or seek to cooperate with the emerging economic powers? If EU member states have been content for the EU to fulfil the role of a forum for negotiation rather than as a distinctive actor when the agenda was shaped by likeminded OECD countries, will they feel equally content when the agenda and negotiations are shaped by a more heterogeneous group of countries? In the more multi-polar international economic order of the twenty-first century, the role the EU assumes will have systemic implications as well as implications for the EU's international policy aims and the level of integration within Europe.

The contemporary context for the debate on the role of the EU in economic diplomacy is shaped by the treaty changes brought about by the ratification and adoption of the Treaty of Lisbon (Treaty on the Functioning of the European Union, TFEU). These pose challenges and offer opportunities for the EU. The challenges include integrating the European Parliament (EP) with the greater powers it has acquired as a result of the Lisbon Treaty into EU decision-making. Greater democratic accountability could strengthen the EU, but there is also a need to ensure EU economic diplomacy is efficient. The TFEU means increased

---

[1]   Through the book the abbreviations EEC, EC and EU will be used depending on the status of the European treaties at the time. When discussing the European Union in general, the abbreviation EU will be used as this is now the common usage.

EU competence in areas such as foreign direct investment (FDI), and thus a greater role for the EU as opposed to the member states. The treaty changes have also disturbed the established practice in decision-making in terms of the balance between the member states in the Council or its working groups and the Commission. A further challenge is how to meet the treaty aims of integrating all the EU's external policies under the common external action and within the European External Action Service (EEAS). Replacing the three pillar structure of the European Union (European Community, Common Foreign and Security Policy and Justice and Home Affairs) with a single system that brings together trade, environment, development and humanitarian assistance with foreign policy holds the promise of a greater role for the EU in international relations, but it also poses the challenge of ensuring coherence across different policy areas.

How Does EU Economic Diplomacy Function?

The volume's approach to this question is an unashamedly practical one. It simply aims to explain the processes by which the EU seeks to decide on a common position and how it goes about representing this common position in international negotiations. For many practitioners and stakeholders both within – but more especially outside – the decision-making processes of the EU are often seen as arcane, complex and not infrequently frustrating.

There are a number of reasons for this complexity. The EU is clearly not typical in that its economic diplomacy must reconcile the positions of the 27 member states as well as many sector interests and conflicting aims between different policy areas. It is therefore necessary to understand how the positions of the member states are aggregated to form a common EU position. For this it is in turn necessary to understand the roles of the various EU institutions, primarily the Council, Commission and European Parliament, and how these shape EU economic diplomacy at different stages in the policy-making and negotiating processes. Compared to other national settings, such as the United States, these institutional factors are probably more important, but EU preferences, like those of individual countries are significantly shaped by sector and other interests.[2]

---

[2]   In addressing this question it is also possible to draw on a fairly extensive literature. In the past much of the analysis of foreign economic policy-making or the process of negotiation has originated in the United States and has been based on studies or observation of US foreign economic policy (Odell, 2000). Whilst valuable, this literature needs to be adapted before it can be applied to the EU, which is not a state and is characterised by even more complex decision-making and negotiation processes. Although it is possible to apply different approaches to all economic diplomacy, the pluralist nature of US decision-making tends to lend itself to rationalist interpretations. The EU being the product of considerable internal debate in a succession of institutions provides more scope for constructivist or institutional interpretations of decision-making and negotiation.

The picture is further complicated by the issue of competence, or whether it is the EU or the member states that have power to determine policy and engage in negotiations with third parties. Competence also varies between policy areas and is sometimes shared between the EU and member states, so that while the EU may have near full competence to conduct external trade policy this is not the case for financial regulation and or even international environmental policy. The search for coherence across policy areas therefore requires coordination between policies in which the EU has competence and those in which the member states retain significant competence, something that adds a further layer of complication.

As in all policy-making, the formal processes often differ from practice. For example, formal procedures may stipulate qualified majority voting for decision-making, but in practice consensus is nearly always sought.[3] Shadow voting may influence decision-making. In other words, in the absence of a formal vote, decisions to proceed with a given policy may be based on what would be the outcome if there were voting. Decision-making and negotiation are also complicated by the fact that *de jure* competence and *de facto* practice varies across policy areas. What may be the case in international trade is not the case in development policy so reconciling policies in different policy areas or horizontal policy coherence as it is sometimes referred to, is also more complicated than in the national context. EU economic diplomacy like that of nation states also evolves over time with treaty changes and developments both within and outside the EU.

One of the contributions of this volume is therefore a comparative treatment of EU decision-making in a number of different policy areas; trade and investment, finance (in particular financial market regulation), environment and development in one volume. The book addresses questions such as who really shapes EU policy and how? How is the EU's negotiating position determined? Who negotiates for the EU and how closely are these negotiators supervised or controlled by the member states or other principals? The volume provides an up-to-date treatment in that it includes an assessment of how the TFEU will affect EU economic diplomacy. As noted above, the TFEU brings external economic relations under one roof with EU foreign policy and – at least on paper – dispenses with the three pillars of the European Union in the shape of the European Community, Common Foreign and Security Policy and Justice and Home Affairs. The adoption of the TFEU, with the creation of the High Representative for Foreign and Security Policy (henceforth HRFSP) and the European External Action Service, has stimulated a great deal of discussion on the EU's role in foreign policy. But the changes could also have

---

[3]   A qualified majority vote under the Nice Treaty, the system in place until 2014, requires at least half the member states, 74 per cent of the voting weights and 62 per cent of the population. This translates into 14 member states, 255 voting weights and 311 million people represented by states voting in favour. Under the Treaty on the Functioning of the European Union (TFEU) or a majority of member states (55 per cent) representing 65 per cent of the EU population must vote for a provision for it to be adopted. Four member states or states representing 35 per cent of the EU population can block a proposal. These voting rules will be introduced in 2014.

important consequences for EU economic diplomacy. At the time of writing, from late 2010 to early 2011, the full implications of the treaty changes were not fully clear. There remained a number of disputed interpretations that affect in particular the comitology process and the respective roles of the Commission and member states in external environment negotiations. Just how the role of the EP will develop is also something that can only be assessed over time.

What Role Does the European Union Play in Economic Diplomacy?

Addressing this question requires rather more analysis than the task of describing how the EU functions in economic diplomacy. It is possible to identify a number of roles. Perhaps the most important distinction is between the role as a distinctive actor and that as one of a number of forums or levels in international economic negotiations. A simple way of illustrating this point is by reference to two of the cases discussed in the following chapters. In the case of external trade policy, it is only the EU representative, the European Commission, who takes part in international negotiations. In the case of international finance, member states represent themselves, sometimes along side the EU, and issues concerning international finance are discussed simultaneously at both the EU and international levels in forums such as the IMF or the Financial Stability Board. So in the case of trade the EU's role is that of an actor, whereas in finance it is more that of a forum.[4]

It is then important to assess what type of an actor the EU is. Does it tend to follow initiatives taken elsewhere, or does it lead or have leadership aspirations? There is the question of whether EU is an instrumental actor that directly influences the positions of third countries in negotiations through the use of market power or bargaining, or more of a normative actor shaping agendas and positions more indirectly as a model for others.[5]

Given the variation between issues the question here is not so much whether the EU is an actor and what kind, but rather when its role tends towards that of a distinct actor and when that of a forum, and whether it is possible to identify

---

[4]   There is a considerable literature on the role of the EU in external relations, much of which assesses the extent to which the EU is an actor in foreign policy. (Bretherton and Vogler, 2008; Telo, 2009; Hill and Smith, 2005; Smith, 2003). This has tended to compare the EU with unitary states, because in most international relations literature the decisive actors are national states. But this comparison is largely an inappropriate comparison (Bretherton and Vogler, 2008; Smith, 2005). In more recent times there have been efforts to extend the analysis of the EU as a global actor to a wider range of policy areas than foreign policy, including the environment, human rights and trade (Telo, 2009).

[5]   This literature builds on the concept of the EU as a civilian power (Duchêne, 1973) and has suggested that the EU differs from other actors by being a 'normative power' (Manners, 2002). There are differing views on what normative power is, but it is seen as related to 'what the EU is' rather than its ability to exercise coercive power (Manners, 2002, p. 252).

the factors that determine this? Equally, it is not so much whether the EU is an instrumental or normative power, but how these are combined with other sources of power such as market power to shape EU economic diplomacy. The purpose is also not to discuss whether the EU possesses the attributes of an actor in international relations, which has been the focus of much of the international relations literature on EU foreign policy, but to analyse the role of the EU in specific areas of international economic relations.[6]

The analytical framework developed in Chapter 2 is intended to help assess the role of the EU in different policy areas. This considers a range of factors including relative market power (a source of structural power), the stage of development of the internal *acquis communautaire* (arguably the main source of normative power) as well as the decision-making procedures within the EU that determine the EU's ability to exercise instrumental power.

Finally, the role the EU plays in international economic negotiations has evolved over time, in part as a result of the internal integration process and in part how the EU member states have responded to external drivers or global challenges. For example, greater coordination or integration in a policy area may come about as a result of member states' desire to pool sovereignty in order to have a greater influence in international economic relations. The volume therefore considers the evolution of EU domestic policies and economic diplomacy in each of the four case policy areas chosen the study.

What Determines the Effectiveness of EU Economic Diplomacy?

The third question the volume addresses is the more challenging one: What determines the effectiveness of EU economic diplomacy? While far more difficult to answer conclusively, this is the question that is clearly the most important for practitioners and interesting for observers. Effectiveness is defined in terms of influencing outcomes and is assessed without prejudice to the balance between the EU as actor or forum. In other words, it may well be that even where the EU does not possess all the attributes of an actor, it can still have an important effect on outcomes. Effectiveness of the EU depends on a number of factors. These include 'domestic' EU factors, such the cohesion or heterogeneity of member

---

[6]   There have been important contributions to work on EU external economic policy in a number of specific policy areas. Here trade has attracted the most attention because of the importance of the EU in this field (Meunier, 2000; Duer, 2008; Elsig, 2002; Kerremans, 2005); Woolcock, 2010). But other areas have also been studied including the environment (Grubb and Gupta, 2000); development (Carbonne, 2008; Orbie and Versluys, 2009) and finance (Sapir, 2007). There is also a considerable literature on the legal basis of EU external policies (Eeckhout, 2004). These studies provide a valuable insight into the issues and the decision-making processes within the EU including the respective roles of the member states and EU. But there has been no systematic treatment of EU economic diplomacy across issues, or much in the way of comparison between the policy areas.

state and sector interests, the stage the *acquis communautaire* (the agreed set of domestic or internal rules) has reached, as well as the institutional capability of the EU. The effectiveness of the EU will also depend on international, extra EU factors, such as the EU's relative economic or market power and what its negotiating partners do. The EU can be efficient in defining its preferences and in negotiations but still have no impact if its negotiating partners are not ready to cooperate. This means that effectiveness will vary from policy area to policy area and depend on the specifics of any given negotiation. Interests within the EU will vary as will the international context and relative economic power of the EU's negotiating partners. Generalisations for all negotiations will be difficult to make. Each of the four case studies therefore includes a more detailed discussion of a particular negotiation or topic to illustrate how effectiveness of the EU could be assessed. These specific cases include some important recent negotiations, so that their coverage has the added advantage of providing some information on the position the EU has taken and why.

Defining effectiveness

Before discussing what determines the effectiveness of EU economic diplomacy, we need to be clear about what is meant by effectiveness and how it might be measured as a dependent variable. First of all we distinguish between efficiency and effectiveness. Efficiency seems best suited to describe the ability of the member states to reach a common position or the capacity of the EU's decision-making procedures to agree on a set of common negotiating aims.

Effectiveness should then be seen as the capacity of the EU to achieve its negotiating aims. It has to be recognised that the various actors in EU economic diplomacy may have different interests in any given negotiation or may have different utility functions. Member state government utility functions are likely to include both the economic/welfare gains to be had from any negotiated outcome as well as political utility in terms of re-election or the retention of power. As rationalist political economy literature suggests, governments may prefer one outcome over another if it helps retain the support of a key interest group. In the EU context member state governments may also be motivated by a desire to retain sovereignty or control over the policy area concerned, which will lead them to resist pressure for a common EU position in response to external drivers for fear that this could lead to *de facto* or *de jure* integration within the EU.

Equally, the various EU institutions will have their own specific interests so that one cannot see them as pure agents. The Commission, as the guardian of the treaties, has an interest in ensuring that negotiations with third countries do not undermine the prospects for EU integration. The Commission will therefore push for common responses to head-off distinct member state responses to external challenges that could make future EU integration difficult. In the 1970s this spurred Commission initiatives in environmental policy. Today the adoption of national levies on banks to pay for future bailouts would pose a threat to common EU schemes and make agreement on cross border supervision of banks difficult. The

Commission may also use international negotiations to promote internal reform in the fashion envisaged by two-level game analyses (Putnam, 1998). Equally, the European Parliament (EP) may seek to use any leverage it has to ratify a specific agreement, such as a bilateral free-trade agreement, as a means of gaining ground in the battle for power with the other EU institutions and in particular the Council.

Assessing outcomes

Assessing the effectiveness of EU economic diplomacy means finding some way of measuring outcomes against EU aims and such as assessment inevitably includes some subjectivity. By definition the EU engagement in negotiations is likely to result in some degree of cross issue bargaining of concessions, so that there may be progress in one issue but not in another. Any assessment of whether the EU has achieved its negotiating aims is also made difficult by the fact that the EU's detailed position will not be public. Although general negotiating aims may be publicly available, these are for the most part drawn fairly broadly so as not to undermine the position of those negotiating on the EU's behalf. Furthermore, as in all negotiations the negotiating aims in EU economic diplomacy are regularly refined in discussions in the various Council working groups, in Council of Ministers meetings or in discussion with European Parliament committees. A further difficulty is that much economic diplomacy is an iterative process. In other words outcomes can only be assessed over an extended period. Thus the 'success' of the EU in promoting a particular policy cannot be judged solely on the basis of one discrete negotiation. A failure in one round of negotiation may need to be seen against the general evolution of policy that could represent a move towards the EU's longer term policy objectives.

In opposition to such a more nuanced approach to measuring effectives one often reads general broad brush statements on the effectiveness of the EU in negotiations. For example, the EU was ineffective in its response to the financial crisis in 2008 or in the Committee of the Parties (COP) 15 in December 2009 in Copenhagen on the post-Kyoto approach to negotiations under the Framework Convention on Climate Change (FCCC). In trade it has been argued that the EU was ineffective in the Cancun WTO ministerial conference in 2003. Generally there is less coverage of negotiations that appear to have been successful for the EU, such as the EU – Republic of Korea FTA negotiations. In order to get away from such broad generalisations and to provide a basis for case studies in the following chapters, what is therefore needed is a framework for assessing the outcomes of negotiations.

The approach adopted here is therefore twofold. First, the evolution of EU economic diplomacy in the policy area concerned is assessed over a period of years and in some cases decades. The same is done for the more specific case studies in each broad policy area. This facilitates an assessment of EU effectiveness over an extended period encompassing numerous negotiations. For example, the Doha Round of negotiations in trade is assessed rather than just the Cancun WTO ministerial meeting, or the climate change negotiations over an extended period rather than just the COP meeting in December 2009. In this way it is also possible to assess the impact of the 'normative power' of the EU in shaping the ideational basis for negotiations. Taking a longer period of reference also enables an assessment of how the stage of development of the EU's internal *acquis,* which evolves over decades rather than years, influences policy. Relative economic or market power can also vary over time. Second, negotiation analysis is applied as a tool by breaking down each negotiation into a number of constituent parts or phases and thus facilitating an assessment of overall performance (Devereau and Lawrence, 2007).

What Is EU Economic Diplomacy?

Before going any further it is necessary to clarify the scope of EU economic diplomacy. First of all this volume is concerned with *European Union* external policies not the policies of the individual member states. It is therefore to be distinguished from *European* economic diplomacy that would encompass the policies of both the EU and the member states. Clearly the role of the member states in shaping EU policy needs to be properly considered and where there are distinct national policies running parallel with EU policy this will have important ramifications for EU policy. Such parallel policies are less of an issue in EU economic diplomacy than in EU foreign policy as a large share of EU external economic policies are either exclusive competence or at least shared EU and member state competence with broadly common negotiating positions.

Economic diplomacy is *decision-making and negotiation in international economic relations* (Bayne and Woolcock, 2007) and is about process rather than the structure of power or the universe of sectoral or national interests. Member state and sector interests however, clearly shape the EU preferences. EU economic diplomacy includes decision-making or how the member states and EU institutions reach (or do not reach) common positions or objectives and then how the EU seeks to promote this agreed EU position in negotiations with third parties.

The term economic *diplomacy* is used because this best reflects the activities of the various actors involved. With increased economic interdependence a much wider range of member state and EU officials have become active participants in international negotiations. Until the 1990s, ministries of foreign affairs, supported by ministries of trade and finance, conducted almost all economic diplomacy. But in recent decades many more services or departments have become directly involved in negotiations with their counterparts in other countries. For example, financial regulators engage in negotiations on international regulatory or prudential standards, sub-central government bodies are also now involved, because international negotiations touch upon their competences, as are non-governmental organisations and epistemic communities. These various actors seek to influence international agreements through persuasion or bargaining. In other words they engage in diplomatic activity.

Economic diplomacy here does not mean economic actions by diplomats, nor is it the consideration of economic or commercial relations in foreign policy, but negotiation on core economic issues. The distinction is important. The consideration of economic factors by diplomats in foreign policy would, for example, include the use of economic inducements or sanctions in order to promote foreign or security policy objectives. Economic sanctions are implemented by the EU, but these are generally determined by common positions adopted by the member states in the CFSP process and are mostly only taken following agreement at a multilateral level in the United Nations Security Council. Nor does economic diplomacy as used here mean the use of foreign services in the promotion of exports or investment. This is more commercial diplomacy and involves, for example, commercial delegations accompanying a head of state or minister on a foreign visit in the search of business or contracts (van Bergeijk, 2010). The EU does not engage in commercial diplomacy, which individual member states still pursue. The EU only promotes trade in the sense that it seeks to remove barriers to trade and investment. Economic diplomacy is becoming more important in international relations because the core economic and trade-related issues have become more important relative to security and foreign policy. During the Cold War, when international relations were dominated by the bipolar security system of the US versus the USSR, a distinction was made between the high politics of international security and the low politics of economic relations. This distinction is no longer made nor valid. Financial crises, and in particular that of 2008–2009, have shown that the foundations of the global economy cannot be taken for granted or treated as low politics. The near collapse of the international financial system and the economic consequences has brought home the importance of stable financial markets to all concerned. Climate change poses the threat of major disruption and instability in various regions and ultimately to the planet as a whole. So equally international environmental policy and especially climate change, now has to be seen as something of major importance that cannot be left to 'low' politics. Underdevelopment, especially in a number of sub-Saharan African countries, also poses a threat to collective security (Cable, 1999).

The purpose here is not to argue for a general securitisation of international economic policy, but rather to make the case that economic diplomacy now assumes a relatively more important role in international relations and therefore requires adequate attention. This is perhaps best illustrated by the way the globalisation process has been driven by the evolution of trade, investment and finance over decades. Policies in these core areas of economic diplomacy have had a profound impact on the nature and pace of globalisation. In other words economic diplomacy has become relatively more important because international economic and economic-related issues have assumed greater relative importance, not because of any securitisation of finance, trade or environmental policy.[7]

---

[7]   This distinction is made because 'securitisation' of trade, finance or climate change is about redefining the issues in terms of security. This inevitably refocuses the debate and analysis on national security as the nation state remains the unit of analysis in traditional international relations. This then risks prejudicing any debate about the role of the EU in economic diplomacy towards a realist interpretation in which the member states of the EU use the EU to further their national economic and thus security interests.

Economic diplomacy has also become more important because in a multi-polar economic system outcomes are shaped more by negotiation and less by a hegemony, hegemonic leadership or clubs of likeminded countries. In international economic relations there has been a multi-polar world for some time. Following the immediate post-1945 period, the US dominated the western economic order, but as early as the 1970s this dominance had been replaced by a 'Club model' that included the European Community (EC) on trade issues, as well as Canada and Japan (Keohane and Nye, 2001). By the 1980s transatlantic economic diplomacy largely shaped multilateral negotiations with other countries following, for the most part, the lead taken by the US and EC in trade, finance, development and the regulation of markets. The end of the Cold War brought many previously centrally planned economies into what had until then been the western system. These were joined by the newly industrialising countries (NICs) such as South Korea that sought membership of the club as their economies developed. During the 1990s larger developing countries, such as Brazil, India and China, that had previously pursued semi-autarkic or import substitution based policies, shifted to a policy of engaging with the multilateral economy and emerged to create a more multi-polar system.

In a multi-polar system negotiation assumes a greater importance than structural power in the sense that the old structures based on OECD leadership are no longer seen as legitimate or sufficient. Agreement now requires consensus or agreement among a larger group of actors. Given the importance of the EU in international economic relations, EU economic diplomacy is therefore important for systemic reasons as well as for the development of the EU. As will be shown in the following chapters, the EU taken as a whole still constitutes the largest market in the international system. How it acts therefore has systemic importance. For the EU, as for individual states involved in economic diplomacy, there are important linkages between domestic and external economic policies. EU external economic relations are both shaped by and shape developments within the EU and within its member states, so economic diplomacy also has important consequences for the future evolution of European integration.

The Case Studies

This volume will compare EU decision-making in policy areas in which the EU has exclusive competence and those in which is shares competence with the member states. The choice also provides scope for comparisons between policies in which the EU decision-making regime has become well established over a period of half a century and those in which the EU is still struggling to establish such regimes. The policy areas chosen provide an opportunity of comparing cases in which the EU 'domestic' or internal *acquis communautaire* is well developed and those in which it is still incomplete. The cases compare areas in which there is a broad consensus on the role of EU level regulation, what we shall call *framework norms,* and areas in which there is no such consensus. There are cases in which the Commission is sole negotiator, cases in which there is a team of negotiators drawn from EU presidency and Commission and cases in which the member states negotiate more or less by themselves. The respective roles of the various EU institutions, Commission, Council and European Parliament also vary between the policy areas.

In the field of *trade and investment* the common commercial policy (CCP) offers a model against which to measure other policy areas. The EEC, the EC and now the EU have had an important role in international trade for some time. The Treaty of Rome (in Art. 113) provided for exclusive competence for the CCP of the EEC, so at first glance it would seem that exclusive competence was an important factor in determining the role of the EU in trade policy. But in reality things are less clear cut. The Treaty of Rome provided no definition of the CCP, so the scope of EC/EU competence in trade has been contested at every turn as pressure from the EU's trading partners has resulted in an ever wider trade agenda. EC/EU decision-making and negotiation processes in trade have evolved over a period of more than 50 years in response to such external drivers as well as domestic developments, in the form of the creation of the common market in the 1960s and the deepening of integration with the Single European Market (SEM) in the 1980s. External trade therefore illustrates how EU economic diplomacy has evolved over time, with a progressive increase in the scope of EC/EU external trade policy and a steady shifting of *de facto* competence to the EC/EU level. This trend is formalised by the extension of exclusive EU competence to all major trade issues as well as foreign direct investment (FDI) in the Treaty of Lisbon. Trade has been a model in a real sense in that the treaty provisions for negotiating international agreements in the shape of Art. 218 TFEU (ex Art. 300 TEC) have drawn on experience in the trade field.

The second case study is EU *financial diplomacy*. Because of the very broad scope of international financial policy the case study focuses on the role of the EU in international financial regulation rather than monetary policy or efforts to coordinate fiscal policies, although the latter are included to some degree because of their links to financial market regulation. There is shared competence in international financial market regulation, with EU competence for internal financial market regulation, but shared competence in the field of supervision of individual financial institutions and in effect for key aspects of EU policy towards the coordination and standards-making in international financial regulation. Compared to trade, international financial market regulation is a policy area in which the EU decision-making regime is still relatively recent or at best still evolving. The EU has been pursuing the aim of a Single Financial Market (SFM) only since 1998, rather than 1968 as in the case of goods or perhaps 1986 in the case of other services. As will be shown in chapter four, financial market regulation is an area in which there is no broad EU consensus on the balance between regulation and market forces. This contrasts with the case for goods markets where the SEM programme was based on a broad agreement on the approach to regulation in the EU. The nature of the external drivers of EU financial market regulation also differs from those in trade in the sense that there is intense pressure to coordinate policy during financial crises, but this is intermittent and often fades with the crisis, whereas in trade there is enduring, but less intense pressure on the EU to develop a common position.

International environmental policy provides an example of a policy area in which there is exclusive EU competence for internal policy, albeit with some important exceptions. This means that the Commission remains the main driver of internal and thus external policies, even though there has been mixed competence in external EU environmental policies. As in trade, but in contrast to financial market regulation, the member states have adopted a pragmatic approach. In trade the member states delegated negotiation to the Commission even for issues of mixed competence. Something similar has happened in environmental negotiations. The difference is that there has (at least to date) been a Troika of the Commission, current presidency and incoming presidency of the Council rather than just the Commission negotiating.[8] But in environmental negotiations, member states have continued to seek to engage in negotiations themselves. International environmental policy is an area in which policy within the EC/EU has evolved over a couple of decades, so it assumes a mid-way position between trade with a well established decision-making regime and financial markets. In international environmental policy, the EU has sought a leadership role, as it has rather less explicitly in international trade. This again contrasts with international finance where the EU has been more of a follower than leader.

The final case study is of *development policy.* This is another area in which competence is shared and one in which the member states have insisted on being able to pursue national policies in parallel with EU development policy. This differs from international environment in which although shared competence applies member states have sought to define one common policy for the EU as a whole. It differs perhaps somewhat less from financial market regulation in which member states also assume the role of actors in their own right. One contrasting feature of EU development policy is that it is a purely external. There is no internal 'development' policy and therefore no internal *acquis.* Like EU foreign policy it is based on efforts by the EU member states to agree on common approaches based on policy statements or objectives rather than a substantive *acquis communautaire.* But in development the need to ensure coherence between various EU external and internal policies is especially important as such coherence is a central importance to its effectiveness. This is the case for all EU policy areas but especially for development.

The Structure of the Book

The approach used in the book is to first provide an analytical framework for assessing the factors that shape EU economic diplomacy. This is done in Chapter 2. The following chapters then consider case studies in trade and investment,

---

8   One of the unresolved issues concerning the TFEU is whether it implies an end to this arrangement and if so for what topics in the environment field, see Chapter 5.

international finance with a focus on financial market regulation, international environmental policy and development. Each case study provides a broad description of the evolution of EU economic diplomacy in the policy area concerned. This draws on the analytical framework in Chapter 2 and provides a comparison of the independent variables identified in that chapter.

Each case then provides a description of the EU process of decision-making and negotiation in the policy area concerned. This includes a discussion of the changes resulting from the Lisbon Treaty so that the volume is fully up to date in terms of the formal changes. Inevitably, much will depend on how the treaty changes are implemented by the various EU institutions, but where possible there is a discussion of the most likely developments based on past practice, the existing treaty provisions and positions of the member states and EU institutions. This descriptive exercise addresses the first aim of the volume, which is to promote a broader understanding of the EU processes and procedures. It also enables a comparison of the decision-making and negotiating procedures in these four core policy areas.

Each of the chapters then applies the framework developed in Chapter 2 to assess the relative importance of the various independent variables shaping the role of the EU. This addresses a number of the hypotheses offered at the end of Chapter 2. This is then followed by the consideration a specific negotiation, or rather series of negotiations, in order to illustrate of how the framework can be used to assess the effectiveness of EU economic diplomacy.

Conclusions

This volume therefore seeks to describe how the EU conducts economic diplomacy, assess the factors that determine what role the EU plays in different policy areas and offers an approach to analysing the effectiveness of EU economic diplomacy. It does not offer any overarching theory, but by applying a common analytical framework to the various policy areas it illustrates how the relative importance of a number of factors (dependent variables) can be evaluated. Much more work remains to done, especially on the detail of how the EU negotiates (as opposed to decides on its negotiating aims).

Chapter 2
A Framework of Analysis

Introduction

This chapter develops an analytical framework for evaluating European Union (EU) economic diplomacy as defined in Chapter 1 and illustrated in the four case studies that follow. It does not claim any specific originality, but draws on the existing literature on the EU as an actor and other relevant contributions on the EU's role in international relations. There are three parts to the framework. The first provides a general typology of EU decision-making and negotiation to guide readers through the description of the decision-making process in each of the case studies. This is really intended for readers who are not familiar with EU decision-making in general or EU decision-making in economic diplomacy in particular.

The second section discusses a number of factors – or independent variables – that shape the role of the EU in economic diplomacy. These factors include 'domestic' factors such as EU competence, decision-making regimes (both formal and *de facto*), as well as external drivers, systemic factors and the EU's relative economic or market power. Sector and member state interests are also included and there is an assessment of EU normative power as it relates to economic negotiations. The case study chapters then use this framework in order to assess when the EU's role is more likely to be that of an actor and when more that of one forum among others.

The third part of the framework provides a breakdown of the phases in any negotiation process. This draws on negotiation analysis and is intended to help when it comes to the third question of assessing the effectiveness of the EU in negotiations. As noted in the previous chapter it is necessary to focus on specific negotiations, rather than any given policy area, in order to assess how effective the EU has been and what factors appear to have been most important in determining effectiveness.

A Typology of EU Economic Diplomacy

The challenge in all economic diplomacy is to find an agreed position among the various ministries, branches of government and stakeholders/sector interests *and* still be able to negotiate at an international level. Finding a common position requires some aggregation of preferences, for example, between protectionist and liberally minded sectors of the economy. In the case of the EU there is also a need to aggregate member state preferences in order to reach an agreement among the 27 member states. How the EU goes about this depends on whether there is exclusive EU competence in the policy area concerned, or whether competence is shared with or retained by the member states.

As a general guide, Figure 2.1 shows a typical decision-making flow chart for EU economic diplomacy. In each policy area of economic diplomacy decision-making will deviate to a greater or lesser extent from this general pattern. Policy initiatives come from the Commission or from a combination of Commission and member states. These proposals are then discussed in working groups. For example for trade policy this would be the Trade Policy Committee (TPC) that brings together senior member state officials. There are equivalent working groups in the other policy areas, such as the Working Group on International Environmental Issues (WGIEI), the Economic and Finance Committee (EFC) (for international financial matters) and the Development Committee for development cooperation. These working groups are also served by specialist committees. Much of the work developing EU negotiating positions is done in such specialist committees and senior working groups before the final political decision to authorise the opening of a negotiation is taken by the Council (Art. 218 (3) TFEU). The Council level decision is taken by member state ministers in the relevant specialist Council, such as the Council of Environment Ministers, the Foreign Affairs Council for trade and development and the Economic and Finance (ECOFIN) Council for financial market regulation. The European Council often provides an endorsement of the overall EU position at the level of Heads of State and Government.

Once the EU position is adopted and the Council has nominated the negotiator, negotiations begin with supervision being provided by the working groups for most substantive issues or the relevant Councils if political level action is needed. The negotiator or agent for the EU varies. Negotiations on issues of exclusive EU competence are conducted by the European Commission, on issues of shared or mixed competence it may be the Commission, or a combination of Commission and Council or – for issues in which member states retain some competence – a representative from the member state government themselves.[1] During negotiations the Council can direct the EU agent to adopt a specific position (Art. 218 (4) TFEU). The Council on the recommendation of the negotiator then adopts a decision authorising the signature of an agreement. The final agreement must be adopted by the Council and in many cases also by the European Parliament (EP). For example, the EP must grant its consent if any change in EU domestic law is required when that law has been adopted using the Ordinary Legislative Procedure (OLP).

Factors Shaping EU Economic Diplomacy

This section presents the key factors (independent variables) included in the analytical framework, which are presented in simplified graphical form in Figure 2.2. It places decision-making at the centre as the concern here is with EU decision-

---

[1]   Following the adoption of the Treaty of Lisbon the Commission is pressing for a further shift towards a position in which it is the sole negotiator for the EU.

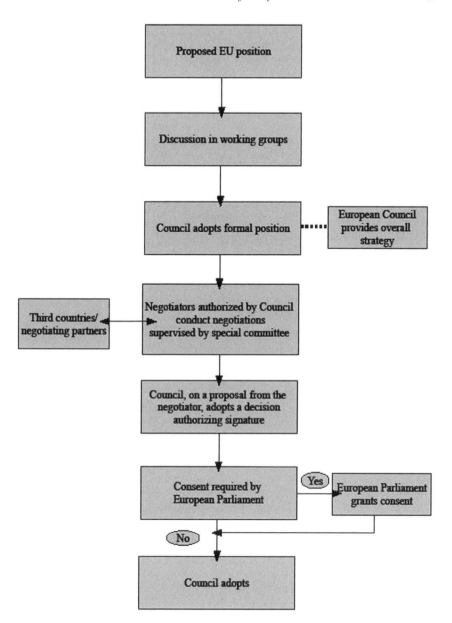

Fig. 2.1   The Basic Pattern of Decision-Making in EU Economic Diplomacy

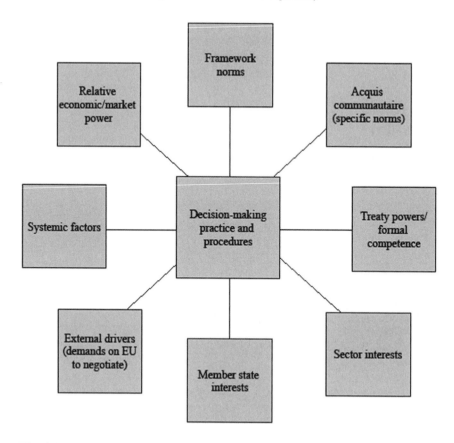

Fig. 2.2   Factors Shaping the Role of the EU in Economic Diplomacy

making and negotiation in international economic relations. EU decision-making is of course, itself a factor in the form EU diplomacy takes and its effectiveness.

Relative economic or market power

The EU's role and possibly effectiveness in international economic negotiations will be greater the larger the EU's relative economic or market power. Equally important is the ability or willingness on the part of the EU to offer or deny access to its market. In the exercise of such market power it is the EU as a whole that counts and therefore the ability of the EU rather than the member states to determine access. This is in line with systemic theories of international relations or international political economy. In practice if the US or the EU engage in negotiations with developing or smaller economies, their relative economic power must be expected to have a significant bearing of the outcome.

Generally measuring relative power in international relations can be problematic. In the case of economic diplomacy the task is somewhat easier in that one can use market size or similar metrics. If one takes market size as a measure of economic power then clearly the more integrated the EU market, the greater the potential economic power of the EU. Perceptions of the value of market size can also shape processes in the EU. For example, pooling of sovereignty by agreeing to create a single market or common policy, have been seen as a means to enhancing the EU's leverage in international negotiations. Greater cooperation in order to have more of a say internationally and to begin to match the predominance of the dollar was, for example, one of the motives for monetary cooperation in Europe in the 1980s and has featured in all EU economic diplomacy.

Relative market power is important because all economic diplomacy is shaped to a greater or lesser degree, and more or less formally, by reciprocity or the view that there should be a broad balance of benefits (or costs) resulting from any negotiation. The issue is generally how such a balance is defined and over what period. In some areas such as trade policy, reciprocity has been and remains, for better or for worse, one of the underlying principles of the GATT/WTO system of multilateral trade negotiations. Relative market size is even more important in bilateral (or other preferential) trade negotiations that have become the dominant feature of international trade negotiations since the late 1990s. In 2009 the EU constituted the largest single market in the world with a GDP in purchasing power parity (PPP) of $14.5 trillion in 2009, just slightly larger than the US at $ 14 trn and equivalent to China, India, Brazil and South Africa put together ($ 14.9 trn). As the case study chapters will show there are equivalent metrics that can be used in other policy areas.

It is not just market size that counts however, but also the ability and willingness to use it in negotiations. In some policy areas the ability of the EU to offer concessions or deny market access has been significantly reduced through internal EU policies or successive rounds of liberalisation and in some cases the fact that EU policies such as market liberalisation are bound under rule based international regimes, such as the WTO. The EU like other countries has also adopted autonomous or unilateral measures, such as the creation of the SEM programme in the 1980s and 1990s. The SEM programme disciplines EU member state government intervention in markets and promotes transparency, the use of international standards and regulatory best practices that effectively facilitate non-reciprocal access to the EU market for third-country suppliers. The general shift to a liberal paradigm during the 1980s has also meant that national industrial policies have been removed and privatisation extended to many sectors of the economy. Nor has the EU developed any EU level industrial policy, with the possible exception of Airbus industries. When market power is measured in terms of the ability to make concessions as part of negotiations seeking mutual gains, the existing level of liberalisation in the EU has therefore reduced the EU's market power. Market power can also be used in the negative sense of threatening to apply restrictions on access to your market in those areas where there are no legally binding constraints on such action. Many EU commitments are binding under international agreements. There is also a sizable group of 'liberal' member states that are opposed to threatening market closure, which given the practice of consensus in EU decision-making could be said to undermine the EU's willingness to use what market power it has.

In international financial regulation the EU's potential to shape outcomes depends on the size of its financial markets. In financial services, as in services in general, the EU has still to achieve the same degree of integration as in goods markets. This means it has not realised its full potential in the sector. Were the EU to have a fully integrated market, its combined share on capital markets would at least match that of the US. Indeed, as chapter four shows the EU financial markets when put together are larger than the US and Japanese markets measured by some metrics, such as bank assets or insurance premiums. Only in equity markets and derivatives was the US bigger in 2007 (Becht and Correia da Silva, 2007, p. 201). The financial sector also shows how the introduction of EU level regulation can be used to enhance EU market power and thus provide leverage in international negotiations. Proposed EU legislation to establish a common regime for banking within the SEM programme in the form of the Second Banking Coordination Directive (SBCD) famously included a debate on what reciprocal access the EU should seek from the USA. This arose because the SBCD facilitated improved access for US and other non-EU banks to the wider EU market and the EU had to decide to what extent it would require reciprocal access to the US financial services markets. A more recent case concerns EU proposals on the regulation of hedge funds (the Alternative Investment Funds Directive or AIFD). In this case US interests saw the introduction of EU level regulations as threatening the existing access to the EU market via member states. Such 'opportunities' to enhance market power through EU initiatives require a consensus of the member states, which due to the general liberal orientation or vested interests of some seldom exists.

In the case of international environmental policy, market size is also important in that access to the EU market can be made dependent on meeting (EU) standards of environmental protection. Such power can be used in different ways. At one end of the spectrum there is the indirect or non-obligatory market power of the EU. This exists when common EU environmental standards shape the expectations of consumers who then demand that imported products also meet such standards. At the other end of the spectrum there is the use of (the threat of) market closure, such as with the use of the border (tax) adjustment measures that would impose an import levy on products produced by countries that do not meet EU expectations in terms of reductions of carbon or other green house gas emissions. Power in negotiations on the environment is also shaped by how important the entity is as a polluter. If one takes the case of climate change, the EU accounts for a relatively small share of global carbon emissions (see chapter five). Whilst action by the EU is essential for any agreement on climate change, other countries have more leverage due to the relative size of their emissions. An agreement including the

EU, but without the US or China, would have no decisive impact on the problem of climate change. Analogous to the trade field, where existing liberalisation by the EU can be seen as reducing its leverage in negotiations, the EU's lead in reducing carbon emissions can therefore also be seen as an autonomous measure that reduces its leverage and thus its ability to shape in international environmental negotiations. In Copenhagen at the COP 15 negotiations the EU had little to contribute to the negotiations, in part, because it had already done much more than the other Annex I countries.[2] On the other hand the case for EU leadership in reducing emissions has been made in the belief that the EU has normative power (discussed below) and can shape outcomes by providing an example or model for the rest of the word.

In development policy it is the EU's role as a provider of official development assistance (ODA) to fund programmes in developing countries that provides it with real economic power. The size of the EU market is also of considerable importance given that the EU takes a very large share of all developing country exports. EU trade policy and its 'internal' policies on agriculture and fisheries are therefore part of the EU policy vis-à-vis developing countries. In recent years the drive for Policy Coherence for Development (PCD) has stressed the importance of EU policies in areas such as trade for development. EU official development assistance is split between the EU and member states with the latter accounting for the larger part (Orbie and Versluys, 2009).

This discussion of the economic power of the EU clearly shows that the EU has substantial economic power even if it is not always able to use this due to a lack of market integration or an ability or willingness to do so (Sapir, 2007). It is also important to consider how the EU's relative economic or market power is changing with changes in the balance of the international economy and the emergence of a more multi-polar system. A relative decline in the EU's economic power will mean less leverage and thus influence for the EU in the future. It will also have implications for the nature of EU economic diplomacy, favouring perhaps, the use of more bilateral negotiations in which the EU can maximise its asymmetric leverage. Reduced market power may also favour strategies of cooperation or relatively fluid (i.e., issue specific) coalition building in order to achieve a critical mass of support from the EU's policy objectives.

Recognition

The literature on the EU as an actor has identified 'recognition' of the EU as a negotiating partner as opposed to the member states, as important (Jupille and Caporaso, 1998). *De facto* recognition as an actor can come as a consequence of market power. For example, from the time the Commission emerged as the

---

[2]   Annex I countries are the developed economies in the UNFCCC negotiations on climate change.

negotiator for the EEC during the Dillon – and especially the Kennedy – rounds of the GATT, the EC was recognised as an actor distinct from the EU member states.

Recognition of the EU as the negotiating partner in any international negotiation is likely to be associated with formal competence, but this need not automatically be the case. In the case of international trade the EEC/EC has not had exclusive competence for all issues on the international trade agenda by any means, but it was still recognised as the negotiating partner, even for issues of mixed competence. The EU has become recognised by third countries as the negotiating partner in international environmental negotiations, even though member states retained the right to engage directly in international environment negotiations.

In financial market regulation there is only partial recognition of the EU even though the position in terms of competence is not very dissimilar to that for environment negotiations in that the EU is competent for internal policy on financial market regulation with the use of Ordinary Legislative Procedure (OLP) for the adoption of EU regulations. On certain topics such as systemic risk, the European Central Bank (ECB) appears now to have been recognised as representing the Eurozone, but not the whole of the EU. But it is the member states with large financial markets that appear to have more recognition than the EU in negotiations on international financial regulation and it is the member states that are represented and thus recognised in such bodies as the Basil Committee on Banking Supervision (BCBS) and the Financial Stability Board (FSB). As chapter four will show the EU has some limited recognition in the International Monetary Fund (IMF) and somewhat more in the G20, where since 2008 the Commission has been included. In the wake of the 2008 financial crisis there has however, been a redoubling of efforts to make EU level policies in financial market regulation more cohesive and the European Commission appears to have strengthened its position vis-à-vis the member state governments somewhat. In development policy, another case where competence is shared, the EU is also recognized as an actor and aid doner, but only alongside the member states.

De jure or formal recognition in international institutions is an indicator of the degree to which the EU has become an actor. The EU is recognised as a legal entity in the WTO, where it has been a fully fledged member along side the EU member states since the establishment of the WTO in 1995. In the field of international environmental policy the EU was recognised as a Regional Economic Integration Organisation (REIO) in the United Nations Framework Convention on Climate Change (UNFCCC). In international finance there is a patchwork of EU representation (Gstoehl, 2008). The Eurogroup and the European Central Bank (ECB) have small roles in the IMF Management Board meetings, but only when the Euro is being discussed. At other times it is the member states that are present, either in their own chairs or as chair for constituencies made up of EU and non-EU countries. In the G7/8 there has been some representation of the EU in the shape of the president of the Commission and the president of the European Council, but for the most part it is again the member state governments, and then only some of them, that have had formal recognition in such bodies. In the various international bodies responsible for financial market regulation there is limited EU level representation. Some such bodies such as the BCBS and the FSB now include the Commission, but not all.

Recognition is not only important as an indicator of EU 'actorness', the form of recognition or representation in international organisations can also have implications for decision-making and negotiation *within* the EU. If the EU is recognised as representing all the member states there will be less temptation for third parties to seek out member state governments. But if the EU is recognised alongside the member states or there is shared competence, the temptation remains for the EU's negotiating partners to engage member states in negotiation.[3] In the field of climate change, shared competence has meant that there have been bilateral negotiations between individual member states and third parties running parallel to negotiations between the EU and third countries, as in the case of The Hague negotiations on climate change in 2000.

The form of recognition or representation of member states in international organisations can also have effects on internal EU cohesion. It has been argued for example, that hierarchical member state representation in international organisations tends to correlate to a relative lack of cohesion within the EU (Reiter, 2009). This is because those member states with privileged representation in international organisations, such as the IMF, World Bank or FSB, resist common EU policies as these would undermine the credibility of maintaining their privileged status.

Systemic Factors and External Drivers

Systemic factors are defined here as broad international pressures on the EU to act, while external drivers are defined as specific demands on the EU to negotiate. Systemic factors would therefore be, for example, the need to maintain an open, rules-based international trading system in order to ensure access for EU exports and investment. The response to such a systemic factor would typically take the form of domestic and external policies. For example, the need to enhance international competition in order to match Japan and the US was a major factor behind the SEM programme in the 1980s. This was combined with efforts to improve access for EU exports of goods and services. The need to ensure access for EU exporters to markets with potential such as India, China and Korea has also been a factor shaping EU trade policy in the 2000s.

In the case of international financial market regulation there have also been systemic pressures on the EU to compete in international financial markets. As will be discussed in Chapter 4, this has led to rather different responses from the member states. Some member states have seen a need to ensure EU financial

---

[3]   The distinction needs to be made here between lobbying the member states in order to shape the EU position, which happens all the time in all policy areas, and seeking to negotiate with a member state.

markets support the general competitiveness of their economies and the EU as a whole, other member states with important financial centres, such as the UK in particular, have placed rather more emphasis on the need for financial markets as such to be competitive. The other systemic pressure on EU financial market policy has, of course, been the desire for stability especially in response to international financial crises. The 2008 financial crisis clearly stimulated a redoubling of the efforts to strengthen EU policies in financial market regulation although it may be too early to say how much of an effect these will have.

In the environment, the need to develop a coherent EU response to global challenges, such as climate change, has had a profound impact on EU policy. Only through developing a common approach have the member states been able to have an impact on the global debate and thus respond to the systemic challenge of global warming. In development policy, the systemic pressure on the EU takes the form of the desire or need to promote development, eradicate poverty and thus improve collective security.

External drivers take the form of demands on the EU to negotiate, either as a result of initiatives by other countries or ongoing negotiations. The pressure to respond to negotiations can come in the form of regular meetings, such as in the shape of G7 (finance ministers), G8 or G20 summits, or when there are regular negotiations under a framework convention, such as in the case of the COP to the UNFCCC. These external drivers then force the EU to decide who is going to represent the EU and whether – and if so what – will be the common negotiating position.

The nature of the pressure on the EU to negotiation will vary in terms of intensity and duration. In the case of international trade there have been demands (in the past mostly from the US) for the EU to engage in more or less continuous negotiation. This began with the Dillon Round of the GATT even as the EEC was finding its feet and continued right through to the Doha Development Agenda (DDA) that was ongoing in 2011. GATT and WTO rounds have lasted between 6 and 10 years (and counting in the case of the DDA). If one includes the periods during which trade rounds were being prepared and agendas shaped, the EU has had to engage in multilateral trade diplomacy more or less continuously since 1958. This has required the EU to develop and maintain an agreed position on an expanding number of trade topics throughout the period. With the exception of the final phases of GATT or WTO rounds, the intensity of these negotiations has not generally been very great, so that the EU has also had time to develop common positions. It will be argued below that this has facilitated the establishment of a *de facto* decision-making and negotiation regime (or *de facto* competence) based on shared expectations about how decisions are made and negotiations conducted.

In environment the external driver in the form of demands on the EU to develop common positions came somewhat later, during the 1980s. There had been early international environmental negotiations, such as the Stockholm UN Conference on the Human Environment in 1972, but at that time the EC involvement was more in the form of ensuring that member state involvement in international negotiations did not undermine the common market. The negotiations on the Convention on Trade in Endangered Species (CITES) and the Montreal Protocol on ozone depleting substances posed the first real challenge for the EU to develop common positions. With Rio in 1992 the need to develop EU policies on biodiversity and climate change began and these topics have been a constant challenge for EU decision-making ever since with preparations for the various COP meetings spanning the period from the 1992 FCCC right up to the present. So like the case of trade the pressure from external drivers has been fairly consistent and only in the run up to key summits very intensive.

In the field of financial market regulation the pressure to engage in negotiations has not been continuous. There has been intense, but intermittent pressure to respond to financial crises, such as the Asian financial crisis of the late 1990s or the international financial crisis of 2008. Outside of these events the pressure to develop common positions has been less, although technical negotiations have been ongoing for decades. The intermittent nature of these pressures means that there has been less opportunity for the EU to establish de facto decision-making regimes. Given the nature of financial crisis and the need for an immediate response, sometimes literally overnight, policy initiatives have generally been led by the member states because of the inevitable delays in the EU policy coordination.

An interesting question is therefore whether persistent but relatively low intensity pressure to engage in international negotiations promotes more effective EU economic diplomacy or whether crises are needed to stimulate a stronger, more effective common EU response? While crises may be seen as opportunities for policy entrepreneurs to bring about advances in EU coordination, the need to respond to markets may necessitate rapid action that is not possible through the EU. On the other hand, in crises or when the pressure from external drivers is intermittent, member states may opt for more *ad hoc* responses. Once the crisis passes so generally does the pressure to coordinate within the EU, as well as internationally.

Member State Interests

The interests of member states will clearly shape EU economic diplomacy. From an analytical point of view there is a difficulty because member state and sector interests will vary from negotiation to negotiation with differences often within a given policy area. It is therefore helpful to differentiate between general member state interests, such as retaining national competence over key areas of policy and the more specific interests in the policy area under discussion. The latter are likely to be concerned with the distribution of the costs and benefits of various EU policy options between member states. Otherwise heterogeneous member state interests may also be aggregated in the *acquis communautaire*. It can be assumed that greater integration and thus agreement on framework and more specific EU norms (see the following section) will tend to mean more homogeneous preferences in external policies based on a common *acquis*.

Of the general member state interests, retaining national competence in certain sensitive areas is likely to apply to many if not all member states. For example a strong link to foreign policy interests in any policy area will tend to mean a more pronounced desire of member states to retain control. EU development policy provides an example of this. Member states retain development policies parallel to those of the EU, in part because they see development aid as a key instrument in their foreign policy vis-à-vis developing countries. So compared to trade and environment policies where foreign policy issues are more remote, there has been less coordination and convergence in EU development policy.

Fiscal policy is another area in which member states are keen to retain national sovereignty/competence, so that any linkage between EU economic diplomacy and tax or fiscal policy will mean member state resistance to developing common EU positions. In climate change efforts to support EC climate change policy with carbon taxes or spending under the Clean Development Mechanism (CDM) in the UNFCCC have been impossible or difficult to agree upon for this reason. As chapter four shows stronger EU level supervision of pan-EU banking and other financial institutions has been constrained by a lack of agreement on *ex anti* financial burden sharing between member state governments for bailouts of any failing bank or other financial institution. This is because of the implications in terms of financial obligations on the member states and thus their fiscal sovereignty.

Member state interests will also play a role in the sense that the political utility functions of governments may lead them to promote or block decisions in EU economic diplomacy for reasons unrelated to the specific policy concerned. Governments can block decisions for electoral reasons, as was the case in agricultural trade during the final stages of the Uruguay Round negotiations. More recently, the British government blocked discussion of EU regulation of hedge funds (the AIFD) until after the May 2010 British general election.

Sector interests

Rationalist approaches to economic diplomacy see sector interests as a key independent variable. Negotiations are seen as involving linkages between issues in value-claiming or value-creating strategies (Odell, 2000; Woolcock, 2011). Sector interests can indeed go a long way to explaining the positions of the EU member states and thus the EU in any given negotiation. In some cases there will be a trade-off between the interests of different sectors in a negotiation, such as between agricultural and manufacturing interests in the DDA negotiations. The costs or benefits of a policy may be more or less dispersed throughout the EU. In environmental policy the costs of measures to tackle climate change are fairly concentrated whilst the benefits are widely dispersed. The same holds for financial regulation. Such sector interests will therefore be important in the political economy of EU economic diplomacy.

As in the case of member state interests, the level of development of the *acquis* is important. Generally speaking the more heterogeneous sector interests are the more difficult it will be to agree on common EU preferences, but if there is a well developed *acquis* that establishes an agreed internal policy this will often provide the basis for the EU external policies. This is at odds with the argument that heterogeneous interests provide scope for issue linkages and thus facilitate international negotiations. In the EU this is less likely to hold if the sector and member state interests are closely associated, because member states tend to have a fairly tight control over the EU agent. It has been argued that member states find it easier to defend the status quo against change, such as that induced by international negotiation, than adopt a common offensive or proactive position (Meunier, 2000).

Normative power

The expectation in terms of norms is that the more the EU member states can agree on common norms the more normative power the EU will acquire and thus the more effective it will be in its economic diplomacy. Compared to market power or the other metrics of economic power, normative power is often abstract and not easily measured, so how should it be applied in this analysis of EU economic diplomacy? When the EU insists on conformance with EU norms before a country can join the EU, it clearly exercises normative power. This sort of case falls under the general heading of the Europeanisation (of the near neighbourhood) (Graziano and Maarten, 2008). Our interest here lies more in EU economic diplomacy vis-à-vis third countries outside of the candidate countries and in most cases even outside the near neighbourhood.

In order to better assess the impact of norms and whether the EU has normative power, the approach here distinguishes between three types of norms. *General norms* such as those set out in Chapter 1, Title V of the Treaty of European Union plus some general norms that relate specifically to economic diplomacy. The Treaty of Lisbon Art. 205 states that EU external action shall be conducted in accordance with the general provisions laid down in Chapter 1 of Title V. This includes support for democracy, the rule of law, human rights, good governance as well as the somewhat more specific objectives of 'sustainable economic, social and environmental development of developing countries with the primary aim of eradicating poverty', the 'integration of all countries into the world economy, including through the progressive abolition of restrictions on international trade', and support for the 'develop(ment of) international measures to preserve and improve the quality of the environment and the sustainable management of global resources, in order to ensure sustainable development' (Art. 21 (2) TEU). This is a clear codification of general norms, but how these relate to economic diplomacy is not always very clear.

In addition to these general norms specified in the treaty, the EU is also seen to represent a post-Westphalian model of international relations. In other words a model in which the national state does not play an overriding or central role. In this respect the success of European integration serves as a model for other regions

(Manners, 2002, p. 239; Hetne, 2008). In the economic sphere it is possible to argue that there has been some emulation of European integration in other regions of the world. The two phases of regional integration in Africa and Latin America in the 1960s and late 1980s, and indeed North America in the 1990s, could be said to have been at least in part inspired by developments in Europe.

Framework norms are defined here as those determining the underlying approach to market regulation or the relationship between authority (i.e., state or EU powers) and the market. One example of a framework norm was the broad consensus reached between major EU member states that provided the basis for the SEM in the 1980s. This was a compromise between, for the sake of simplification, the Anglo-Saxon *laissez faire* policies that were embodied in the deregulatory and liberal paradigm of the 1980s on the one hand, and French *dirigisme* on the other. The compromise reached was something closer to German *Ordnungspolitik* in which free markets operate within a framework of rules designed to ensure that key social, environmental, competition and prudential policy objectives are satisfied. Agreement on this framework norm facilitated the extension of the *acquis communautaire* in goods markets during the 1980s and early 1990s. The internal consensus also enabled the EU to play a far more proactive role in multilateral trade negotiations in the Uruguay Round during the 1980s and 1990s. Agreement on key issues at the European level that were also being negotiated on at the international level also gave the EU normative power. Other examples of framework norms would be the consensus that has been achieved over the past couple of decades in environmental policy and in particular on the target of low carbon or ecological growth. As chapter five will show, the absence of agreement on the framework norms for financial markets has created difficulties in the creation of a single financial market and denied the EU normative power in international negotiations on financial market regulation equivalent to those in goods markets.

Specific norms or standards are defined as those codified in EU legislation or regulations and other decisions that together go to make up the detail of the *acquis communautaire*. A specific norm would therefore be a particular regulatory provision or standard that has been adopted as a common EU measure. In economic diplomacy the EU may use such specific norms as the basis for common offensive or defensive positions.

By distinguishing between the different types of norms it is possible to make operational the concept of normative power, assess the degree to which the EU poses it and consider how much it has shaped the policies or approaches of other countries. It is also important to ask whether the norms the EU promotes are distinctive EU origin norms and whether they need to be for the EU to have normative power? Norms that the EU is promoting in international negotiations are seldom the result of a purely internal EU debate. Trade provides a number of examples of how EU policies and the EU *acquis* are based on norms developed elsewhere such as in the OECD. In international financial markets one has a very good example of how the EU is applying norms developed in international discourse rather than in the EU. Indeed, this is one of the declared aims of EU policy in financial market regulation. Chapter 5 on international environmental policy will also show how the EU is promoting carbon trading as a market based instrument to reduce carbon emissions, an idea developed originally in the US.

It seems clear that it is not essential to have distinctive EU norms for the EU to poses normative power. The EU by implementing norms that have been agreed in other forums has a considerable impact on the likelihood of the norms becoming international practice. But for the EU to be recognised as an actor may require distinctive norms. The concept of an actor in international relations is closely associated with identity, which seems to speak for distinctive norms. Again the case studies shed light on this point. What appears to be important in shaping the EU's role in economic diplomacy is not so much distinctive norms, but whether the EU leads in the application and thus interpretation of what are often internationally agreed principles. By definition, internationally agreed principles leave scope for different interpretations or differences in their application. Early implementation may therefore provide scope for the EU to exercise normative power by shaping the way the international rules are applied.

Institutional factors

If the EU possesses market or normative power there remains a question of whether it can apply this power effectively in international negotiations. This raises the question of the ability of the EU to reach a common position and to negotiate effectively. Here the efficiency of decision-making becomes an important factor in the effectiveness of economic diplomacy. EU economic diplomacy can be expected to be more effective when there are well established regimes governing decision-making and the conduct of negotiations. Given the nature of the EU with the need to reconcile 27 member states the decision-making regime is likely to be more important than in countries in which the reconciliation necessary is of differences within the national economy, various government departments or at most different states or provinces within a federal system. In order to include such institutional factors in the analytical framework this section looks at formal competence, *de facto* procedures (or de facto competence) and the policy autonomy (of the EU agents)

Formal competence

The expectation is that formal EU competence for a policy area will make for more effective EU economic diplomacy. Figure 2.3 provides a simplified overview of EU competence for the four policy areas covered in Chapters 3 to 6. Where there is EU competence, it will be the European Commission that has right of initiative, something that provides the Commission with the means to drive and shape policy. As a relatively unified actor the Commission is one EU body that could develop a common strategic approach to negotiations. Note however, that EU

Policy area	Internal policy	External policy	Negotiator
Trade (and investment)	Exclusive EU competence Title IV Chapters I-III TFEU	EU exclusive competence Art 207 TFEU for the Common Commercial Policy	European Commission
Financial market regulation	EU competence for the adoption of regulatory standards (Art 63 TFEU), but some member states competence Art 65 TFEU	Shared competence with member states playing a large role	Mostly member states, but Commission for topics that are EU competence
Environment	Mostly EU competence Art 192 (1) TFEU, but with some areas reserved for member states Art 192 (2) TFEU	Shared Art 191 (4) and last paragraph TFEU	Commission or Troika (current and next presidency, with Commission)
Development policy	Not applicable	Shared Art 209 (1) TFEU provides for EU competence, but Art 209 (2) and 211 state this is without prejudice to member states' competence	Commission and member states in parallel

Fig. 2.3   A Overview of European Union Competence

competence does not mean the Commission decides. EU competence generally means that the EU method or what used to be called the Community method of decision-making will apply. With the 'Community method' 'policy design and brokering is delegated to the Commission which also manages the interface with "abroad"'(Wallace et al., 2005, p. 79), but the Council and European Parliament share decision-making powers.[4] The 'Community method' broadly corresponds to the formal system of decision-making that used to be called co–decision-making and after Lisbon is now termed the Ordinary Legislative Procedure (OLP) (Art. 294 (TFEU). See Figure 2.4 for a diagrammatic outline of the OLP process. With the 'Community method' the Commission deals with the external dimension and therefore has the right of initiative, as in the case of trade and will make proposals on the EU negotiating position to the Council. When there is EU competence in external policy, it is the Commission that negotiates and coordinates policy.

In the case of trade there has been exclusive EC/EU competence since the treaty of Rome, but this has not meant EU trade diplomacy has always been

---

[4]   There is an extensive literature on EU decision-making. See for example Pollack, Young and Wallace, 2010; Wallace, Wallace and Pollack 2005.

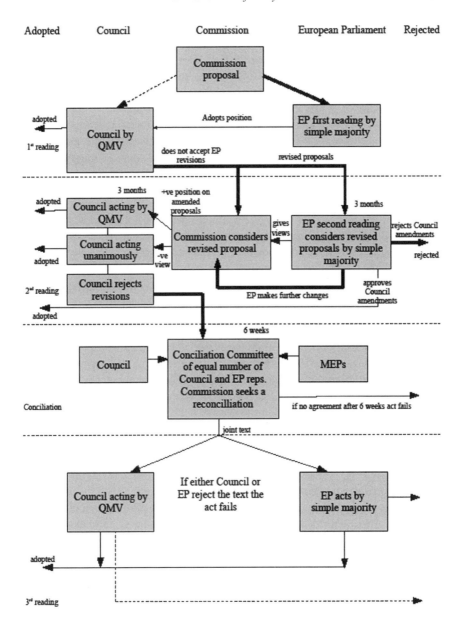

Fig. 2.4   The Ordinary Legislative Procedure

straightforward.[5] The greatest difficulties in EU trade diplomacy have come equally in sectors in which there is EU competence as in sectors of shared competence. Decision-making in areas that were shared competence until the TFEU increased the scope of the CCP, such as services or intellectual property, was no more difficult than in areas of exclusive competence. This suggests that formal competence is but one of a number of factors at work.

In international financial market regulation the question of EU competence is complex. In some areas, such as capital movements there has been EU competence for some time under Art. 63 TFEU. Access to EU financial services markets has been negotiated in the General Agreement on Trade in Services (GATS) and was handled as a shared competence trade issue. The European Court of Justice (ECJ) decision of 1/94 clarified that services were shared competence. When it comes to financial market regulation there is EU competence for the domestic EU market so following the principle of implied competence one would expect the EU to have competence in international negotiations on financial regulation.[6] But as Chapter 4 shows the prudential carve out in EU legislation on financial markets has meant that national governments or regulators have retained control over market supervision and in practice competence for negotiating financial market regulatory policy internationally.

The area of finance is also complicated by the linkage between different policy areas that is necessary for effective financial market regulation. When some policy areas are EU competence (such as capital movements) but others (such as fiscal policy) are not, decision-making is again based on shared competence. In the case of financial markets the issue is further complicated because it touches on policy areas in which the member states are very jealous of their sovereignty. As Chapter 4 shows, the picture is further complicated by the fact that the European Central Bank (ECB) has a small but possibly increasing role in international financial negotiations and played an important role in the EU's response to the financial crisis. The ECB is of course fully independent. The EU response to the financial crisis also involved fiscal policy.

In environmental policy there is EU competence, but a number of qualifications on the use of exclusive competence have in effect meant that international environmental policy has to date remained shared competence. Since the Lisbon Treaty, the Commission has argued that Art. 3 TFEU effectively extends implied competence to all external environmental negotiations, but this is contested by some member state governments. To date the EU has dealt with competence issues in international climate change negotiations pragmatically. There has been agreement on the need for a single voice in negotiations and either the Commission, presidency of the Council or what are called 'negotiation leaders' have conducted negotiations for the EU. As Chapter 5 shows this did not always function

---

[5]   See for example Hodges and Woolcock, 1996 on the EU's difficulties reaching a common negotiating position during the Uruguay Round of the GATT.

[6]   For a discussion of implied competence see Eeckhout (2004) pp 58

smoothly. In a practical sense the EU seems to have moved towards accepting a *de facto* competence for the EU with a single negotiator, but the ability of member states to intervene in their own right, especially at heads of government level, is clearly seen by the Commission as undermining EU credibility. The position is therefore rather different from that of trade. As in the case of financial markets, the issue of competence becomes a real difficulty when environment is linked to other policy areas, such as energy and especially fiscal/tax policy. In development policy competence is again shared and, in contrast to the other policy fields, there appears to have been very limited willingness to move towards greater EU *de facto* competence.[7]

Where there is EU competence for internal policy, but there is shared competence for external negotiations, such as in the case of the environment, the Commission can still be the driver in EU economic diplomacy especially where the EU's position in external negotiations is significantly shaped by domestic policy. This has been the case in climate change. Where competence is shared for internal policy, or where there are important exclusions from EU competence, as in the case of financial markets, the Commission has not emerged as the driver of external policy. In the case of development, both Commission and member states are engaged in development policy.

The picture with regard to formal competence is therefore far from clear cut. In all policy areas, including trade there has been a good deal of shared competence. Even where there is exclusive EU competence in a policy area, linkages with other policy areas coming under member state competence are usually necessary for effective policies or as a result of the nature of the international agenda. This suggests that the key to understanding EU decision-making and negotiation may lie in the practice or *de facto* competence.[8] It has been argued that an important determinate of EU 'actorness' is whether it has cohesion in decision-making and that one measure of such cohesion is whether there are institutional rules of the game (Jupille and Caparoso, 1988). It is to this issue that we now turn.

Decision-Making in Practice (or De Facto *Competence)*

EU decision-making could be expected to be more cohesive and thus the EU more efficient in reaching a common position and effective in negotiation where there are well established *de facto* rules of the game. Competence influences the formal decision-making procedure, that is, whether qualified majority voting of unanimity, but in practice decision-making in many aspects of EU economic diplomacy

---

[7]   It remains to be seen what impact the institutional changes brought by the Treaty of Lisbon and the creation of the European External Action Service, which integrates much of EU development cooperation, will have. See Chapter 6.

[8]   For a similar view based on a comparison of the EU's role in the International Criminal Court and the climate change convention see Groenleer and Van Schaik (2007), p. 992

is by consensus even when the formal requirement is for a qualified majority decision. Clearly when qualified majority voting is a legal possibility, member state governments will be under more pressure to seek an agreement in order to avoid being outvoted. Shadow voting may also take place.[9] But if consensus is the practice it suggests there is a need to consider *de facto* rules and the expectations of the member states, Commission and other actors about how decisions are taken. In theoretical terms this would point towards regime theoretical considerations (repeated negotiations and the shadow of the future acting as a constraint on member states using blocking or delaying tactics). Alternatively constructivist or socialisation approaches could be used to explain the cohesion within the various decision-making bodies (Checkel 2005; see also Elsig, 2008, on the effects of enlargement).[10]

In the field of trade, decision-making procedures have evolved over half a century. In the Trade Policy Committee the established practice is that there is a commitment to find a common position that can be accepted by all.[11] There is also a trend towards a greater 'brusselisation' of the process, with more decisions and more institutional capacity shifting from the member state level to Brussels (Woolcock, 2010). This is of course not the same as decisions shifting into the Commission. It is also worth noting that in trade the member states have always had equal representation within the GATT and the WTO. The only hierarchical representation has come when trade has been discussed in the G7 or G8 processes, but such summits have never been serious negotiating forums for trade.

In the case of financial market regulation the EU institutional structures are not so well established. The Eurogroup is still of relatively recent establishment and only covers those member states within the Euro. Whilst decision-making on internal EU financial market legislation follows established practice, the voluntary cooperation between national regulatory bodies that is supposed to inform this is not well established and all the EU decision-making procedures went through a reform in the 2000s with the Lamfalussy process. By the time the financial crisis hit these reforms were still being implemented. The crisis precipitated a redoubling of efforts to strengthen the EU level regulatory and supervisory framework, but this will, if anything, come in time for the next crisis. As the section on recognition

---

[9] Shadow voting is when there is no formal vote but the sense of the meeting through discourse suggests that there is or is not the requisite support for a qualified majority or, more simply, unanimity.

[10] There is no definitive theory that explains the mechanics of socialisation in EU decision-making, but there is a reasonable amount of evidence that it exists. For our purposes the issue is how important well established decision-making procedures are rather than what form socialisation takes and what conditions make socialisation more likely. The premise here is that continuity in decision-making structures will tend to socialise the participants whether through role playing or normative suasion (Checkel, 2005).

[11] This is similar to the use of cohesion by Groenleer and Van Schaik (2007) who discuss the difference between rational-choice institutionalism and sociological institutionalism in assessing EU actorness.

above pointed out, there is a hierarchy among the member states when it comes to representation in international financial institutions, with some having full membership and others not. Policy cohesion is also difficult because negotiations on financial market regulation take place in numerous forums with EU decision-making practice varying from forum to forum.

Procedures in international climate change negotiations have been established for some time, but not as long as in the case of trade. There also appears to have been a progressive strengthening of the EU dimension over time. Choices of who negotiates for the EU have been based on pragmatism and the expertise of the negotiators. Detailed negotiating positions are often shaped by experts from specialist Council working groups and it is not uncommon for lead negotiators to be nominated from such working groups based on their expertise rather than their nationality or institutional (Commission or Council) origins. Member state membership of international environmental organisations is not hierarchical.

EU decision-making in development policy has been anything but established, with repeated reorganisations even within the Commission. The TFEU and the establishment of the European External Action Service, which includes development policy, are but the latest cases of reorganisation.

The Autonomy of the Negotiator

EU economic diplomacy involves negotiation in order to seek international agreement in line with the EU's policy and negotiating aims. As the principal-agent literature suggests the degree of autonomy of the EU negotiator will therefore also be a factor (Jupille and Caparoso, 1998; Kerremans, 2005. The expectation would be that more autonomy means greater flexibility and thus a greater capability to conclude agreements. Limited autonomy means tight control by the member states (or sector interests) and the prospect that the EU's ability to conclude agreements will be undermined. Negotiation theory argues that tight constraints on the agent of the EU would however strengthen the EU's negotiating position.[12]

Negotiations in economic diplomacy are almost always mixed value-creation and value-claiming. Value-creation is where negotiators seek compromises in order to reach an agreement with mutual gains. Value-claiming is where one partly seeks only to get concessions or claim value from the other. Only in very rare cases do countries pursue pure value-claiming strategies. So negotiators are nearly always in the business of trading concessions. This requires of course some flexibility to accept an outcome that is less than the optimal for one sector interest or group even if the overall benefits for the EU are greater (Odell, 2000). In the case of the EU, negotiations cannot practically be carried out by all 27 member states, so agents are designated by the Council to negotiate. Flexibility to enable value-

---

[12]   For example, EU negotiators can argue that they are unable to make any concessions because of opposition from the Council or European Parliament and thus bring pressure on a negotiating partner that stands to gain from an agreement.

creation through bargaining of concessions in negotiations therefore concerns the relationship between whoever is negotiating for the EU and the member state governments or other principals.

The principal-agent relationship in EU economic diplomacy differs from policy area to policy area. This is not unusual and is the case for most state actors. For example, decision-making and negotiation in financial policy tends to be carried out by a fairly small policy elite, with ministries of finance and central banks retaining a fairly large measure of autonomy. Over the years, trade policy has become more open, in the sense that more stakeholders participate in the process. International environmental policy has always been more open to inputs from a range of non-governmental organisations with environmental lobbies leading the way. In the case of the EU the issue of competence again plays a role. Three general forms of principal-agent relationship in EU economic diplomacy have been identified; full delegation; supervised delegation; and coordination (Pisani-Ferry, 2005). Again this typology is only a general guide and the relationship between negotiator and member states or other principals such as the European Parliament is often more complex.

Full delegation of powers is where the negotiator has full discretion and authority to negotiate and take decisions. This is only really the case in exceptional circumstances in EU economic diplomacy. The ECB has such full delegation of negotiating authority when it engages in EU monetary policy for the Euro and thus in influencing EU policy such as in Euro exchange rate policy. The only other case of full delegation, in this case to the Commission, can be found in the field of competition policy where the Commission has full autonomy in the enforcement of competition policy, whether in the form of the external reach of EU competition laws via the so-called effects doctrine or in the form of applying bilateral agreements.[13]

Supervised delegation is the norm for most EU economic diplomacy. In this the agent is delegated with the task of conducting negotiations, but under supervision by the member states. The agent may be the Commission, the presidency or any other agent delegated to negotiate. Art. 218 (TFEU) provides a general procedure covering EU negotiation of international agreements. This grants the Council powers to nominate the negotiator or the head of the Union's negotiating team, within the parameters set by the treaties. In the case of trade and investment, EU economic diplomacy functions by means of supervised delegation to the Commission. For international environmental negotiations it has been mostly delegation to the Commission or a presidency-led troika consisting of the current and incoming presidencies of the Council and the European Commission in the case of climate change. In the case of financial market regulation, there is very little delegation and member states tend to conduct negotiations in the various

---

[13]   The Commission cannot however, conclude bilateral cooperation agreements in competition policy. In 1991 the Commission concluded such an agreement with the US Department of Justice, but this was successfully challenged by the some member states as exceeding Commission powers (Damro, 2006).

international bodies that determine international standards for financial markets and rely on coordination to support any common EU position.

Continuity

In policy areas of shared competence, such as external environmental policy the EU lead negotiator has changed with the rotating presidencies. Although the Commission is present in the troika, and some continuity can be achieved through the addition of the incoming presidency, this turnover of negotiators has made for inconsistencies in the approach to negotiations. Some member states have provided a strong lead, while others have tended to stick to speaking notes, usually drafted by the Council Secretariat or Commission. Both can have implications for the effectiveness of negotiations. When strong member states lead it is difficult to retain consistency because of the differences in priorities and negotiating styles. Negotiation also requires the building of trust between negotiators and this is hard to achieve when the EU rotates its chief negotiator. When weaker member states have the presidency and stick to agreed texts, flexibility is lost. Consistency is easier to achieve where the Commission adopts a strategic view of negotiations, provides the negotiator and has the benefit of a strong institutional memory.

A Predilection for Negotiation

Somewhat more speculatively it might be argued that the EU has a predilection for the use of value creation negotiating strategies, that is, seeking compromise positions that result in both parties benefiting to some degree. The EU is seldom if ever ready to walk away from a negotiation or to use purely value-claiming strategies. Perhaps the only case in which the EU has maintained tough stances and been willing to see negotiations fail has been in trade negotiations. Whilst value-creation strategies generally favour cooperation and compromise, they are not always pursued by the EU's negotiating partners. Negotiators with a clear mandate including clear red lines (zones of an acceptable agreement) can seek to maximise outcomes using value creating strategies, but if a minimum level of progress is not made, they will have to walk away. With a range of views within the Council, there are always likely to be member states that are not ready to break off negotiations. A second factor is that in internal negotiations the EU functions by member states being committed to continue negotiating until agreement is reached. This culture may well carry over into international negotiations. Third, continuous control of EU negotiators rather than clearly defining negotiating limits and then leaving the agent some slack to negotiate, means negotiators will always have to refer back to the Council rather than walk away.

Coherence

It is often argued that the EU needs to have more coherent external policies if it is to have an influence in international affairs. Coherence can take a number of forms. There is vertical coherence between EU policies and those of the member states and horizontal coherence between policies at the EU level (Carbonne, 2008). Vertical coherence has of course much to do with the *acquis* and competence, and has been discussed above. All countries face the challenge of horizontal coherence and complete coherence is probably impossible to achieve. Coherence or the lack of it can, however, affect EU economic diplomacy in different ways. First, clear cases of incoherence would undermine the credibility and effectiveness of EU policy. For example, promoting development aims, while continuing to restrict agricultural imports from developing countries could be said to be incoherent. The case of EU fisheries policy, in particular buying fishing rights off certain least developed countries that deprive artisanal fisheries of their catches, while voicing support for the promotion of food security and sustainable development in the countries, has also been criticised as a clear case of incoherence (Bretherton and Volger, 2008). Second, efforts to ensure coherence can complicate policy-making, requiring extensive inter-service consultation within the Commission or the External Action Service and within the various member state administrations. Such complications can then increase the friction or inertia of EU policy-making, so that the EU becomes even more ponderous in negotiations than it is already.

Much of the debate about coherence has centred on EU Common Foreign and Security Policy (CFSP). But there has also been a growing debate in other areas and in particular in development policy, where there have been considerable efforts made to promote Policy Coordination for Development (PCD) since the Maastricht treaty. See Chapter 6 for a case study of PCD. The issue of coherence is likely to assume a more central role following the ratification of the Treaty of Lisbon, which places most EU economic diplomacy (trade, environment and development) together with EU foreign policy.

Conclusions on the Factors Shaping the Role of the EU

In this chapter it is not possible to cover in detail all the factors that shape EU economic diplomacy in specific negotiations. These will in any case vary from case to case as different member state and sector interests impinge on decision-making and negotiation. The aim is to provide an overview of how factors vary across some of the main policy areas covered by EU economic diplomacy and how they might be expected to shape the EU's role in economic diplomacy. Figure 2.5 summarises these.

Issues Relating to the Negotiation Process

All of the factors discussed above will have some impact on EU decision-making and negotiation. In order to better assess their relative importance and how each might affect the effectiveness of EU economic diplomacy it is helpful to break down the negotiating process into a number of phases. This makes it easier to see which factors have been important and when. The outcomes of negotiation and

	Trade	Finance	Development	Environment/ Climate change
External drivers	Fairly significant; steady pressure over long periods	Intermittent with crisis	Relatively low importance except in near neighbourhood	Steady increase in pressure due to global externalities
Economic power	Significant; largest single market, but in relative decline	Significant; third of global capital market	High; provides 55% of official dev. assistance and largest market access for developing country exports	Market, potential funder, but smaller emitter than US or China
Recognition	High and long-standing	Limited as Member States have major role	Mixed; Member States provide more funds, but EC determines market access	High, established in last couple of decades
Normative power	Agreed framework norms, but only partially distinctive specific norms	Limited, no consensus on framework norms, tended to follow int. norms	Limited, only general norm of regional integration is distinctive	Significant, strong EU policy based on a consensus on framework norms
Decision-making regime	Well established procedures, tried and tested	Relatively weak procedures until very recently	Weak due to repeated changes in decision-making	Established over last 15 years
Coherence	Trade relatively autonomous of other policy areas	Major issues of coherence within finance	Coherence central to effective policy but elusive	Some autonomy but links to fiscal policy, energy and potentially trade

Fig. 2.5   Factors Shaping EU Economic Diplomacy in Core Policy Areas

thus the effectiveness of EU economic diplomacy can be assessed by considering the following stages in any negotiation.

Preparation is the first and often vital stage in any negotiation. A party to any economic negotiation should ideally be in a position to determine the national, or EU interest on the basis of a cost–benefit analysis, for a range of potential outcomes. Well-prepared trade negotiators will have the benefit of research that provides indications of the potential gains and losses from a range of potential policy outcomes. Equally, a well-prepared negotiation will be one that makes extensive soundings with sector interests in order to determine the domestic preferences, as well as ideally gather intelligence on the preferences of key negotiating partners. In the case of the EU preparation clearly includes the development of a common EU position, so that if the EU is able to establish a common position, or negotiating mandate in advance of any negotiation, this would be an indication that the EU is effective. Complete knowledge of the costs and benefits of various potential outcomes is impossible and all negotiators operate under a degree of bounded rationality, the better prepared a party is however, the more likely they are to be able to defend their interests. It is generally assumed that the more informed the parties are the more able they are to engage in mutually beneficial 'value-creating' negotiating strategies. A lack of information and high levels of uncertainty about gains or losses will tend to result in negotiators adopting defensive strategies (Odell, 2000).[14]

Another early stage in a typical negotiation is *framing*, or identifying the problem to be resolved. This can have a profound effect on any negotiation. A case in point is climate change. If the debate about climate change is framed as one about saving the planet from global warming and its consequences, the nature of the negotiation will be very different to one framed as sharing the burden of the long-term costs of reduced carbon emissions. Framing therefore implies a proactive forward looking approach. If the EU is capable of promoting a common approach to framing this would be a sign of effectiveness and requires rather different capabilities from those required to respond to an external driver urging the EU to act.

Agenda setting is more concerned with the detail than framing. For example, getting targets for carbon reductions included in climate change negotiations is about agenda setting. Agenda setting will determine whether negotiations are comprehensive and cover a wide range of issues or more limited. The addition and subtraction of issues in any negotiation will have an impact on the outcome of bargaining. Here the measure of effectiveness of EU economic diplomacy will be whether the EU is successful in getting its preferred issues onto the agenda. In so far as the EU has explicit aims in agenda setting these can then be measured against outcome. Normally the general negotiating aims of the EU are known or can be derived from EU policies even if detailed negotiating positions are not, so assessing effectiveness will involve a comparison of the EU mandate with the agenda as it emerges.

The choice of a *negotiating forum* can have an important bearing on the nature of negotiations and the likelihood of a successful outcome. EU effectiveness can therefore be assessed in terms of whether the EU is able to get its forum of choice. An awareness of the different forums within which negotiations can take place will also be necessary for this. For example, if the EU is unsuccessful in promoting a comprehensive trade agenda in the multilateral setting of the WTO, it may opt for bilateral negotiations in a form of forum shopping or strategic use of different forums. If we measure the EU effectiveness in shaping the trade agenda only with reference to the multilateral negotiations of the WTO, we neglect the fact that the EU may be successful in pushing its comprehensive agenda in other forums. On the other hand, if the multilateral level was the EU forum of choice, resorting to the bilateral level could be seen as an indication that EU economic diplomacy has been ineffective.

---

[14]   In reality of course the status quo can result in increased costs, but negotiators tend to be risk averse.

When it comes to the *negotiations proper,* it will be necessary to try and establish what the specific EU negotiating aims are and to consider the degree to which these have been achieved. Clearly any assessment must recognise that most economic diplomacy takes the form of mixed negotiating strategies that include both value-creating and value-claiming strategies (Bayne and Woolcock, 2007). Only when the EU adopts a clear value-claiming strategy – in other words when its negotiating objectives require concessions by other parties while not accepting any concessions – would it be possible to make a simple comparison between the EU's initial position and the outcome. If the EU is seeking 'x' in concessions from the other party and gets 'x' then one can say the outcome matches the EU aims. But because economic diplomacy in general and EU economic diplomacy in particular almost always involves a mixture of value-creation and value-claiming strategies, there is inevitably a degree of compromise on both sides in order to achieve joint gains. Rationalist models of negotiation offer a number of means of assessing outcomes. For example, if the EU is willing to trade concessions in agricultural market access and levels of agricultural EU subsidy against tariff liberalisation in manufactures by China and Brazil in trade negotiations, there is a range of potential final outcomes, some of which will be closer to the EU's preference and some closer to that of China and Brazil. So assessing outcomes can be done by judgements about where the final outcome lies. It is important to note that effectiveness here could be measured in terms of results compared to negotiating aims or alternatively some measure of economic benefit. In assessing the effectiveness of EU economic diplomacy one must however, recognise that the EU negotiating aims may be sub-optimal in economic terms.

As noted above there are certain structural features of the EU approach to decision-making that result in a predilection towards continued negotiation and a bias towards value-creation rather than value-claiming. The practice of seeking a consensus combined with divergent views on how to respond to developments during negotiations, means the EU may find it difficult to agree on what is acceptable as an outcome for the 27 member states. This is indeed, one of the reasons for the long discussions in the Council meeting in location during negotiations. To put it another way, it is just as difficult to reach consensus on breaking off a negotiation as reaching a consensus on the final deal even if the likely outcome appears to be outside the original EU 'win-set' (Putnam, 1988). The likelihood of a small number of member states wishing to continue negotiating rather than to have the EU walk away from negotiations is fairly high. An additional factor is that various interests may wish the EU to show leadership. The Commission and environmental interests have sought to retain EU leadership in climate change. The Commission has also effectively promoted EU leadership in trade and in financial markets and the Commission with support from some member states would also like to see the EU fulfil a leadership role in the post financial crisis re-regulation of markets. In order to lead there have to be ongoing negotiations so the EU is reluctant to see negotiations break down.

An assessment of the outcome of a negotiation should not stop with the agreement, but should extend to *implementation*. An agreement can be negotiated and still not serve a party's interests because it is not implemented or not effectively enforced. Results in terms of achieving economic aims also generally depend on what happens after an agreement is reached. For example, in addressing non-tariff barriers to market access, trade agreements will typically establish a joint committee to monitor progress with implementation. It will therefore be important to consider how effective the EU is in establishing procedural means of following through on any agreement. This can be done through formal dispute settlement provisions as well as through consultation in joint committees or councils established for this purpose. The assessment of the effectiveness of EU economic diplomacy should also include the EU's performance in its own implementation and enforcement. If the EU negotiates an agreement, but cannot get it adopted by the member states, obtain the consent of the European Parliament or get the provisions implemented by the member states, this is clearly not an effective policy. Non-implementation will also have an adverse effect on the EU's credibility in negotiations and as an actor.

A negotiation analysis approach to assessing the effectiveness of EU economic diplomacy cannot remove all the difficulties associated with measuring effectiveness. In each of the above categories there will be problems measuring outcomes. But a structured breakdown of these key phases in any negotiation will provide a better guide than broad brush assessments. It also enables a better assessment of the EU's relative strengths. For example, it may be that EU normative power has an impact on framing and agenda setting in any negotiation, but not in the negotiating phase. The EU may find it hard to respond to rapid changes during a negotiation phase, but may be more effective in following through on agreements to ensure they are effectively implemented.

Some Hypotheses to Be Considered

Some Generally Held Views

From the literature and the general debate on EU policy-making, it is possible to distil a number of underlying assumptions or expectations about EU economic diplomacy. The first is that the EU effectiveness depends on competence. It is often argued for example, that the EU is only effective and recognised as an actor if it has exclusive competence. This view is similar to the one that the EU needs to become an actor in its own right if it is to have any impact in international relations.

A second generally held view is that the EU is more of a normative power than an instrumental power. The relative weakness of the EU as an instrumental power that can convert economic or market power into results in negotiations is then explained by the third general view that the EU is hampered by a lack of flexibility during negotiations due to the need for the EU to reach agreement internally before it can respond to developments during negotiations. To what extent are these assumptions valid? This section argues that while they touch on important aspects of EU economic diplomacy, these general views over simplify.

Some Alternative Hypotheses

1. The EU does have considerable economic/market power, but this is in relative decline. There are also clear limits to the EU's ability and willingness to use market leverage in negotiations. This suggests the EU cannot rely on market power, but must use other means to pursue its ends that are likely to place greater demands on economic diplomacy/negotiation (e.g., optimisation of existing market power through forum shopping, coalition building, and use of persuasion).

EU economic diplomacy is affected by the EU's relative economic or market power. The nature of many economic negotiations is such that reciprocity plays a role in one form or another. The discussion above suggests and the case studies in Chapters 3 to 6 confirm that the EU does indeed have significant economic/market power, but the EU's overall position may be in relative decline due to the growth of emerging markets. There remains some scope to compensate for this through the addition of new competences such as foreign direct investment as a result of the Lisbon Treaty or greater integration of financial markets. Shifts in relative market growth will also determine the EU's position. More dynamic internal economic growth would enhance the EU's position. Perhaps as important however, is the EU's ability and willingness to use its market power. Progressive liberalisation of goods and services markets combined with binding obligations under various agreements means the EU is limited in its ability to use market leverage. EU leadership in promoting rules on behind the border issues and the environment has also resulted in unilateral policies that promote transparency and regulatory 'best practice' in the EU that further reduce the ability of the EU to use market leverage. A coalition of member states willing to block the use of aggressive use of market leverage is also quite likely, especially when member states are targeted by the lobbying of the EU's negotiating partners.

2. Formal EU competence is not essential for the EU to be recognised as a negotiating partner. Effective economic diplomacy depends on a well established, tried and tested regime of decision-making (or de facto EU competence) more than any other institutional factor. Coordination of member states that engage in economic diplomacy may be an option, but only when member states have equal status in international negotiations.

In terms of recognition the cases discussed in this volume suggest that formal EU competence is not essential in order for the EU to be recognised as a negotiating partner in preference to the member states. Competence is clearly one factor, but evidence from trade shows that the EU can achieve recognition even when there is shared competence. When it comes to the institutional arrangements the key factor is not competence, the type of principal-agent relationship or formal voting requirements, but how well established decision-making and negotiating procedures are. But hierarchical representation of member states in international organisations or negotiations do appear to correlate to poor internal policy cohesion.

3. The EU is more likely to develop common policies and to negotiate when the pressure on it to act is enduring and of relatively low intensity. Intermittent but intensive pressure is likely to result in ad hoc coordination between the member states.

External challenges on the EU to respond to third country initiatives or systemic threats such as a financial crisis or global warming are significant factors in EU economic diplomacy. Where the pressure on the EU to negotiate is consistent, but not intense there is a greater likelihood that decision-making regimes will develop. Where the external drivers are intermittent but intense, decision-making regimes in which the member states have confidence are not established so that individual member states respond.

4. The EU has normative power when there is a consensus on framework norms. This also facilitates a proactive economic diplomacy and the development of more specific norms or standards for market regulation. But normative power is unlikely to be enough to shape outcomes. Distinctive norms are not essential for the EU to exercise normative power, so an 'identity' is not therefore necessary for the EU to have an impact in economic diplomacy.

The EU has normative power, but it is important to differentiate between general, framework and specific norms if one is to assess their impact. It is difficult to show any impact of the EU on general norms, although these may have an impact in the longer term.

5. Policy coherence is likely to be a double edged sword. On the one hand, incoherence undermines EU credibility and thus the effectiveness of EU economic diplomacy. On the other hand, the need for policy coherence means more time consuming inter-service and inter-institutional debate within the EU that is likely to undermine effectiveness.

It is not possible to generalise about member state and sector interests as these vary from policy area to policy area and case to case. However, where member states hold jealously to national sovereignty in specific policy areas such as fiscal and foreign policy, this can limit the effectiveness of EU economic diplomacy in other policies because of the importance of horizontal coherence for effectiveness. Where policy coherence is decisive for effective EU economic diplomacy such checks pose barriers to pragmatic decision-making which is ultimately necessary for the effectiveness of EU economic diplomacy.

Chapter 3
EU External Trade and Investment Policy-Making

Introduction

External EU trade policy is an area in which the EU has played a significant role for some time and therefore provides a template against which to measure other policy areas. This is true for any analysis of EU economic diplomacy as well as in a formal sense in that Art. 218 (TFEU), which sets out general procedures for EU participation in international agreements, is modelled on the treaty provisions and practice developed in the field of trade.

Although Common Commercial Policy (CCP), as it is formally referred to in the treaty, was established as exclusive EEC competence in the treaty of Rome, the EEC and subsequently the EC and EU did not acquire a leading role in international trade policy-making and did not become a key actor overnight. With the completion of the customs union the EEC gained market power that it was able to use to some effect in getting the US to reduce tariff protection in the 1960s. But in tariffs the EEC was obliged to adopt a common policy in the shape of a common external tariff if it was to establish a customs union. In most other, non-tariff areas of trade policy there was no common EEC policy. In these areas it took years if not decades for the EU to develop an equally important role. This chapter therefore first summarises how EU policy has evolved over time as background for the rest of the chapter. It argues that the positions of the EEC, EC and then EU shifted from being largely inward-looking and defensive in the early years to the adoption of a more outward-looking support for a rules-based multilateral system in the 1980s and 1990s. EU external trade policy, like other aspects of EU economic diplomacy, now appears to have reached a decisive juncture. The multilateral approach adopted by the EU during the 1990s and 2000s is undergoing something of a re-evaluation in the light of the EU's limited success in promoting a comprehensive agenda in the World Trade Organisation (WTO). The EU is also promoting strategic relations with a number of major trading partners and thus spreading the focus of its trade policy and trade relations that had for many years been focused on the US.

Trade policy is an area in which the EU has long been seen as important, but the internal decision-making processes and how the EU goes about negotiating international trade agreements can still be difficult to understand for those not directly involved. The changes that the Lisbon Treaty promise for EU decision-making in trade have even caused some long-standing practitioners to wonder how things will work in the future. The second section of this chapter therefore provides a practical description of how the 27 member states of the EU go about reaching common positions on trade and includes a discussion of the likely effects of the changes the Lisbon Treaty will bring.

The chapter then applies the analytical framework developed in chapter two to the case of external trade in order to assess the relative importance of the different factors in shaping the EU's role. As such it provides a first test of the framework in this core area of EU economic diplomacy. The analytical framework in Chapter 2 has set out the key factors, but in any given case the circumstances, member state and sector interests and the strength and positions of its main negotiating partners will vary. An assessment of the effectiveness of EU trade diplomacy also requires consideration of how the EU positions and those of its main trading partners have changed over time. In order to facilitate such an assessment the chapter therefore includes a specific case study of some issues in the Doha Development Agenda (DDA). Space limits the scope for a full assessment of the EU's effectiveness in such an extensive negotiation as the DDA, so the discussion here is better seen as an illustration of how an assessment of effectiveness could be undertaken.

Before proceeding, a brief word on definitions is needed. Clearly the chapter is concerned with EU external trade policy, so does not cover factors shaping trade and investment within the EU, which is determined by the integration process in the shape of the Single European Market (SEM) programme. As will be shown below, the advancement of internal integration and thus the *acquis communautaire*, will have important implications for external trade policies. The term *trade policy* is used to describe all those policies that form the substance of international trade negotiations. It therefore reaches well beyond the narrow definition of trade that is sometimes used in the sense of market access or measures at the border. For at least 30 years international trade negotiations have addressed behind-the-border or regulatory issues. Liberalisation from the 1980s onwards has further reduced the role of border measures and increased the relative importance of regulatory issues. The definition of trade used here includes investment. With the Lisbon Treaty, foreign direct investment (FDI) is now included in the CCP. The definition of trade used here also includes all those domestic regulatory issues that affect trade in goods and services that are included in negotiations, such as environmental and food safety regulation, state support for agriculture, industry or the financial sector as well as – to a lesser degree – labour standards.

The Evolution of EU External Trade Policy

As noted in Chapter 1, the EEC's external role evolved within the framework of a US-led and then OECD Club–led approach to economic diplomacy. Only in recent years, with the emergence of China and other emerging markets, has this approach been seriously challenged. The other major trend in trade policy has been a progressive move towards a more comprehensive agenda. Initially trade policy under the General Agreement on Tariffs and Trade (GATT) was focused on tariffs. In the 1970s the agenda was extended to include non-border measures and in the 1980s to services, investment and intellectual property. In each instance the extension of the international trade agenda was at the initiative of the USA. As the EC has had to respond to these initiatives, its trade policy was to a significant degree shaped by responses to US initiatives.

Priority to Building Europe

Initially the common external tariff (CET) of the EEC, an inevitable by-product of the customs union, shaped the *acquis*. As the EEC exports a very wide range of products, it tended to have a flatter tariff profile. This was confirmed with the CET that harmonised tariffs and also tended to flatten tariff peaks. In comparison the US approach to tariff reductions after the 1934 Reciprocal Trade Agreements Act had been to negotiate sector by sector commitments. This left more tariff peaks, even if average tariffs were relatively low. When the EU and US engaged in tariff negotiations, the EU therefore favoured linear reductions that reduced all tariffs or ideally a formula based approach that reduced tariff peaks more. In other words the EU *acquis* in the shape of the CET and Customs Union shaped EU external tariff policy. In the early years, the EEC's trade policy was also subservient to integration needs, so that, for example, the EU defended the Common Agricultural Policy (CAP) when this was challenged by US initiatives in the Kennedy Round of the GATT. But the creation of a customs union gave the EEC real market power, which it used effectively to bring down US tariffs, using linear reductions, during the Kennedy Round of negotiations between 1963 and 1968 (Duer, 2008).

Defensive Policies in the 1970s

During the 1970s, the US again initiated a new round of multilateral trade negotiations in the shape of the Tokyo Round 1973–1979. Although the customs union was complete by the late 1960s, there was no genuine common/single market. EU member state governments intervened to promote national champions. France still had fairly comprehensive indicative planning, Britain had an interventionist industrial policy and Italy and Belgium intervened selectively to promote national industries. Germany had a social market economy and had no explicit industrial policy, but various measures provided support for domestic producers. There was therefore no agreement on framework norms in terms of the balance between state intervention and markets. Even though a majority of member states favoured some form of intervention, there could be no agreement on an EEC industrial policy because national champions were competing with each other and there was no support for centralised intervention at an EEC level. The one area of common policy remained the CAP.

During the Tokyo Round of the GATT, European Community (EC) trade policy was shaped by a need to defend the 'policy space' for member states to pursue such national champion strategies and the status quo in the CAP. The EC was effective in these defensive aims. US efforts to subject agriculture to GATT disciplines were again blocked, as were US efforts to establish effective multilateral disciplines for national subsidies, national preferences in government procurement and technical regulations that favoured national champions.[1] Member state views differed naturally, but the majority favoured such a defensive stance. In terms of how this was done the member state governments were pragmatic in the sense that they allowed the Commission to negotiate, thus ensuring a single voice, on issues that were both EC and member state competence.

The Shift to More Rules-based Multilateralism in the 1980s

The international trade policy agenda in the 1980s was again shaped by US demands on the EC to negotiate in a comprehensive round of negotiations that included services (US financial service sector pressure), protection of intellectual property rights (pressure from the US pharmaceutical sector) and investment (pressure from the US information technology sector among others). India also sought to shape the agenda by resisting these new issues and stressing liberalisation of textiles and clothing. The EC's initial response was defensive because the economies of the member states were in recession in the early 1980s, but by the mid-1980s there was more support from member states for a positive response to the US initiative (Hodges and Woolcock, 1996). This then necessitated a common approach and as before the member states agreed that the Commission would be the sole negotiator on all topics even if the new issues proposed by the US were either member state or shared competence.

During the Uruguay Round of the GATT (1986–1994), domestic developments within the EC helped bring about a major change in its external trade policy. European industry came to the view that it could no longer compete internationally on the basis of national markets and called for the end of the fragmentation of the European market. This market-led development combined with a general shift in policy towards more support for a liberal paradigm for trade and industry within the EC. A consensus emerged that favoured market liberalisation within an agreed regulatory framework. This principle found expression in the New Approach to market integration based on mutual recognition and thus competition among rules, but with harmonisation of the essential minimum requirements. Underlying the idea of the New Approach was thus a consensus that there should be more competition, but within a broad framework of norms that support essential social, safety and environmental objectives. The result was the Single European Market (SEM) programme, which had the effect of liberalising trade and investment, but also resulted in a considerable strengthening of the *acquis communautaire*. The

---

[1]   Qualified most favoured nation codes were negotiated in the Tokyo Round covering technical barriers to trade, government procurement and subsidies and countervailing duties, but these were weak agreements that had limited impact on the scope for national industrial policies.

deepening of the EC market combined with agreed domestic policies on issues ranging from telecommunications liberalisation, through technical regulations for goods to agreed rules on subsidies both strengthened the EU's market power and the domestic basis for common external positions.

The continuation of *de jure* member state trade protection under Art. 115 EEC (which provided for national quotas on goods entering the EC) and *de facto* protection in the form of 'voluntary' export restraints (VERs) on Japanese and other Asian Newly Industrialising Country (NIC) exports to specific member states, became impossible with the removal of internal border controls in the SEM. When goods could pass freely between member states, there was no way to police national quotas and there was no agreement to replace national quotas with EC quotas (Hanson, 1998). The only VER negotiated at an EC level was for Japanese car exports and this was phased out in 1991. This trade liberalisation was accompanied by a shift, also due to the SEM, away from the use of member state discretionary power to intervene to support national champions that distorted competition within the EC, to a rules-based European level regime for all the non-tariff barriers. This shift in the internal policy then contributed significantly to a shift in the EC's external position and to it becoming a supporter of a multilateral liberal rules-based approach.[2] This in turn enabled the EC to play a more active role in trade so that the outcome of the Uruguay Round negotiations was largely shaped by a duopoly of the US and EC within the wider OECD club.

Member state positions had played a more obvious role in shaping EC trade policy in the 1970s and 1980s than during – and especially since – the Uruguay Round negotiations. As the *acquis* became stronger, member states' positions counted less, as the EC position was based more and more on the agreed EC policy. But a well established *acquis*, such as in agriculture, also made policy reform difficult because member states with vested interests in retaining the status quo could block reform thanks to the use of consensus in decision-making (Meunier, 2000). The resistance to reform in agriculture during the 1970s and 1980s was possible because France could count on the support of Germany and other smaller member states, such as Ireland. The beginning of reform in the CAP therefore had to wait until Germany shifted to a more liberal position, which only happened after German unification and after Ireland had been bought off with promises that income support in the form of the so called 'blue box' subsidies would ensure Irish farmers would not be worse off as a result of the McSharry reforms of 1992. The McSharry reforms began the process of decoupling support from price support and thus export subsidies and trade. At a critical stage in the Uruguay Round negotiations in 1989 and 1990, the Federal Republic of Germany had not wished to undermine France by shifting policy because it needed French support for German unification (Hodges and Woolcock, 1996).

---

[2]   Inevitably there were other factors such as a desire to contain the unilateralist tendencies in US trade policy by stronger multilateral rules.

The ideological position of the member states on trade has also shaped the evolution of EC policy. Whilst simplistic generalisations should be guarded against, some member states have historically been more influenced by liberalism and others by more by mercantilism. Thus Sweden, Denmark, Britain and the Netherlands, joined since the eastern enlargement by the Baltic States and the Czech Republic, tend to adopt a generally liberal approach to trade. France, Italy, Spain, Greece and Poland tend to be more mercantilist in that they will seek both more reciprocity in negotiations and are more ready to use contingent protection such as anti-dumping. Germany tends to assume an important swing position. Although not historically liberal, the social market economy of the Federal Republic anchored liberal ideals more firmly in policy than in many other member states. These general normative positions also tend to affect the member state approaches to negotiations, with liberal member states being more ready to make concessions. For the liberal frame of mind a 'concession' on market access means an economic benefit. In negotiating terms, this tends to mean that liberal-minded member states have a bias in favour of value-creation in negotiation and the more mercantilist member states a bias towards value-claiming. The more mercantilist minded member states will be less ready to make concessions until they are sure that these are matched by the EC's negotiating partners.

Proactive Policies from the Mid-1990s

Thanks in large part to the SEM and agreement on framework norms for trade in goods, by the mid-1990s the EU had assumed a more proactive, offensive position on multilateral trade than at any time since the founding of the EEC.[3] The Commission led in pushing for a new round of trade negotiations from the mid-1990s (Britten, 1996). By the mid-1990s, the EU was developing proposals for a comprehensive multilateral trade agenda. This included topics that were broadly supported by trade policy makers in a range of countries, such as investment and trade facilitation, as well as topics the EU wished to add like competition policy and government procurement (European Commission, 1996). The EU also articulated a policy of encouraging partner countries to form regional agreements from the mid 1990s.[4] In other words, the EU was seeking to assume more of a leading role in trade and to be proactive in framing and shaping the multilateral agenda rather than being dragged rather reluctantly into negotiations by the US. In this it was the Commission that shaped policy. The EU pressed the US to support a new round, which the Clinton Administration did rather reluctantly at the WTO ministerial meeting in 1998. In 1999 the Commission proposed the EU adopt a moratorium on any further negotiations of preferential agreements in order to focus on the new

---

[3]   European Union (EU) is used in place of European Community for the description after 1990.

[4]   See for example the conclusions of the Essen European Council of 1994 in Maur, 2005, p. 1567.

multilateral round. At the time the EU had a good number of outstanding FTA negotiations, so it is important to stress that the moratorium applied only to new FTA negotiations. The launch of what was to be the millennium round in Seattle in 1999 failed, however, due to a lack of agreement on the core agenda among the major WTO members, US reluctance to commit to new liberalisation, a growing determination of developing WTO members to have a say in the negotiations and a general increase in the awareness of trade issues in the political debate that was reflected in opposition from various non-governmental organisations (NGOs) (Bayne, 2000).

In the new multilateral round, the DDA that was ultimately launched in 2001, it was the EU that was the most consistent promoter of a comprehensive round, even if, as will be shown later, it was not always successful.

Decision-Making and Negotiation

Decision-making in external trade policy is broadly in line with the Community Method. In other words, the European Commission has right of initiative. But it varies somewhat between three different forms of trade policy. There is decision-making at the level of international trade negotiations that deal with market access and rules. Second, there is decision-making on so-called autonomous trade policy of the EU, such as unilateral measures opening the EU market to least-developed countries (LDCs) under the General System of Preferences (GSP) scheme. Finally, there is decision-making in the use of trade remedies as in the day-to-day trade decisions on anti-dumping or safeguards to 'protect' EU industries from unfair import competition or deal with unexpected import surges that can injure EU industries.

For international negotiations, the proposals are discussed by the member states at a working group level and then go to the Council for decisions. The Commission then negotiates in cooperation with the member states, and it is the Council that decides whether the agreement negotiated by the Commission is satisfactory. With the Lisbon Treaty, the European Parliament must now also be informed on the same basis as the member states and must then grant its consent to the final agreement. The Ordinary Legislative Procedure (OLP) is used to determine the legislative framework for external trade, so that autonomous measures must now be adopted using the OLP. EU trade policy has been characterised as technocratic in that national and Commission officials do much of the work (Woolcock, 2000). These trade officials are for the most part fairly well insulated from populist and protectionist pressures, although such pressures are fed through the member state governments into discussions at the EU level. The benefits of this technocratic mode of policy-making have been that trade policy has not been highly politicised, and decisions have, for the most part, been based on broad definitions of national and EU interests. There has been limited capture of the policy process outside of the agricultural sector. Another advantage of the technocratic character of EU trade policy is that national officials have had the flexibility to be pragmatic in dealing with issues of competence and have tended to focus on results rather than questions of sovereignty.

The costs of technocratic policy-making are, of course, that decisions have tended to be taken by a fairly small trade policy elite which, though formally accountable through national governments and thus national parliaments, has not in practice been subject to a great deal of scrutiny. Member state parliaments have been either disinclined or unable to follow the detailed deliberations on trade policy issues that would be necessary to provide effective scrutiny. In trade as in much economic diplomacy, the devil is in the detail, and national parliamentary systems have found it difficult to follow this given that the negotiations take place in fora that are twice removed from national politics. There is first the EU level at which common positions are developed, and then the negotiation between the European Commission and third parties either in the WTO or in a regional or bilateral negotiation. The EP has not been able to fill this 'democratic deficit', at least to date, because of its limited powers. The Lisbon Treaty may change this. Other measures have been undertaken to reach out to the NGO community in the shape of the Civil Society Forum run by the European Commission since 2000.

International Trade Negotiations

The Treaty of Lisbon (TFEU) simplified and streamlined the formal structure of EU trade diplomacy and codified much of what was existing practice. With the TFEU virtually all aspects of EU trade policy, including trade in goods and services as well as trade related aspects of intellectual property rights (TRIPs) and now foreign direct investment (FDI), come under exclusive EU competence. Henceforth there will be much less shared competence. The TFEU does not however, mean the end of shared competence altogether, because agreements are still likely to contain elements that are not exclusive EU competence such as non-trade related intellectual property rights or transport issues.

The TFEU introduces a uniform procedure for all international negotiations in Art. 218 TFEU. Before this most recent treaty change, there were different procedures for multilateral trade negotiations in Art. 133 (TEC) and bilateral negotiations of association agreements under Art. 300 (TEC). The association agreements were a very important part of EU trade relations with developing and neighbouring countries. Under the previous system, the formal decision-making provisions under Art. 133 provided for qualified majority voting (QMV), but unanimity for association agreements under Art. 300 (TEC). Exclusive competence for the EU means broadly that the Community method applies. It does not, as many assume, mean competence for the European Commission; EU competence means decision-making involves all three main EU institutions, Commission, Council and European Parliament. As will be shown below however, the Commission clearly has acquired considerable *de facto* competence and shapes the EU negotiating strategy.

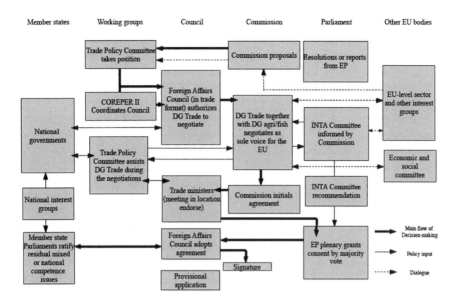

Fig. 3.1   EU Decision-Making in External Trade Policy

Setting the EU Agenda and Objectives

The formal decision-making and negotiation procedures of the EU are set out in Figure 3.1, which shows how the Commission has right of initiative (Art. 207 TFEU). It is thanks to this right of initiative and to the institutional capacity of the Commission in the Directorate General for Trade (DG Trade) and other directorates that the Commission has been able to shape the strategic choices for EU external trade. For example, it was proposals from the Commission that shaped the EU policy on a new comprehensive multilateral trade round in the 1990s, that brought about the *de facto* moratorium on new bilateral free trade agreements in 1999 in order to focus on pressing the EU case for a comprehensive multilateral trade round (Lamy, 2004) and that proposed the shift back towards a more active policy of negotiating free trade agreements in 2006 (European Commission, 2006).

The Commission proposes the EU's negotiating aims after consulting with the different DGs of the Commission.[5] This provides an opportunity to ensure coherence in EU policy and for the various services, such as industry, environment, social, agriculture and development policy, to have a say in the Commission proposals. Broadly speaking, DG Trade has a liberal leaning in trade compared to some other departments that may sponsor particular industries or have differing ideological tendencies or interests. The Commission, through DG

---

[5]   The Commission's right of initiative is not absolute however. The Council may at anytime direct the Commission during a negotiation.

trade, also consults with sector interests at the EU level. There is a clear preference for engaging in discussion with EU-level interest groups and the Commission will tend to discount national private sector lobbies as non-representative of the wider EU interest (Woll, 2007). In proposing the EU position, DG Trade will also draw on past precedents. There is seldom anything new in trade policy, so that the position the EU has held on a particular topic in the past will be the starting point for any new proposal. The large institutional memory of the Commission also helps to minimise the transaction costs of policy development.

The Commission's proposed negotiating mandate or position is considered by the member states. In the first instance this takes place in the Trade Policy Committee (TPC) (formerly known as the 133 Committee after Art. 133 in the treaty that set out the procedures for trade policy-making). The TPC, in its full 'titulaire' format, is made up of the top trade officials from each member state government. In some cases, these will come from the ministry of business (Britain), in some from the ministry of economics (Germany), in some from foreign affairs (Sweden) and in some from the ministries of finance (France), depending on which ministry leads on trade. The full TPC meets once a month on Fridays in Brussels, but meets at the level of deputies each week, also in Brussels. The deputies are more likely to be Brussels based trade officials based in the member state permanent representations who follow EU trade policy. The TPC can also sit in different specialist formats, to cover topics such as services. The TPC, or rather its predecessors in the shape of the 133 Committee and before that the 113 Committee, has facilitated intensive dialogue between the member states and the Commission on trade topics. A socialisation process within the 133 Committee also led to the development of shared norms and values. With successive enlargement and now 27 member states, there is less time and ability for dialogue between the member states and the dynamic of the TPC has changed from a dialogue between the member states to more of a dialogue between the Commission and the member states with more business being done outside of the TPC. [6]

The formal authorisation of the EU's negotiating position is by the Council following a consideration of the issues in the TPC (Art. 207(3) and Art. 218 (2) TFEU). The European Parliament does not authorise negotiations, unlike, for example, the US Congress. The EP would like, however, to have some say in setting the EU objectives, because without it the EP has little prospect of influencing the EU during a negotiation.[7] As there is no EU council of trade ministers, decisions on trade are taken within the Foreign Affairs Council (formerly the General Affairs and External Relations Council (GAERC)). External trade is therefore

---

[6]   On the impact of enlargement on EU trade policy formulation see Elsig, 2009.

[7]   In its report on the Lisbon Treaty, the International Trade Committee of the EP (INTA) argued that it should be entitled to set preconditions for granting its consent to the outcome of any trade negotiation through the renegotiation of the Inter-Institutional Framework Agreement between the Parliament and the Commission. European Parliament 2008/2063(INI)27 May 2008.

distinct from other EU policy areas such as environment or finance where there is a specialist Council of Ministers responsible. The normal practice is for foreign affairs issues to be discussed first, and then for the Foreign Affairs Council to sit in a trade format. This arrangement has functioned because there is seldom much difference between the positions of the member states in the TPC and the Council, although the TPC may of course leave politically sensitive issues to be finalised by ministers. COREPER II the Committee of Permanent Representatives to the EU prepares Council meetings and is the key body for coordinating member state positions across all policy issues. In external trade policy however, the TPC has tended to retain control of the substance. This is due to a desire on the part of the TPC to do so and to the fact that the member state ambassadors or deputies who sit on COREPER are generalists and do not normally seek to duplicate work done by the more specialist, senior trade officials in the TPC.

Negotiating

The Commission then negotiates for the EU (Art. 207 TFEU).[8] In trade, the Commission representative is the sole negotiator. This means DG Trade on all issues except agriculture on which DG Agriculture leads. This separation between agricultural trade and other trade issues is a reflection of the degree to which agriculture has been treated as a special case. Negotiating sessions can be led by Commission officials at Director level or even Heads of Unit level as well as by the Director General or Deputy Directors General of DG Trade with the Commissioner for Trade providing the ministerial level input in bilateral or multilateral meetings. In working groups of the WTO/bilateral negotiations or other technical negotiations, the EU is again represented by the Commission in the form of DG Trade specialists. The TPC 'assists' the Commission during negotiations (Art. 207 (3) TFEU). The TPC is the key interface between the Commission negotiator and the member state trade representatives. Note that it is the specialist trade departments in each member state and not the foreign services that coordinate national inputs, unless the trade department happens to be located in a foreign ministry. The TPC functions by consensus. There are very seldom any votes. If the proposed Commission line does not gain sufficient support, the Commission will withdraw it and come back with something that can gain a consensus. Shadow voting does take place in which the Commission will press ahead with a particular line if it looks like there is a qualified majority of member states in favour. If member states are unhappy with developments, such as if they wish to maintain a more defensive position than that proposed by

---

[8]   This remains the case despite the TFEU, which in Art. 218 provides that the Council decides whether the Commission or the High Representative for Foreign and Security Policy shall negotiate for the EU in any international agreement. But this is without prejudice to Art. 207 (TFEU), which states that the Commission negotiates with the assistance of the Council.

the Commission, they will 'politicise' the issue and push it up to COREPER or ultimately the Council.

In recent years, the Commission appears to have gained more *de facto* competence for external trade policy, meaning that it tends to shape policy and the member states approve or disapprove and seek modifications. In the earlier decades, perhaps up to the 1980s, *de facto* competence was more shared with the member states shaping policy through dialogue in the Art. 113/133.[9] There are a number of reasons for this shift towards more *de facto* Commission competence. First, more and more trade policy is based on agreed EU domestic policies. Where there is a well-established *acquis*, such as on technical regulations, government procurement or services, this provides a common basis for external trade policy. Progressive liberalisation has also meant that there is less to discuss, for example, successive rounds of tariff negotiations have reduced tariffs on industrial goods to a trade weighted average of only about 3.5 per cent. These developments have resulted in some member states committing fewer resources to trade policy formulation. Trade policy has therefore undergone a 'Brusselisation' process with more decisions being taken in Brussels than in national capitals. The Lisbon Treaty, with its increased EU competence and greater role for the European Parliament, in part at the expense of national parliaments, tends to confirm this trend.[10]

In the past, the European Parliament has not played a major role in trade. Under the so called Luns-Westerterp procedure, there was agreement that the Commission should inform the EP in good time for it to consider the outcome of any trade negotiation. The Commissioner for trade has for some time attended meetings in the EP to report on trade policy and negotiations, and during the 1999–2004 period Commissioner Lamy pursued a policy of treating the EP as if it had more power. Until 2005 monitoring of EU external trade was carried out in an EP committee which also covered industry and energy and which could as a result give only limited attention to trade. In the 2005–2010 Parliament, a specialist International Trade Committee (INTA) was established. This was in anticipation of the EP playing a larger role following the adoption of the constitutional treaty. But the committee was not one of the more senior EP committees and did not attract a great deal of interest among Members of the European Parliament (MEPs), who sought places in committees such as the budget or foreign affairs committees. In recent years, and in particular between 2005 and 2010, the Commission has begun to intensify its consultations with the EP now through the INTA and provided INTA with the same information it provided to the TPC, again in anticipation of

---

[9]   Another definition of *de facto* competence for the EU would be the control of information concerning trade negotiations and retention of institutional memory by Commission trade officials rather than by member state officials.

[10]   The role of national parliaments has been reduced because there remains only a residual of shared competence issues in the (current) trade agenda that would require ratification by the national governments. The added powers granted to the European Parliament could then see it assume a more important role in scrutinizing EU trade policy.

the TFEU. The Commission's motives here were to ensure the EP was adequately informed, but also to head off any difficulties with EP assent for agreements. Before the TFEU the EP had powers to give its assent to certain trade agreements. See discussion on the adoption of results below. The TFEU requires the Commission to 'report' to INTA (TFEU Art. 207 (3)), which would appear to give the INTA a lower status than the TPC which is to 'assist' the Commission in negotiations.

It remains to be seen how the enhanced powers for the EP under the TFEU will affect EU trade policy. Clearly the INTA Committee and the Parliament as a whole will have to be taken more seriously by all involved in EU trade policy. This is something the Commission is more comfortable with, since increased powers for the EP are likely to be at the expense of the Council rather than the Commission. With the Commission as negotiator, it will be the Council that will be obliged to share its powers of control or scrutiny with the EP. But there are a number of reasons for believing that change will not be fast or especially dramatic. First, the institutional memory and technical capacity of DG Trade and the member state representations in the TPC far exceeds anything the INTA is likely to be able to develop in the foreseeable future. As trade policy concerns detail, effective scrutiny of the Commission is only possible if its expertise, or *de facto* competence in the sense of knowing the material, can be matched. Second, the INTA Committee at present does not meet as often as the TPC (which meets each week), so the dialogue between the Commission and the TPC will remain more intensive. Clearly informal links may be established between the Commission and the INTA. Third, the member states will resist any diminution of their role, and it is the Council that still retains the power to authorise negotiations and thus set the objectives for EU policy. Unless the EP can get some say over objectives, its ability to hold the Commission to account will be limited. This is not to say that the EP cannot focus on the more political aspects of trade policy and make it consent conditional upon it being satisfied on these.

In external trade negotiations, the Commission is the sole voice (agent) of the EU. Contrary to past practice, member state representatives are rarely present in the room in formal negotiating sessions and do not speak. During negotiations there will normally be regular meetings of the Commission and member state representatives to finalise details of the EU's position and consider how to respond to developments in the previous session before the Commission goes into a negotiating session. The level of member state representation will depend on the importance of the meeting. Thus, at WTO ministerial level meetings, the member state ministers responsible for trade and probably agriculture and possibly some other areas will be present. At other times it will be senior trade officials from the member states, and at more routine technical meetings in Geneva it will be the Geneva based representatives from the member states.

A good deal of work in trade negotiations takes place outside formal negotiating sessions however. The Commission negotiators will meet with their counterparts from third countries informally. In such instances it is difficult to distinguish between information exchange and negotiation with positions being tested informally. At such times there can be tensions between the interests of the member states in retaining control over the Commission's position and the interests of the Commission in exploring possible compromises or trade-offs (linkage) between issues without committing the EU as a whole. With its increased powers under the TFEU, the European Parliament in the form of the INTA Committee is also seeking a greater say. The expectation is that the Commission will report developments to the member states, but the Commission's influence as an actor is enhanced by the fact that it has some control over what information it passes on to the member states. The Commission cannot however, stray very far from the agreed line, because the EU's negotiating partners will also talk to member state representatives and thus inform them of the Commission negotiating tactics and positions. One infamous case of the Commission straying too far from the agreed line as understood by some member state ministers was the Brussels GATT Ministerial meeting in 1990. This was supposed to complete the Uruguay Round negotiations, but the negotiations collapsed when the Commission appeared to offer more on agriculture than some member states were ready to give (Hodges and Woolcock, 1996).

The European Commission therefore leads in EU trade diplomacy. It is responsible for research on the costs and benefits of any trade negotiation and prepares the draft negotiating position. It is the EU's representative in all the technical working groups or exploratory meetings with negotiating partners. The Commission drafts the EU's negotiating aims and conducts the negotiations. Through trade representatives in the various EU delegations around the world that report to DG Trade, the Commission can also gather information about the domestic positions, strengths and weaknesses of their negotiating partners. In the field of trade, the Commission has therefore established a very strong position over the years and has acquired significant *de facto* competence. The strength of DG Trade is illustrated by how it was able to remain outside the European External Action Service when this was established in 2010. As noted above, one of the aims of the Treaty of Lisbon was to bring all external policies under a single heading. Art. 207 (1) TFEU requires that EU external trade policy is in line with the principles and objectives of the Union's external action. In the application of the new treaty however, DG Trade has managed to remain outside the EEAS, which means that the institutional memory and technical capacity of DG Trade will not be diluted in the EEAS.[11]

---

[11]	In the reorganisation brought about by the TFEU, there was a question as to whether trade desks occupied by officials from DG Trade should report to directly to DG Trade as in the past or through the European External Action Service (EEAS). The Council Decision on the organisation of the EEAS (8724/2010) of April 2010 leaves the issue of instructions from the Commission (i.e., DG Trade) to EU delegations. In practice there appears to have been an agreement that DG Trade will continue to be able to communicate directly with the trade people in EU delegations.

Adoption of the Results

Although the Commission speaks for the EU, the member states always follow the key stages of any negotiation and are often present in the location. Member state ministers are generally present for the final negotiating sessions at which the key bargaining or issue linkage occurs between the EU and its trading partners. Effective communication between the Commission and member states generally ensures that the latter are able to endorse the EU's position immediately, so there is minimal risk of an agreement being initialled by the Commission but then rejected by the EU, what Putnam has termed involuntary defection (Putnam, 1998). In Geneva, for example, there are meetings between the Commission and the member states before each negotiating session. Given the different negotiating groups in the Doha Development Agenda negotiations for example, this has meant more than 1000 co-ordination sessions a year. The Council – and since the TFEU – the European Parliament then adopts the results of a negotiation that have been concluded by the Commission. Formally, the Council does so by a qualified majority vote for those parts of any agreement that are covered by exclusive EU competence. Since the TFEU, this means almost all issues covered in trade negotiations. In practice however, consensus within the Council is sought on important decisions. Because the member states follow each development in the negotiations, issues concerning the distribution of costs and benefits of any reciprocal concessions will have been dealt with during the negotiations. Any side payment for a particular country to ensure that member state's support for the final package is generally also dealt with as part of the negotiating process. This is one reason the EU can sometimes take a long time deciding its position. Whilst this can be frustrating for the EU's negotiating partners, the benefit is that, at least to date, there has been very little risk of defection or rejection of the agreement by the member states. This may change with a greater role for the European Parliament.

Prior to the TFEU trade agreements included quite large elements of shared or national competence. For the adoption of these agreements, there was a formal requirement of unanimity. This gave member states that were opposed to any agreement more power to veto it in the Council, because there was no danger of being in a minority position in any shadow voting. The shared or member state competence elements of any agreement also had to be ratified by the national parliaments. The EU practice in such cases was and remains to have those parts of the agreement covered by exclusive EU competence applied provisionally while awaiting the ratification of the full agreement by all member state national parliaments. Provisional application is decided upon by the Council on a proposal from the Commission (Art. 218(5) TFEU). There has seldom been any doubt that the national parliaments will ratify agreements. Ratification by national parliaments has often been little more than a time consuming rubber-stamping exercise. But there have been cases of member states linking ratification of a trade agreement to concessions on other internal EU issues. Such tactics could then hold up final ratification by the whole EU but not block it. After the TFEU, the extension of EU competence to cover all major trade issues and foreign direct investment means the scope of provisions requiring ratification by member state parliaments has been reduced. The practice of provisionally applying trade agreements pending formal ratification of the non-exclusive competence elements seems set to continue.[12] But member state ratification is still necessary in a few limited areas, such as non-trade related aspects of intellectual property rights, provisions on transport policy included in a trade agreement or any additional non-trade provisions in agreements. The argument has also been made that unanimity should be used for key decisions affecting issues of continued shared competence during a negotiation if such decisions are irreversible. For example, a decision to include or exclude intellectual property rights from an agenda.[13]

The TFEU confirms the role of the EP in the adoption of all trade agreements. Under the pre-Lisbon arrangements, the *de jure* position was that the EP had to grant its assent if an agreement: (i) established specific institutional frameworks; (ii) had budgetary implications; or (iii) required changes to EU legislation adopted by co–decision-making (i.e., when the Council and the EP were co-legislators). The EP also had to give its assent in the case of (iv) Association Agreements. In practice, however, the expectation was that the EP's assent would be requested for all major trade agreements. It was for example, understood that the results of any WTO round of negotiations would be put to the EP as would bilateral trade agreements such as the Economic Partnership Agreements (EPAs) with the African Caribbean and Pacific (ACP) states. The TFEU confirms that *all* trade agreements will require the *consent* of the EP. Art. 218 TFEU (ex Art. 300 TEC) extends the conditions requiring EP consent to include 'agreements covering fields to which …. the ordinary legislative procedure (OLP) (i.e., co-decision-making) applies. Art. 207 (TFEU) then states that OLP applies to measures defining the 'framework for implementation of the common commercial policy'. The EP must therefore grant its consent to all trade agreements by a simply majority of MEPs.

Just what use the EP will want or be able to make of this veto power depends on the composition of the EP, what say it has had in setting the aims of any trade agreement and the specifics of the agreement concerned. Generally speaking, the position of the major party groups in the EP has meant a fairly stable majority favouring trade liberalisation. In the 2010–2015 EP, the support of the European Peoples Party (EPP) and the Alliance of Liberals and Democrats (ALDE) could well be sufficient to ensure a simple majority in favour of a trade agreement and these party groups are generally inclined to free trade. The Socialist Group is

---

[12] The precedent for future trade agreements under the TFEU is the provisional application of the EU Republic of Korea Free Trade Agreement. Here the EP made its support for provisional agreement conditional upon the adoption of flanking measures in the shape of legislation introducing a bilateral safeguards provision, rather than any attempt to withhold its consent for provisional application.

[13] This argument was made at the time of the 2004 Framework Agreement on the DDA.

likely to be more concerned about adjustment costs for EU industries and thus workers, but is generally also in favour of market opening. The EP has in the past interested itself in more general issues such as human rights, labour standards, environmental sustainability and development issues rather than the detail of tariff schedules or other parts of an agreement that can impact on specific sectors. In general, then, the EP can be expected to push for the inclusion of such provisions in trade agreements. But the increased powers of the EP are also likely to attract the attention of interest group lobbying that could force the INTA and perhaps the EP plenary sessions to deal with more detail and to address the balance between sector interests and between sector interests and consumer or user interests. A case in point was the lobbying by a few German and Italian car producers on the issue of duty draw back for Korean automobile producers in the EU- Korea FTA. The way the EP manages such lobbying will be decisive for its future role in EU external trade policy.

The ability of the EP to wield its veto power has in the past been limited by the fact that it had no say in authorising the negotiations and thus specifying in advance conditions for granting its 'assent' to any agreement. The EP has also only been able to pass judgement after all the negotiating partners – all 154 in the case of the WTO – and all EU member states, have accepted the agreement. In these circumstances the nuclear option of rejecting an agreement has not been viable. The EP's ability to shape negotiations was also limited by the fact that the legal basis under EU law for the adoption of any agreement was generally not decided upon until the negotiation was complete. This was a by-product of the pragmatic approach of the member states to accept the Commission as sole negotiator, but without prejudice to the question of formal competence. Ambiguity over the legal basis for the final adoption of an agreement then encumbered EP involvement. The TFEU strengthens the EP's powers by requiring its 'consent' to all trade agreements but does not provide the EP with powers to authorise negotiations. Thus, whilst the Commission must report to the INTA, and the EP will be asked to give its consent to trade agreement, it is not clear from the treaty that the EP will play a significantly different role in EU trade policy in the future.

The Legislative Framework for EU External Trade

There are few major legislative acts required in EU external trade. The major legislative acts will be acts implementing the results of trade agreements, autonomous trade policy measures – such as the unilateral granting of preferences for least-developed countries under the General System of Preferences (GSP), 'GSP plus' or everything-but-arms schemes – or EU legislation implementing WTO rules on trade remedies such as anti-dumping or safeguards measures. Prior to the TFEU such legislation was adopted using the consultation procedure in which Commission proposals were adopted by the Council through regulations with only, at best, a brief consultation with the European Parliament. With the

TFEU, the Council and European Parliament share legislative powers to adopt 'the measures defining the framework for implementing the common commercial policy' through the OLP (Art. 207(2) TFEU). Figure 2.4 provides a diagrammatic summary of the OLP. It is not the intention here to discuss the OLP in detail. This has been done elsewhere. But it is necessary to say how its use will change EU trade policy.

Clearly the use of OLP for trade legislation gives the EP greater power in an area in which the Council previously had full control. This will enhance the democratic accountability of EU trade legislation. For example, trade preferences for developing countries and EU's legislation applying trade remedies (see following section) will now come under co–decision-making. But the OLP will also take longer than the adoption of Council regulations using the consultation procedure. In the past it has been possible to get legal acts adopted within a matter of weeks, which with the OLP could take many months and perhaps more than a year. But not all provisions that had previously been adopted by Council regulation need to go through the OLP. Art. 290 (TFEU) provides for delegated acts for detailed measures, such as those implementing an agreement or making adjustments to schedules. Delegation here is to the Commission. An important question is therefore what will be defined as essential elements of the common commercial policy and thus require the OLP and what non-essential and thus subject to delegated acts. During the 2005–2010 EP legislative period, the EP assented to 18 pieces of trade legislation, and there were 21 acts covered by the consultation procedure. During the same period, the Council adopted no fewer than 271 legal acts directly concerning trade under Art. 133 (TEC) and 281 trade-related acts under Art. 300 (TEC). If the EU is to remain effective in implementing trade agreements there is clearly a need for the non-essential issues to be delegated to the Commission. A complicating factor here is that this would strengthen the Commission at the expense of the Council, which brings us to the question of trade remedies and anti-dumping in particular.

Trade Remedies

The rules for EU trade remedies are set by international agreement, whether in Art. VI (anti-dumping) or Art. XIX (safeguards) of the GATT (1994), or in bilateral agreements. But these rules provide considerable scope for each WTO member when it comes to their implementation in national or EU legislation, which will after Lisbon now be adopted using the OLP as trade remedy measures seem certain to fall under the heading of essential elements of the common commercial policy.

Figure 3.2 shows the decision-making process for EU anti-dumping actions. Anti-dumping is the more important trade remedy and so is illustrated here. Safeguards and the Trade Barriers Regulation have been much less used, and countervailing duties hardly ever, although there may be pressure to use these other trade remedies if emerging markets such as China begin to promote national

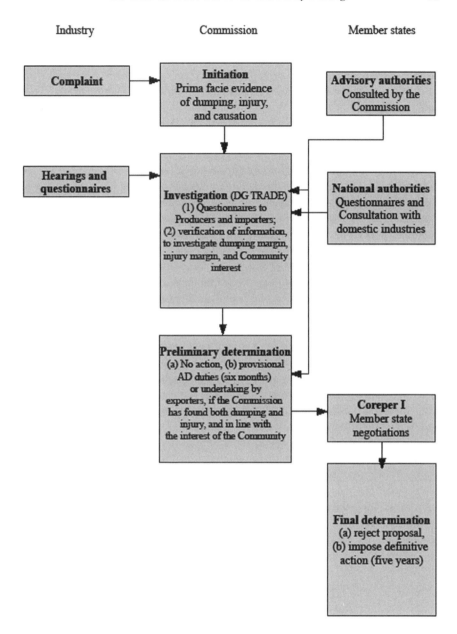

Fig. 3.2   **EU Decision-Making for Anti-dumping Measures**

champions through subsidies. For anti-dumping, the Commission is responsible for all the technical work assessing whether the conditions to apply anti-dumping duties have been satisfied, such as whether dumping has occurred and whether it poses a threat of serious injury to EU industry. In an exception to the general rules on comitology for the CCP, the Council has had power to adopt definitive anti-dumping duties.

The process begins with a complaint from companies affected by alleged dumping or sales below the cost of production by a foreign supplier.[14] The Commission then makes an initial assessment. If it finds there is a case to be answered, the Commission proposes an investigation, but before it can proceed the member states must give the green light in the Anti-dumping Committee. The hurdle for positive decisions on anti-dumping actions has been brought down from QMV to a simple majority vote in 1994 and to a simply majority of those voting in 2004. The first change was by way of a *quid pro quo* for the support of more protectionist member states for the adoption of the Uruguay Round negotiations in the GATT. The second change was made because the same more protectionist member states feared that member states joining the EU in 2004 would tend to abstain on decisions concerning the use of trade instruments that did not affect them and thus make it difficult to obtain a simple majority.

Unlike decisions taken by the TPC or the Council during negotiations, voting is regularly used in anti-dumping actions. In this the positions of the member states tend to be influenced as much by whether they are liberal or more protectionist as by the details of the case itself. The more liberal member states will tend only to vote for an investigation when there is clear evidence of dumping; the more protectionist member states tend to vote in favour of the initiation of an investigation in all cases.

Once an investigation has begun, the Commission has considerable discretion. In addition to determining whether dumping is occurring and threatening serious injury, as required by Art. VI of the GATT (1994), the Commission must also decide whether the imposition of anti-dumping duties is in the 'community interest'. Assessment of the Community/EU interest involves balancing the benefit for EU producers of imposing duties against the costs for users of the imported products and the consumers. This Community/EU interest test is not (yet) a WTO obligation. When the Commission finds evidence of dumping, it can impose preliminary duties. Finally, the Commission can negotiate price undertakings, in other words an agreement that the foreign suppliers of products that have engaged in – or been accused of – dumping remove the margin of dumping by increasing the export price.

The Commission has come in for considerable criticism over its application of trade remedy provisions. Before 2005, this was mostly from liberal interests who saw the Commission use of discretion as a form of contingent protection.

---

[14] There is a heated and complex debate over what constitutes dumping, which we cannot go into here.

Under the first Barosso Commission of 2005–2010 there was then criticism that the Commission was blocking or refusing to recommend investigations. Indeed, there was a low level of definitive anti-dumping duties applied during the 2005–2010 period.[15] This reduction was probably partly due to changes in the structure of trade. As companies have become more and more international, with production sites in a range of countries, they have become proponents of free trade and opponents of anti-dumping duties that add to their costs. But the reduction in the use of anti-dumping measures also reflected a shift in the normative bias of the Commission towards a more liberal stance and thus one less inclined to use contingent protection.

With the TFEU, any renewal of EU anti-dumping or other trade remedy legislation will now use the OLP. The EP has been critical of the existing practice and argued that the exception from general comitology rules that allows a Council vote to implement trade policy is inconsistent with Art. 291 (TFEU) on the delegation of implementing powers to the Commission. The EP also argues that the voting in the Anti-dumping Committee politicises what should be an objective, legalistic process. The member states sought to retain the existing procedure and thus the privileged position of the Council in implementing trade remedies. At issue was not whether the EP should have powers to intervene in specific cases, but whether the Council will lose some of its power to the Commission, with Council and EP sharing oversight of the Commission's implementation of policy. Under the previous system there had been an exception to the general comitology arrangements under Council Decision 1999/468 for trade instruments that allowed for decisions on anti-dumping and anti-subsidy (countervailing measures) to be taken by the simple majority of member states voting. The outcome of a heated debate resulted in new comitology arrangements being adopted in March 2011 governing the use of Art. 290 and 291 TFEU (European Parliament and Council, 2011). These replace the previous five types of committee with just two: the examination and the advisory procedures. In the examination procedure the committee's response to Commission proposals will be decided by a qualified majority. If the decision goes against the Commission, the issue can go to an appeals committee. This was introduced to satisfy the EP that there would be a more political level discussion of controversial issues.

In the case of anti-dumping if a simple majority of the (examination) committee opposes the Commission proposal it is submitted to an appeal committee. Until September 2012 the appeal committee will also take a decision by a simple majority.

---

[15]   The number of definitive anti-dumping duties applied or acceptance of price undertakings fell from 19 in 2005 to 12 in 2007. Some increase is expected to follow the recession in 2009 due to the effects of the financial crisis, but these levels are still low compared to previous years. See Commission Staff Working Document; accompanying document to the 27th Annual Report from the Commission to the European Parliament on the Community's Anti-Dumping. Anti-subsidy and safeguard activities COM(2009/573); SEC (2009) 1413 26 October 2009.

After this date, the appeal committee will presumably act by a qualified majority as in the case for other policies. In other words, it appears that an exception has been made for trade instruments that allows for decisions (to refer a decision to the appeal committee) to be taken by a simple majority of member state representatives in the examination committee. The agreement was clearly a compromise between the Council that sought to retain the powers the member states had in the Anti-dumping Committee and the EP that wished to ensure uniform application of the simplified commitology rules across all policy areas. The advisory procedure is for the type of issues that were dealt with in the previous advisory committees under the old comitology rules and simply require the Commission to take utmost account of the opinion of the committee. For the examination procedure, both the EP and Council have scrutiny powers for comitology regarding delegated acts under legislation adopted by OLP (co-decision). In other words, either can require the Commission to review and amend or withdraw any measure adopted if the Commission exceeds its powers.[16]

Having described the decision-making procedures for international trade negotiations, EU trade legislation and the use of trade remedies, the next section turns to an analysis of the key factors that shape EU trade diplomacy.

Factors Shaping EU Trade Diplomacy

As noted in the analytical framework in Chapter 2, reciprocity has underpinned trade policy, at least to date, so that the larger the domestic market relative to that of one's trading partners, the greater the negotiator's power by virtue of his or her ability to offer, withhold, or withdraw, access to this market. Binding commitments to tariff reductions and other liberalising measures in recent decades have reduced the scope for offering or withholding market access concessions, but there remains room for discretion in many fields of trade.

Economic Power

From the beginning, the European Economic Community (EEC) possessed market power through the creation of a customs union, a fact recognised by the original six member states. The EEC was then able to use this power to bring about reductions in US and other countries' tariffs during the Kennedy Round of the GATT (Duer, 2008). After a stagnation in European integration during the 1970s, the creation of the Single European Market (SEM) meant that EC trade policy held the key to a wider and deeper market. This leverage enabled the EU along

---

[16] One point of detail of relevance to trade policy is that if an appeals committee reaches no opinion the Commission can adopt anti-dumping measure but cannot adopt a multilateral safeguard action. This seems to suggest that a qualified majority of member states in an examination procedure would be required for the Commission to adopt such a safeguard measure.

with the United States (and to a lesser degree other members of the 'quad'), to shape the international trade regime throughout the Uruguay Round of the 1980s and early 1990s. But during the 1990s the EU's relative market power in the field of trade did not increase. The US economy grew faster over the decade thanks to productivity gains from the rapid application of information technology and from debt-financed consumer led growth. In the 2000s relatively fast economic growth in large emerging markets with relatively high bound tariffs, such as China, India and to a lesser degree other emerging markets, has reduced the EU's relative market power.

Market power in trade negotiations is determined by market size but also by the EU's ability and willingness to use it. The EU has negotiated away or unilaterally ceded much of the market power it holds in the form of the ability to offer concessions. As a full participant in successive multilateral trade rounds, the EU has bound tariffs for industrial goods in the order to 3–4 per cent, but higher rates for agricultural products. The generally liberal nature of the SEM could also be seen as constituting a degree of unilateral liberalisation vis-à-vis third countries (Hanson, 1998). The SEM significantly enhanced transparency and introduced a rules-based system of regulation within the EU that made the EU market more open to competition from suppliers within the EU, but also from those outside. Furthermore, there is no qualified majority among member states, let alone a consensus in favour of threatening to close the EU market. Liberal member states see strict definitions of reciprocity as economically counterproductive.[17]

As noted above, since the mid-1990s it has been the EU that has sought to shape the international trade agenda. It was the EU that made the running for a new multilateral trade round and pushed for a comprehensive WTO agenda by using its remaining negotiating leverage (in agriculture) in an effort to make progress in areas, such the 'Singapore agenda' items of investment, government procurement, competition and trade facilitation (Woolcock, 2003). The EU has largely failed in this effort to lead in shaping the multilateral trade negotiations due to opposition from developing countries and emerging markets (to proposals on investment and government procurement) and indifference or opposition from the US (to multilateral rules on competition). The EU's economic power was therefore not sufficient. Systemic factors, such as the structural changes in the international trading system that have favoured the large emerging markets, are clearly one factor here. Indeed the relative decline in EU economic power could be seen as a factor shaping the EU reversion to a more active use of bilateral negotiations after 2006 (Evenett, 2007; Woolcock, 2007). Bilateral negotiations enable the EU to maximise its economic power. The significant size of the EU

---

[17] The 2010 revised Commission strategy for trade hints at a somewhat more aggressive approach to trade with emerging markets such as China, but the suggestion of withholding access to the EU market is limited to specific policy areas, such as public procurement. The strategy does not imply anything like a consensus in favour of using the threat of market closure to enhance negotiating leverage. See European Commission (2010 (a)).

means that bilateral negotiations will inevitably mean an asymmetry that favours the EU, especially in negotiations with developing countries. A decline in the EU's relative economic power could therefore partially explain its lack of success in multilateral negotiations and the shift back to preferential agreements.

Recognition

There can be no doubt that the EU is recognised as the actor in trade diplomacy. From the time the Commission emerged as the negotiator for the European Economic Community (EEC) during the Dillon – and especially the Kennedy – rounds of the GATT, the EEC was recognised as an actor distinct from the EU member states. It was also the European Community (EC) – in the shape of the Commissioner responsible for external trade – not the member states, that participated in the 'quad' during the 1980s. The picture has been different in the bodies such as the OECD, which was important in shaping the club norms and policies during the 1970s and 1980s, where the member state governments were recognised alongside the Commission. Today, the EU in the shape of the Commissioner for Trade is recognised as the actor when trade is discussed in the various forums and groupings inside and out of the WTO. In the case of trade formal, *de jure* recognition was established when the EU became a signatory of the WTO in 1994. Member states are also members of the WTO, which is a member driven organisation in which all members have one vote, but it is only the EU that speaks for the member states. It is also worth noting that member state representation in the WTO is non-hierarchical, in other words all EU members are the same status. This is consistent with the hypothesis that non-hierarchical representation in international organisations fosters greater cohesion between the member states.

Recognition of the EU as the negotiating partner in any international negotiation is likely to be associated with formal competence, but this is not automatically the case. Although the EEC had exclusive competence for the CCP from the beginning, there was no agreement on many trade issues. As the international trade and investment agenda deepened new issues were added, such as technical standards and government procurement in the 1970s and services, investment and intellectual property in the 1980s, for which the EC did not have exclusive competence. Member state governments argued that these issues remained mixed or member state competence, but they were pragmatic when it came to negotiation and agreed that the Commission should negotiate as a single actor/voice for the EC. Thus on services, TRIPs and investment negotiations in the Uruguay Round, the Commission was recognised as having negotiating authority by the EU's negotiating partners, even though there was no *de jure* exclusive EC competence in these policy areas.

In successive Intergovernmental Conferences (IGCs), the European Commission argued for an extension of exclusive EC competence for trade to cover all topics under negotiation, but the Member States resisted, even as *de facto* competence was shifting to the EC. What resulted was an Echternach procession (Bourgoise, 1995) in which the EU appeared to take two steps forward towards greater EC competence only to then take one back. In the Maastricht IGC (1991), the scope of EC competence was constrained and any prospect of a greater role for the European Parliament checked. In the Amsterdam IGC (1996) there was some forward movement in the shape of the enabling clause in Art. 133(5)(TEC), which provided that the Member States (acting unanimously) could extend EC competence to any topic or sector of trade without there having to be a formal treaty change. But the enabling clause was never used. In the Nice IGC (2001), EC competence was extended to services, but some sensitive sectors (health and educational services and those services relating to cultural diversity) were excluded.

Interpretations of the treaty provisions by the European Court of Justice have also shaped the evolution of competence. Initially, the ECJ tended to favour the extension of exclusive competence in decisions such as the AETR decision of the ECJ. Subsequently, the ECJ limited the further extension of competence in the 1/94 decision on the legal basis for the adoption of the results of the Uruguay Round (Eeckhout, 2004; p 59).

Systemic factors

External factors have been important in shaping EU trade policy. A broad systemic factor shaping EU decision-making and negotiation is the need to compete on international markets and to ensure access to markets that offer potential in terms of trade growth. For example, access to the US market during the 1960s was crucial for EU trade growth and competitiveness, while in the 2000s, the crucial issue was more access to the large emerging markets of China and India. The shift towards a policy of negotiating bilateral trade agreements with emerging markets in Asia, namely ASEAN, India, etc., in the Global Europe Strategy of 2006 can therefore also be seen as a response to systemic changes in the form of a shift in market potential away from the OECD countries towards the emerging markets.

External drivers

In the case of international trade, there have been demands (mostly from the US) for the EU to engage in more or less continuous negotiations. During the 1990s, US leadership weakened, and during the 2000s the US shifted to a more self-serving policy of competitive liberalisation (Evenett and Meier, 2007).[18] This gave the EU an opportunity to bid for leadership during the 1990s and 2000s, which has driven the need to agree on common positions. With the exception of the final

---

[18]   Competitive liberalisation was the idea that the US would use any level/forum of negotiation in order to promote liberalisation of market access for the US. It had been around since the mid-1990 but was only really applied once the G.W. Bush administration obtained Trade Promotion Authority in 2001. Its significance is that while the negotiation of free trade agreements during the Uruguay Round was seen in Washington, D.C., as a means of showing the way for multilateral agreement, competitive liberalisation saw free trade agreements as a possible alternative to multilateral agreement.

phases of important negotiations, such as GATT or WTO rounds, the EU has also been able to develop these positions under normal (i.e., non-crisis) conditions. In other words, EU trade policy has been able to evolve in response to steady external pressure. It will be argued below that this has facilitated the establishment of *de facto* decision-making and negotiation practices and procedures that embody shared expectations about how decisions are made and negotiations conducted.

Normative Power

As pointed out in the discussion of the analytical framework in Chapter 2, the EU has been seen as a normative power. But what does this mean in terms of trade policy? Measuring the EU's ability to promote the general norms set out in the General Provisions on the Union's External Action (TEU Art. 21) – such as security, the rule of law, human rights and peace through trade policy – is likely to be inconclusive. Assessing the impact of trade policy on 'encouraging the integration of all countries into the world economy, including through the progressive abolition of restrictions on international trade (Art. 21 (2) (e) TEU) is easier, and the EU's policies in terms of offering duty-free and quota-free access to the EU market for least-developed countries (LDCs) could be said to be pursuing this aim.

Another form of general norm is the idea that the EU represents a form of post-Westpfahlian model (Hetne, 1998). Since the mid-1990s the EU has favoured region-to-region negotiations. This strategy aims to provide an added incentive for regions in Africa or Latin America to integrate by bringing EU market power to bear in the shape of offering enhanced access to the EU market if regions move towards greater integration. A simple observation of EU policy shows that this attempt at furthering regional integration has not been very successful. While many negotiations have begun as region-to-region negotiations, the only region-to-region agreements to date (2010) which could be said to have been completed successfully are the EU–Cariforum comprehensive Economic Partnership Agreement (EPA) of 2007 and the EU–Central America agreement in 2010. But Cariforum/Caricom was already well advanced in terms of regional integration and agreement was greatly facilitated by the existence of the Caribbean Regional Negotiating Machinery (CRNM), something that was set up initially to enable the Caribbean states concerned to negotiate as one with the US. It is difficult to find much evidence of success in any of the other region-to-region negotiations. The EU–Mecosur negotiations broke down in 2004 (one of the few instances in which the EU has walked away from a negotiation, although talks were restarted in 2010). The EU opted to negotiate with individual members of the Andean Community (Peru, Columbia and Ecuador) rather than with the Andean Community as a whole. It has now moved to do the same with individual members of ASEAN (Thailand, Singapore and Vietnam) rather than with ASEAN; although there may be an overarching EU–ASEAN agreement, the real substance appears likely to come in the form of bilateral agreements. In the case of the other Economic

Partnership Agreements (EPAs) with the ACP states, the EU preferred to press ahead with bilateral agreements in order to meet the deadline of the end of 2007 set by end of the GATT waiver for preferential agreements under the Cotonou Agreement. This meant giving up, at least in the short term, the aim of using the EPAs as a means of promoting regional integration in each of the ACP regions. The reasons for the failure of the region-to-region policy need not delay us here, but are clearly related to the lack of willingness or preparedness of the EU's partners to move towards regional integration as defined by the EU. Whilst in a general sense European integration has clearly been emulated in other regions, the more immediate application of trade agreements to promote concrete integration does not appear to have succeeded and the dictates of trade policy have led the EU to press ahead with bilateral agreements.

The analytical framework suggests that the EU's framework norm takes the form of the broad consensus that liberal markets should function within a regulatory framework of agreed rules covering essential social or environmental objectives. During the process of negotiating the SEM the EU member states effectively reached such a consensus. The emergence of this broad consensus does seem to have resulted in the EU adopting a stronger, more influential role during the Uruguay Round. Here then appears to be a case of EU normative power. This approach is mostly implicit in EU policy, but has found expression in the shape of the rather narrower concept of 'collective preferences' (Lamy, 2004). In his definition of 'collective preferences', Lamy included multilateralism, environmental protection, food safety, cultural diversity, public provision of health and education, precaution in risk assessment and welfare rights.

In EU trade diplomacy specific norms are largely codified in the *acquis communautaire* for goods and services, and the EU has had some success in getting these norms adopted internationally. The Uruguay Round agreements on technical barriers to trade, subsidies and countervailing duties, government procurement and services, all reflect elements of the EU *acquis* (Woolcock, 2008). In the DDA however, the EU has been less successful for reasons related to its limited market power discussed above and the nature of the agenda discussed below.

Distinctive EU Norms?

The *acquis communautaire* is rightly considered as the common domestic basis for EU trade policy. But is the *acquis* really distinctively European or EU? An analysis of the path dependency of some of the key provisions in the *acquis* shows that these owe a great deal to norms developed in a wider international context in the OECD (Woolcock, 2008). Norms that the EU is promoting in international negotiations are seldom purely the result of an internal EU debate. This point can be illustrated with reference to the Singapore issues that have become closely associated with EU interests in current trade negotiations. These norms are in good part derived from norms developed within the OECD during the 1970s and 1980s. This does not, of course, mean that the EU does not have normative power in relation to such specific norms. By taking norms, such as those developed for government procurement in the OECD and applying them in the EU as well as promoting their wider use in bilateral free trade agreements, the EU can still project considerable normative power. But adopting norms developed in international forums does not seem to fit with another often cited attribute of EU *actorness*, namely the existence of a distinctive EU identity.

The Acquis Communautaire

The *acquis* has been very important in shaping EU trade policy. The normative consensus on specific legislative provisions or standards in the EU provides the common basis for EU trade negotiators across most trade and investment issues. It is also possible to find a direct impact on the content of EU trade policies. In agriculture the CAP required protection and export restitutions in order to sustain a system based on price support schemes for different products. EU agricultural trade policy only shifted to a somewhat more liberal position following CAP reform during the Uruguay Round in the case of the McSharry reforms of 1992. In the 2000s one can also find a close correlation between the *acquis* in agriculture and EU agricultural trade policy. For example, the reforms in Agenda 2000 programme and the 2003 mid-term Review of the CAP facilitated a more flexible position in the DDA.

In manufactures, EU trade policy became more liberal and rules-based as a result of the SEM. The negotiating position of the EU during the Uruguay Round on topics such as subsidies, technical barriers to trade, government procurement and services reflected the current stage of the SEM programme. For example, the EU negotiating position on government procurement only included purchasing by public utilities once the corresponding directive had been adopted as part of the SEM. The EU negotiating position on services reflected the two-phased approach used within the EU in which financial services, telecommunications and business services were liberalised first followed only later by sectors such as postal services, health and education. Thus in agriculture, manufactures and services the content of EU trade policy positions was significantly shaped by the stage the *acquis* had reached. This argument can be extended to the current DDA negotiations. Thus the desire to have a comprehensive agenda in the DDA reflects the developed and comprehensive nature of EU integration (Young, 2007; Woolcock, 2003).

Decision-making Procedures

Rather than the question of formal competence what seems to have contributed to efficiency in trade decision-making in the EU has been the existence of well-established institutional arrangements. Over more than 50 years, the EEC and then the EC has developed a decision-making regime in which the participants share common expectations of how trade policy will be made. Within the Art. 113 and then the 133 Committees, senior trade officials appear to have gone through the kind of socialisation process described by constructivists and began to identify with EU aims in trade policy rather than just member state aims. Decision-making in EU trade diplomacy has become easier because more and more trade policy is based on the domestic *acquis*. There are few areas where there remains a need to aggregate the various member state positions. When it comes to negotiation there have been setbacks and periods of difficulty when the Commission did not have the full confidence of the member states, but as time has moved on the system of supervised delegation used appears to have worked more smoothly. With time there has also been a shift towards more decision-making in Brussels, with some member state governments reducing the resources they commit to trade policy, sometimes to the detriment of policy-making in terms of properly holding the Commission to account. This can be seen in the steady growth of the influence of the Commission thanks to the strength of DG Trade and other Directorates General in the field of trade policy. The Lisbon Treaty, by granting the EP more powers, also adds to the trend towards more decision-making in Brussels, but poses a challenge for the future in how to integrate the EP into the established decision-making procedures.

The pragmatic response to the need to negotiate mixed competence trade rounds meant that the Commission assumed role of the agent, but also that the member states as principals could veto any Commission position thanks to the shared or mixed competence factor. A system of supervised delegation was therefore developed that satisfied the member states because they had tight control over the Commission, but which nevertheless enabled the EU to speak with one voice. This form of supervised delegation worked well when there was mutual trust between the Council and the Commission, but failed when there was no trust. The ability of the Commission to negotiate was dependent on member state confidence that the Commission would not ride rough shod over any member state interests during a negotiation. When this confidence was not present, member states intervened to control the negotiations.

Coherence

Vertical coherence between EU trade policy and member state policies has never really been an issue since the member states gave up national trade policies. In terms of horizontal coherence, trade policy has clearly been shaped by internal EU preferences in the shape of the *acquis*. EU trade policy decision-making has remained relatively autonomous thanks to the strength of trade policy compared to other external policy issues and to the strength of DG Trade compared to other Directorates General. DG Trade's approach to external policy has in turn been shaped by the prevailing influence of reciprocity in international trade negotiations. Such trade principles appear to have been more effectively promoted by DG Trade than competing concepts of development by DG Dev or environmental principles are promoted by DG Env. The relative autonomy of trade compared to other external policies has been underlined by the fact that DG Trade has remained outside the EEAS.

The Case of the EU in the Doha Development Agenda (DDA) Negotiations

The DDA, the latest multilateral trade round, is central to EU trade policy, but makes for a complex case study, even in summary form. This section therefore focuses on two issues, agriculture and the so-called Singapore issues of investment, competition, transparency in public procurement and trade facilitation, to illustrate EU trade diplomacy. Agricultural trade has been an issue on which the EU has always had strong defensive interests. In contrast the Singapore issues were a central element of the EU's offensive interest in a comprehensive multilateral round. Neither agriculture nor the Singapore issues are however, the most important issues in terms of trade flows. Agriculture accounts for about 9 per cent of world trade, but a declining share of EU trade, where it fell to just 6 per cent of EU trade in goods in 2007 from 9 per cent in 1995. The trade impact of agreement on the Singapore issues is difficult to qualify, but market access issues such as the tariff negotiations under the non-agricultural market access (NAMA) and commitments on national treatment for service providers are probably of more immediate importance to EU business.

Agriculture

The EU has been defensive on agricultural trade since the US pressed for reform of the CAP in the Kennedy Round in the 1960s. In the Tokyo Round the EU negotiating position was to defend the fundamental principles of the CAP. Given the continued use of price support for agriculture in the EU this meant maintaining export subsidies in order to be able to reduce stocks, such as butter mountains and wine lakes, when EU prices were above world prices. Again it was primarily the US that pressed the EU to remove export subsidies, as these were seen as unfair competition for US exports on third markets. During the Tokyo Round the EC maintained strong opposition to liberalisation due to a combination of entrenched vested interests and the *de facto* application of consensus in the Council decision-making that enabled France, with support from some other Member States, to resist reform (Meunier, 2000). The political economy of agricultural trade policy in the EU appeared to show the classic form of rural voters having a disproportionate impact on policy. In negotiating terms this made for a narrow EC 'win-set' and thus strengthened the EU position vis-à-vis the US that in the end accepted a round without any real agreement on agriculture for broader strategic/foreign policy interests related to the Cold War (the NATO twin track policy of deploying cruise and Pershing theatre nuclear weapons in western Europe while seeking nuclear arms reductions with the Soviet Union (Winham, 1986).

The 'success' in resisting pressure for concessions during the Tokyo Round shaped the EC's position during the 1980s. Those defending the CAP could argue that a tough negotiating position paid off and could do so again. The mandate for the Uruguay Round therefore stated again that there should be no concession on trade that would undermine the fundamental principles of the CAP (Hodges and Woolcock, 1996). Path dependency therefore shaped the EC's negotiating position going into the Uruguay Round, but the experience of the UR had other lessons for EU policy makers. From the 1988 Montreal GATT Ministerial meeting onwards the EU was isolated on agriculture as the Cairns Group of agricultural exporters combined with the US to pressure the EU to make more concessions. Up to 1991 the defensive position of the EU remained in place for very similar political economy reasons to the Tokyo Round. To this one must also add a *de facto* German agreement not to isolate France on agriculture at a time when Germany was seeking French support for German unification. In October 1991 the German position shifted in favour of reform and cleared the way for the McSharry reform proposals that provided some scope for EC concessions in negotiations by reducing price support. After a fairly long drawn out negotiation, which was delayed first by the need to implement reforms and then elections in France, an agreement was finally reached which was considerably closer to the EC's starting position than that of the US 'negotiating' position of total elimination. This suggests the institutional factors that gave the EU a narrow win-set and a defensive claiming negotiating position were still important.

This lengthy historical background is important because it is not possible to understand the EU's position on agricultural trade without an understanding of what went before. The EU was under pressure to negotiate on agriculture for a number of reasons. Agriculture in the DDA was part of the inbuilt agenda following the commitment made in the UR to further negotiations starting in 2000. The 'peace clause' agreed in the Uruguay Round that precluded challenges of WTO members' agricultural policies also ran out in 2003. Given this position, the Commission proposed and the member states accepted that agriculture should form part of a wider comprehensive round. In seeking to link agriculture to a wider comprehensive round in which the EU had offensive interests, the EU was simply following the established practice from previous multilateral rounds. The rationale for issue linkage in multilateral rounds was that this could facilitate value-creation in negotiations in which all parties stood to gain. The EU's aim was to ensure domestic agreement by ensuring that any concessions on EU defensive issues (on agriculture) would be balanced against concessions by others on EU offensive interests (essentially tariffs on industrial products in the large emerging markets, access to services markets and the Singapore issues). As negotiations in the DDA soon showed, this framing of the negotiations as a round of reciprocal concessions, albeit with less than full reciprocity demands on developing countries, was at odds with the perceptions of the developing country members of the WTO which were that a development round should provide developing countries with greater relative gains.

In contrast to the EU's position going into the Uruguay Round, the Commission's preparatory work for the DDA sought to create scope for negotiating concessions in agriculture. This took the form first of the Agenda 2000 reforms of the EU budget that were mainly driven by the need to prepare the EU for Eastern enlargement, but which meant reducing agricultural support to a manageable level and by further reductions in price support on top of limited reductions made in the McSharry reforms. The text adopted by the WTO in Doha in 2001 was an example of constructive ambiguity that enabled a round to be launched by not tying down exactly what would be negotiated. The real negotiations on what should be covered by the DDA did not therefore take place until late 2002 and early 2003 when the modalities for negotiation for agriculture and the other issues were to be essentially agreed along with the question of whether the Singapore issues should be added, which India had blocked in Doha.

In the DDA, the main pressure on the EU to make concessions came more from the emerging market WTO Members such as Brazil and a range of other developing country agricultural exporters. The US still sought an end to EU export subsidies, but these were becoming less important as the EU reduced levels of price support and shifted towards decoupling support from trade by providing more direct income support for farmers. Indeed, as the 2002 US Farm Act showed the US was moving along similar lines to the EU. During the spring of 2003 agricultural exporting countries sought a clarification of the EU position on agriculture, before agreeing to the final agenda of the DDA. The EU did not wish to make concessions on agriculture, the sector in which it had most market leverage, until it had at least got agreement on an agenda for the DDA that matched the EU's comprehensive agenda (Kerremans, 2004). In the run up to Cancun, the EU and US negotiated a joint text on agriculture in the belief that this would provide leadership and clear the path for agreement on the agenda. This was in itself remarkable as the US and EU had been at loggerheads over agricultural trade for much of the previous 40 years. The fact that a common position was possible reflected the degree to which EU reforms had slowly brought the EU close to the US position. But the joint position was rejected by the leading developing countries and provided the catalyst for the creation of the trade G20 group of developing countries, led by Brazil and India, in order to counter any renewed EU–US duopoly.

On the 'domestic' front, the Commission pushed through further reform of the CAP at the July 2003 mid-term review of the CAP. These reforms went further than many had expected by bringing about greater decoupling of domestic support from trade and thus provided more scope for EU concessions on agriculture in the DDA.[19] But at the Cancun WTO Ministerial meeting in September 2003 this greater ability to negotiate on agriculture was not enough to deliver for the EU on linkage.

In Cancun, the EU pressed to get its comprehensive agenda accepted but without success. Negotiations broke down even though the EU had indicated, some argued too late, that it would be willing to drop one or more of the Singapore issues of investment, competition, government procurement and trade facilitation from the agenda. In August 2004 there was agreement on a framework in Geneva, which effectively reduced the ambition of the DDA to a more conventional negotiation on reciprocal market access focused on non-agricultural market access (NAMA),

---

[19]   For a debate on the institutional politics of this decision see Swinbank, 2007.

agricultural market access and subsidies and services, with less emphasis on services but with trade facilitation still on the agenda. At the Hong Kong WTO Ministerial meeting in December 2005 the EU made more concessions in the shape of a conditional agreement to phase out agricultural export subsidies by 2013. The EU subsequently agreed to quite significant reductions in agricultural tariffs and agricultural subsidies on the condition that there was also agreement on modalities for opening goods markets (and services) in the emerging markets. The negotiation therefore became one based on reciprocal market access between the EU, the US and other OECD economies on the one hand and the major emerging markets of India and Brazil on the other. China as a recently acceded member (RAM) was under somewhat less pressure to make further concessions. By the end of 2008, agreement on the modalities of an agreement had been reached with tiered reductions in agricultural tariffs and subsidies as well as the ending of export subsidies.[20] With many of the issues resolved in the form of the modalities of the pre-final text negotiations broke down on the issue of special safeguard measures for agriculture with India and the US disagreeing on what level of imports would trigger a safeguard action.[21]

The Singapore Issues

The Singapore issues in the DDA also have a history. Investment, competition (in the shape of restrictive business practices) and public procurement all featured in the debate on the International Trade Organisation (ITO) in the late 1940s. The US tried unsuccessfully three times to get investment onto the GATT agenda before finally partially succeeding with the Trade Related Investment Measures (TRIMs) in the Uruguay Round. The US also pushed government procurement on the trade agenda in the 1960s. This ultimately led to its *de facto* inclusion in the Tokyo Round and the Uruguay Round and the adoption of the plurilateral Government Purchasing Agreements (GPAs) in 1979 and 1994. Competition was not part of previous trade rounds largely because the US opposed international agreements on substantive issues concerning competition and favoured unilateral efforts or less binding obligations to cooperate in bilateral agreements or in the OECD.

At the end of the Uruguay Round there was a broad expectation that investment would form an important part of any future negotiations. With the WTO a rules-based system had been established for trade, but this did not extend to investment, which was in many respects more important for globalisation. This was reflected by an elite policy community made up of trade officials and international investment lawyers that had been engaged in OECD deliberations on investment

---

[20] See the Chair's text of the Agricultural Negotiating Committee of 2008 at http://www.wto.org/english/tratop_e/agric_e/chair_texts08_e.htm

[21] There are different interpretations of what sort of share of the DDA had been agreed. There are those who argue that it was 90 per cent and nearly done, and those who argue that this is far too high a figure.

for years. The EU supported inclusion of investment in a new comprehensive round of the WTO rather than the alternative venue of the OECD, favoured by the US, because most of the remaining barriers to investment were in developing countries. In the end negotiations were sought both in the OECD and the WTO. In the OECD these led to the MAI negotiations, which failed in 1998 following disagreement between the EU and US and strong opposition from civil society NGOs (Henderson, 1999). At the Singapore WTO ministerial in 1996 a Working Group on Trade and Investment was established, but no agreement reached on the scope of any future agreement.

The collapse of the MAI negotiations had a profound effect on the EU's chances of getting investment included in a comprehensive WTO negotiation. The assumptions of the investment policy elite proved to be no longer valid. Following the MAI affair, business and government were no longer willing to make the case for investment rules and the NGO community was encouraged to challenge any inclusion of it in the WTO. In the EU therefore there remained a mandate to negotiate on investment along with the other Singapore issues, but not much support from the main interest groups that would normally be expected to support such an agreement and strong opposition from civil society.

Public procurement had been put on the trade agenda in the 1960s by the US in an attempt to gain access to key European and Japanese markets in telecommunications and power generation equipment that were significantly shaped by contracts from public utility companies that tended to buy national. The SEM programme had produced a comprehensive EU regime. This ensured transparency in public contracts and introduced best practice in the award of contracts. As such it was unilateral liberalisation, because third parties also benefited from better information on EU contracts and the competition enhancing nature of the introduction of best practice. The EU scheme was also comprehensive in that it covered all purchasing entities at all levels of government including even private entities that are subject to some public control through licensing or the granting of special or exclusive rights by government or regulatory agencies. The coverage of the EU regime was therefore much wider than that offered by other WTO members and offered, in effect, unilateral benefits for third countries. The EU support for the inclusion of public procurement in a comprehensive agenda for the WTO round could therefore be seen as a means of gaining equivalent access to emerging markets as well as promoting best practice in developing countries for development purposes and as part of the EU's general aim of ensuring that the WTO kept pace with globalisation of markets.

The inclusion of competition policy in the EU agenda for a comprehensive round appears to owe much to its promotion by competition and trade officials because it was EU practice. In 1996 the Commission assessed the case for an international competition policy (European Commission, 1996). The approach offered by the Commission appeared to be an extension of the existing EU approach, namely that an international dimension to competition policy was required to ensure that private restraints on trade do not develop to replace public restraints on trade, in the shape of tariffs or other border measures, as the latter are liberalised. This was the basis for the growth of EU competition policy as the common market was created. The fact that the Commission has full delegated powers for competition also helps to explain its push in this field. There was not much interest in the inclusion of competition from interest groups. Businesses, especially larger firms, were against international competition policy because it threatened a further layer of control on the international operations of companies and many civil society NGOs especially development NGOs were opposed to all Singapore issues, without much discrimination between them, as being impositions on developing countries. European consumer organisations were the only interests to favour stronger international discipline.

Of the four Singapore issues, the one that had clear support from business all the way through was trade facilitation. Originally pushed by international business in the shape of the ICC out of a desire to reduce the costs of conducting global business, trade facilitation became the one issue the developing countries were willing to see retained on the agenda.

The reasons for the EU to seek inclusion of the Singapore issues on the agenda therefore seem to be numerous. Perhaps most important was a desire to ensure that the further development of the WTO to match developments in the global economy were compatible with the EU norms. The second half of the 1990s was the peak of the liberal paradigm and the advance of globalisation. The EU approach to globalisation was that liberalisation should be accompanied by appropriate rules for investment, competition and, to a lesser degree, procurement. Path dependence also helps to explain the EU inclusion of these issues. All had been included in previous WTO rounds or in OECD level negotiations and so formed part of the wider trade agenda. EC competence did not appear to have been very important. The EC had competence for competition, procurement and most of what would be covered by trade facilitation (with the exception of funding) but not for investment.[22] Nor were the issues put on the agenda at the behest of interest groups, indeed business was rather lukewarm on the Singapore issues as a whole and NGOs, especially development NGOs strongly against their inclusion.

Explaining the Evolution of the EU Negotiating Position

The EU advanced the argument for the Singapore issues at the WTO Singapore ministerial in 1996 and Working Groups were established on each. Although these working groups show some elements of consensus, for example on the desirability of transparency in public procurement or for the eventual move towards greater cooperation in competition policy when firms operate internationally, there was

---

[22] Note, however, Art. 56 (TEC) and Art. 63 (TFEU) required the freedom of capital movements within the EU and vis-à-vis third countries and thus constituted a form of unilateral liberalisation. All pre-December 1993 member state controls on investment were however grandfathered in, i.e., allowed to remain in place.

no support from the major developing countries for their inclusion in the DDA. In some cases this was based on concrete concerns about market opening, but in most cases the developing country opposition was based on a concern that initial modest moves towards cooperation were simply a 'foot in the door' that would lead to greater commitments, or on a desire to play safe in the absence of knowledge of the costs and benefits of including such rules.

The text adopted in Doha in 2001 that launched the round was an example of constructive ambiguity in that it enabled a round to be launched, but did not specify exactly what would be included. This was to avoid a rerun of the Seattle ministerial that collapsed because it tried to tie down the details of the agenda from the start. In Doha India insisted on an explicit consensus on the agenda as a means of blocking the inclusion of the Singapore issues.[23] The discussions on the agenda therefore ran parallel with those on the modalities for agriculture as well as non-agricultural market access (NAMA) and services. The EU came under pressure to agree to modalities on agriculture before it had any commitment on the Singapore issues.

In order to ensure it retained leverage, the EU had to delay decisions on modalities until Cancun. At the Cancun meeting, the Singapore issues were discussed first, but there was no agreement on their inclusion. Faced with a breakdown in negotiations, the Commission negotiators agreed to drop two of the four Singapore issues and clearly investment and competition were the least popular. But this appeared to come too late to save the negotiations, which were then somewhat abruptly brought to a close by the Mexican chair. What made the Commission agree to drop two of the Singapore issues before there had been any agreement on agriculture or NAMA? One explanation would be that there was not strong support for the Singapore issues in the EU. Although agreed in principle, there was little interest in jeopardising the whole round and with it the prospect of greater access to emerging markets for industrial goods and services by keeping in issues that business did not support (competition) or was not very excited about. Second, there was no support among the member states in the Art. 133 Committee or Council to break off negotiations even though the EU's negotiating aims in terms of a comprehensive round were in jeopardy. This reflected the EU predilection for keeping negotiations going and its desire to lead in multilateral trade. Third, the lack of support from the US for the inclusion of the Singapore issues meant the EU was rather isolated in pressing hard for the Singapore issues, although Japan supported it. Progress in the Uruguay Round had been achieved thanks to US–EU cooperation; without US support the prospects for the EU prevailing were slim.

---

[23]   GATT practice had been that a consensus exists if no delegation present objects to what has been tabled. This clearly leaves scope for many developing countries to simply abstain, rather than risk the displeasure of the major powers.

EU Effectiveness in the DDA

This section aims to illustrate how the effectiveness of the EU in the WTO might be assessed using a negotiation analysis approach. Because of the scope of the DDA this has been done for agriculture and the Singapore issues only, but the conclusions that follow suggest some general findings.

In terms of preparation for the negotiation of these two topics, the EU could be said to have been effective. In agriculture, the EU prepared by introducing reforms in the CAP that helped ensure the EU had more flexibility than previously in the Uruguay Round when it was quickly isolated as the main barrier to progress. The preparation took the form of the Agenda 2000 and 2003 mid-term reviews of the CAP. The latter went further in delinking subsidies from trade than many had expected and both the trade and agriculture commissioners worked to bring this about (Lamy, 2004). In the case of the Singapore issues, the EU's domestic preparation was reasonably thorough. As early as the mid-1990s, the EU was preparing its position on competition policy. In the case of public procurement, the EU was well prepared because of its domestic regime in procurement. This was not the case in investment however, where limited EU competence for investment meant the EU did not have a full position.

When it comes to framing, there is a need to look at the round as a whole. Here the EU does not seem to have been very successful. It was not able to frame the negotiations as a comprehensive round covering a range of regulatory issues as well as market access issues and agriculture. This EU attempt at framing failed to convince either the leading emerging markets or the USA. In a reflection of the shift towards a more heterogeneous power structure in world trade, developing countries were successful in challenging the EU's attempt at framing and matching this with development as the key issue.

On the question of more detailed agenda setting, the EU also failed to get the Singapore issues onto the final DDA. These issues were included on the list of topics for the WTO's work programme from 1996 and the EU managed to keep the issues alive at the time the DDA was launched in Doha. But India's insistence on an explicit consensus on the agenda enabled it to effectively veto the EU's efforts to move the Singapore issues forward. One must also not underestimate the impact of the lack of US support for the EU agenda. At the Cancun meeting in 2003, the EU was forced to accept that it could not keep all the Singapore issues despite having had two further years to try and persuade the Indians and others of the case for keeping them. Agriculture was already on the inbuilt agenda for the negotiations. The core topics of market access, export subsidies and domestic support were also *de facto* set because of the precedent from previous negotiations. Within agriculture, the EU had some effect in shaping detailed aspects of the agenda. For example, it managed to ensure that export credit and food aid were brought onto the agenda as part of the debate on export credits. The EU went to some lengths to get geographic indications (GIs) on the WTO agenda and succeeded in this by linking GIs to the issue of notifications of the use of biological resources (WTO,

2008). This enabled the EU to form a coalition with many developing countries to counter the blocking coalition of the US, Australia and Canada and reflects a flexible EU approach to coalition building in trade.

The EU's effectiveness in negotiations must raise some doubts. The overall aim of linking concessions in agriculture to the Singapore issues or to a comprehensive and ambitious round failed. The joint paper produced with the US on agriculture could be seen as an example of the EU not recognising how the balance of influence in the trading system had really changed. Or to put it somewhat differently there was a belief in some parts of the EU that a joint EU–US leadership was necessary to make progress in the round. Once negotiations began after the framework agreement on 2004, the EU repeatedly made concessions in order to keep the round moving. It did so in order to provide leadership, but received very little back in mutual concessions from the other major partners. In general, EU decision-making during the negotiation appears to have functioned and the Commission was able to retain the support of the member states for its tactical decisions during the negotiations.

How effective the EU is in implementation cannot of course be judged on the DDA results. But there has never been any doubt about EU implementation of previous agreements. The EU has never failed to implement an agreement (involuntary defection). This is because the member state ministers endorse the final outcome of negotiations. On enforcement the EU has as good record on its own enforcement of agreements as any WTO member. EU domestic support for agriculture remained within the limits set in the Uruguay Round, and there have been few cases of the EU not complying with agreements concluded during the Uruguay Round. The two main cases were non-compliance with dispute settlement panel decisions on beef hormones and the ban on genetically modified products, which were found to be in contravention of the SPS Agreement.

Overall then, the effectiveness of EU trade policy in the DDA has been rather mixed. But one would need more case studies to assess the overall effectiveness. Equally a case concerning a bilateral negotiation could produce very different results. During 2010, the EU succeeded in completing FTA negotiations with the Republic of Korea, which could be seen as giving the EU a lead in FTA policy over the US. So agriculture and the Singapore issues cannot be generalised for the effectiveness of EU trade diplomacy as a whole. The intention here was to illustrate how one might assess effectiveness.

Conclusions

This chapter has shown that the analytical framework can be used to assess the relative importance of the various factors that determine the role of the EU in trade diplomacy. It has shown that in trade the EU possesses the attributes identified in Chapter 2 as being necessary to play an effective role as an actor in economic diplomacy. It therefore provides a good illustration of how the framework can be applied.

The conclusions from trade suggest that the EU is fairly efficient in decision-making and negotiation. The case of the DDA illustrates how the EU has the capacity to prepare well for negotiations. The comparatively smooth decision-making suggests that the EU has improved over the years in terms of its internal cohesion. During the DDA negotiations, friction between the Commission negotiators and member state and sector interests was contained enough to ensure the EU retained a cohesive position. The EU also had clear strategic aims in the negotiations. It was not reacting to other country initiatives, but had strategic objectives favouring the use of leverage it had in agriculture in order to promote a comprehensive multilateral round that it promoted over an extended period from the mid 1990s through to 2004/2005. A comparison with the trials and tribulations of the Uruguay Round process point to an improvement in the EU's decision-making processes, although the Uruguay Round was more comprehensive and thus more controversial. The effectiveness of EU decision-making is primarily thanks to the well-established procedures in place. This decision-making regime functions because all the participants share common expectations about how decisions are made.

In negotiations, the Commission also appears to have considerable autonomy, another criterion for an actor. In the case of agriculture the Commission had to work on domestic reform in order to have some flexibility, so its autonomy was limited. But bearing in mind that agriculture has been a case of capture for many years, the EU's commitments to reduce tariffs and domestic subsidies and eliminate export subsidies represent a significant shift in policy over the decade. An alternative explanation is that EU agricultural trade policy is merely following trends in the CAP reform. The case of the Singapore issues also suggests that the Commission had considerable autonomy. The push for the Singapore issues was, for the most part, not based on intense sector lobbying. Indeed, even on tariffs for goods, there has been only general business lobbying. Indeed, one could argue that one of the weaknesses of the EU negotiating position was that it had the autonomy to make concessions when others such as the US or India did not because of more constraining domestic win-sets. An associated weakness of the EU is its predilection to continue negotiating even when it appears to be making limited progress. The EU made concessions in Cancun and again at the Hong Kong WTO ministerial, without much reciprocation from its negotiating partners. This suggests that the EU had clear negotiating aims, but no clearly defined BATNA (best alternative to a negotiated agreement). In other words, it did not appear to have a lower threshold beyond which it would simply walk away from the negotiation.

The EU has had normative power in the field of international trade that derived from a consensus on framework norms in the shape of the SEM, as well as specific norms codified in the *acquis communautaire*. It has been argued that framework norms enabled the EU to pursue a proactive multilateral trade agenda in the late 1980s and to aspire to a leadership role in multilateral trade in the late 1990s. But normative power was not sufficient to enable the EU to shape the

DDA agenda. This may have been simply that normative power was not enough or because the momentum gained from the SEM was lost by the mid-2000s. If one considered bilateral negotiations, there may be a more positive view on the effects of normative power.

When it comes to market power, the EU enhanced its market power thanks to deeper integration in the 1990s, but this probably peaked during the 1990s. The EU's market leverage in reciprocal trade negotiations is also in relative decline due to the degree to which it has already liberalised and the emergence of faster growing economies (China, India and Brazil) that have higher levels of protection. The EU's lack of success in the DDA could therefore be due to insufficient market leverage, where market leverage is a combination of market size and what the EU can offer in terms of market access concessions. In other words, efficient decision-making and normative power are in themselves not enough without market power.

The consequences of these conclusions, if correct, are something that cannot be discussed in any detail here. A relative decline in market power would suggest the EU needs to consider an instrumental use of coalitions with whichever countries share EU objectives. Alternatively the EU could follow the bilateral route in order to maximise market leverage or consider threatening to close EU markets. The Global Europe strategy of 2006 represented a shift (back) to bilateral negotiations. This was consolidated with the reformulation of EU trade strategy in 2010. The 2010 strategy also introduces the idea that the EU may consider restricting access to the EU market, such as its public procurement market if emerging markets fail to offer more on government procurement. Finally, if the EU decision-making regime in trade diplomacy is to remain effective it has to now include the European Parliament.

Chapter 4
The European Union in International Financial Regulation

Introduction

EU economic diplomacy in the field of international finance and monetary relations has moved centre stage in the wake of the international economic and financial crisis of 2008. Financial diplomacy is a complex field because of the linkages between monetary, fiscal and financial market policy. For the EU, this adds to the challenge of developing coherent policies because competences and the role of the EU vary between these different policies. In general there is much less *de jure* or formal EU competence in the area of finance and less informal of *de facto* competence than in the trade case discussed in the previous chapter. Until the financial crisis, there was also no clear trend towards greater *de facto* competence, albeit long term and progressive, as in the cases of trade and climate change, which are discussed in the next chapter.

Financial diplomacy is characterised by a particularly high degree of endogeneity of markets in decision-making. In other words, policy decisions can have particularly important effects on financial markets. All economic diplomacy shapes and is shaped by markets, so there is a degree of endogeneity in all policy, but in finance these effects are greater and more immediate. In a financial crisis, speed in decision-making is important. At times there can be a need to reach agreed positions over the course of a weekend before financial markets open the next Monday morning because interbank lending has dried up or because delay would exacerbate uncertainty and nervousness in the markets leading to a loss of confidence that exacerbates the crisis. This need to act quickly poses special challenges for the EU because, given that member states remain competent in many areas of policy, any action requires policy coordination between them. There need to be pre-existing agreements on how to deal with crises and who will make decisions, as well as an understanding that reaching an EU position takes time that decision makers do not have in a crisis.

Another characteristic of financial diplomacy is the need for policy coherence between the different policy areas. As the financial crisis illustrated, effective policy responses require action in monetary policy to provide liquidity, refinancing of the banking system in the short term, followed soon afterwards by expansionary fiscal or monetary policy to mitigate the negative impact on the real economy and ensure that there is no extended recession that would undermine efforts to establish financial stability. Then in the medium term comes the need to reform financial market regulation. Policy coherence in financial policy is made difficult by the fact that EU competence varies across the various policy areas and institutions concerned.

In monetary policy, the European Central Bank (ECB) is a supranational body and is solely responsible for monetary policy within the Eurozone. When the ECB acts in international financial diplomacy, it does so with full delegated powers. Even here, of course, the picture is complicated by the fact that not all member states are members of the Euro and that there are important EU central banks, such as the Bank of England outside the system. In the financial crisis, the ECB acted autonomously to increase liquidity as early as August 2007, a policy the Bank of England did not follow until later. By setting the Euro interest rate, the ECB also acted, in coordination with other central banks, to provide an economic stimulus to counter the deflationary effects of the crisis. The interest rate set by the ECB then influenced the exchange rate of the Euro. Although there are treaty provisions for the Economic and Financial Affairs Council (ECOFIN) to decide on exchange rates, these only apply to the Euro's participation in formal exchange rate regimes, which is unlikely to be the case in the foreseeable future.

In fiscal policy member states are competent and 'represent' the EU in any international discussions or negotiations on policy coordination in the G7/8, G20 or IMF. Thus, fiscal coordination efforts to stimulate the international economy and trade following the financial crisis were primarily in the hands of the member states, and any EU role relied upon coordination between them. Internally, fiscal policy is shaped by various reporting mechanisms and the Stability and Growth Pact that sets targets and criteria for member state policy. In this area, the crisis has rekindled the debate on European economic governance, in other words, greater policy coordination.

With regard to financial market regulation, which is the focus of this chapter, the picture is one of shared competence between the EU and member states. The EU has competence for the realisation of a single financial market (SFM) within the EU. This means a Commission right of initiative and the adoption of EU-level regulatory provisions by Ordinary Legislative Procedure (OLP). There is also EU competence for capital movements both internally and on capital controls between the EU and third countries. But member states have retained competence for the supervision of financial institutions and thus how regulatory standards adopted at the EU level are implemented by banks and other financial institutions. As will be discussed below, the financial crisis has led to some strengthening of EU-level coordination of this supervision. Member state governments or the member state regulatory/supervisory agencies are also recognised as actors in the international bodies that discuss financial regulation and standards, whether this is the IMF, the Financial Stability Board (FSB) or the specialist standards setting bodies such as the Basil Committee on Banking Supervision (BCBS) and other equivalent bodies for securities and insurance markets.[1]

---

[1]   In the wake of the financial crisis and the strengthening of the FSB, the European Commission became a member alongside the European Central Bank thus strengthening

Due to limitations of space, this chapter focuses on the case of the EU in financial market regulation. Given the medium- to long-term nature of policy in financial market regulation, such a focus provides an opportunity to assess the various factors that shape the EU's role and make a comparison with the other cases discussed. Nevertheless, financial market regulation is shaped by conditions in EU monetary and fiscal policy coordination. The chapter therefore covers aspects of these policies in so far as they affect financial market regulation and discusses EU decision-making in these areas, but there is no coverage of the detailed debates on economic governance or responses to the crises in various member states that became a general Euro crisis in 2010.

The chapter shows that the EU has considerable potential market power in financial markets and that, unlike in the case of goods markets, this is not yet seriously challenged in the short term by the rise of emerging markets. But this market power has not been fully utilised because of a number of largely internal EU constraints. These take the form of fragmented decision-making structures and a lack of the kind of *de facto* EU competence that has been established in other policy fields (Posner and Véron 2010). The EU domestic *acquis* in financial markets has also lagged well behind that for goods, which has deprived EU financial diplomacy of a common internal policy base. Underlying differences between member states on how to regulate financial markets (as well as monetary and fiscal policy) have also meant no consensus on framework norms. If the internal foundations for EU financial diplomacy are weaker than in the case of trade in goods and services, the external forces demanding action are stronger. EU member states had to respond to a full-blown financial crisis in the autumn of 2008. As the section below on the EU response to the crisis shows, this has led to greater effort in strengthening EU policy coordination, but it remains to be seen whether the effect of the crisis as an external driver has brought about a significant and permanent shift towards greater cooperation and thus a greater role for the EU in financial market regulation.

As in the previous chapter, this chapter first summarises the evolution of EU policy. This provides a background to the description of the policy-making process in the EU, followed by a section that applies the analytical framework from Chapter 2 to the case of financial market regulation. There is then a case study in the EU's response to the financial crisis. The case study is a means of illustrating the EU decision-making processes and for assessing whether the general hypothesis developed in Chapter 2 explain the relative importance of the factors shaping the EU's role.

The Evolution of EU Policy

Integration in the field of finance has been limited or delayed compared to other policy areas. In monetary policy, the EEC was able to operate under the US dollar–

the EU-level involvement.

based system of Bretton Woods until the early 1970s. The 1970s and 1980s saw the introduction of Franco-German-led attempts to promote exchange rate stability in the shape of the snake and the European Monetary System (EMS). But it was with the Delors Committee of Central Bank Governors, established in 1988, that the push to create a common currency in the shape of the Euro really began. The case for the Euro was that the halfway house of the EMS was vulnerable to the pressure from currency markets, that pooling sovereignty would enable the Euro and thus the EU member states to have more of a role in international monetary policy and, most importantly, that the benefits of a genuine single market would not be fully achieved without monetary integration.

The Maastricht Treaty provided the legal basis for the creation of Economic and Monetary Union, including the criteria that were effectively to guide EU fiscal policy, the establishment and role of the European Central Bank (ECB) and the decision-making procedures governing monetary policy. The independence of the ECB was guaranteed. Indeed, the Treaty on European Union (TEU) granted the ECB a greater degree of independence than the US Federal Reserve and other central banking systems in that it was anchored in a treaty rather than national legislation that can be more easily changed. The primary role of the ECB was therefore to determine monetary policy for the EU, or for member states within the Eurosystem, with price stability as the main policy aim. With responsibility for financial flows within the Eurosystem, the ECB also has an interest in capital movement and the smooth functioning of the payments system because barriers to capital flows or rigidities would make the system less responsive to monetary impulses. But the ECB was not given responsibility for regulating financial markets. It did, however, develop a role in promoting cooperation between the various member state central banks and regulatory/supervisory bodies that were directly concerned with financial market regulation. After 2001, this coordination took place within the Bank Supervision Committee of the ECB. The ECB saw itself as having a role in monitoring the overall stability of the financial system. This flowed from the ECB's responsibilities for the stability of the Euro and it provided the basis for the ECB's role in the more formal provisions on systemic risk that were to be adopted in response to the 2008 crisis. Finally, the ECB has developed an important informal coordinating role thanks to its participation in all key decision-making bodies concerned with international finance, both within the EU and internationally. Internally, the European System of Central Banks/ECB provides a natural focus for coordination between all central banks within the EU, both those within the Euro and those outside. The ECB sits on the EU's important Economic and Finance Committee (EFC). The president of the ECB is present in all key discussions among member state ministers concerning financial matters and attends regular hearings in the European Parliament. Internationally the ECB is present in the IMF, the Financial Stability Board, the key banking regulatory committees and the G20.

In terms of fiscal policy, the Maastricht Treaty set out the targets for convergence criteria of fiscal deficits of no more than 3 per cent – and public debt of no more than

60 per cent of GDP. These provided the basis for the targets codified in the Stability and Growth Pact (SGP) of 1997, which was intended to set the framework for member state fiscal policies. Member states retained sovereignty over fiscal policy of course, with peer review based on Broad Economic Policy Guidelines (BEPG) and reports submitted by the European Commission as the means of enforcing conformity with the SGP. The Council (ECOFIN) can decide on the basis of a recommendation from the Commission whether a member state has an excessive fiscal deficit and there are provisions for sanctions. By late 2004, a number of Euro member states were violating the SGP, including France and Germany. Efforts to force France and Germany into line with the SGP, both by the European Commission and smaller member states which had been obliged to comply with the disciplines, including a case brought to the European Court of Justice (ECJ), were to little effect. As a result, the SGP rules were eased in 2005 to make them more flexible. Germany, however, still supported the SGP targets and strict discipline on member states fiscal policies. By 2007 France and Germany were again back within the guidelines, but with France arguing that the SGP was too rigid and that the EU needed to develop a more active form of economic governance that would enable the EU member states to respond, through closer cooperation, to changes in economic developments. This difference between fiscal austerity on the one hand and a more active economic governance on the other was to shape the EU's response to the financial crisis as shown in the final section of this chapter. It shows a lack of consensus on the framework rules for fiscal policy within the EU.

The Eurogroup was established in 1997 as an informal meeting of finance ministers from those member states participating in the Euro. Over the years the Eurogroup has assumed a more important role, both in terms of internal EU policy coordination, but also in terms of certain external functions, such as when the Euro is discussed within the IMF. In 2005 the member states in the Euro elected a president to represent the group for a period of years. Previously the presidency/ chair of the group had rotated and had been taken by the EU presidency if that was a member state within the Euro or the next Euro member state to hold the presidency when this was not the case. The Eurogroup has now been recognised in the Treaty on the Functioning of the European Union (TFEU).

EU Financial Market Policy: A Comparison with the Market for Goods

The treaty provisions concerning financial market regulation grant the EU competence for the free movement of capital and services (including financial services) within the single market. But the establishment of the *acquis communautaire* in financial markets has lagged the single market for goods and even that for some other services markets, such as telecommunications. The SEM Programme of 1986–1992 included directives aimed at bringing about a single market in financial services. There was the Second Banking Co-ordination Directive (SBCD) of 1988 which set out the principle that banks would be regulated by their home country (home country control) and that regulators in the member states in which these banks operated would recognise the regulatory control of the home state regulatory authority. This idea of a 'single passport' was also applied to investment services and insurance. But the single market in financial services was much less successful than in the case of goods. First, the treaty (see section below) provides a prudential carve out for national regulators to control (i.e., supervise) market operations of financial service providers coming from other member states. The scope to retain these national controls was not significantly restricted by the SEM directives of the 1980s, and many national regulators were not ready to recognise home country regulation in prudential matters. Second, and related to this point, the mutual recognition implied with home country control was not effective because there was no broad equivalence of norms and standards. There remained important differences between the national regulatory standards despite the EU legislation because of the flexibility in EU directives. Third – and again borrowing from the experience of the single market in goods – the policy-led initiatives in financial markets were not matched by private sector initiatives in the form of cross border operations, mergers or acquisitions. Compared to the goods market, financial services and banks, especially, remained relatively nationally oriented. Comparing banks with companies in the manufacturing sector in the late 1990s, only about 25 per cent of banks' operations were in other EU member states, compared to 66 per cent for manufacturing firms (European Commission, 2009 (j)).

Member-State Level Responses to International Competition

In the goods sector, it had been the pressure of international competition that led to an ending of the fragmentation of the EU market, which was seen as undermining European competitiveness. In financial markets there was also pressure from international markets, but the response was more national than European. The international pressure in financial markets came in two forms: competition from other major financial centres, such as New York, and changes in financial markets. There was a progressive increase in the internationalisation or globalisation of capital markets as well as a steady rise in the development of innovative financial 'products' such as the securitisation of various assets that undermined the divisions between market sectors (banking, insurance and investment services) on which regulatory policies had been based. National regulatory policies responded to these challenges by seeking to develop more specialist regulatory agencies. These sought to ensure financial centres could compete, whilst ensuring prudential security by developing and maintaining the expertise needed to keep pace with the increased sophistication and complexity of financial markets. Thus bodies such as the Financial Services Authority (FSA) in Britain and the Bundesanstalt fuer Finanzdienst-leistungen (BfF) were created. The key issue was what balance to establish between competing with other financial centres, which often meant a 'light touch' to regulation, and maintaining effective regulatory control.

EU-level regulatory co-operation remained *ad hoc*. Furthermore, the national approaches reflected deep-seated differences in national preferences. The regulation of finance and capital markets is inextricably linked to the nature of 'capitalism'. Britain, with its liberal tradition and the well-established position of the City of London as an international financial centre, emphasised flexibility through the use of general principles of regulation and a light touch in regulatory policies in order to be able to respond to developments in global markets and thus retain the competitive position of the City. Indeed, one could argue that British policies have long favoured 'the City' over manufacturing (Soskice, Vitols and Woolcock, 1991). In France there was also a desire to compete with London and other financial centres, but the French regulatory culture was based on clear rules including prohibitions. In Germany there was recognition of the need to reform regulation of financial markets in order to ensure that German companies had access to capital at competitive rates and to promote Finanzplatz Deutschland. The central BfF was established in Frankfurt to replace the fragmented Laender-based regulation in order to more ably respond to the challenges posed by the international integration of capital markets. The BfF wished to strengthen Germany's ability to compete as a financial centre, but policy was also shaped by opposition to radical moves towards 'Anglo-Saxon capitalism', i.e., a large capital market shaped by the principle of shareholder value and thus short-term financial interests, over 'Rhineland capitalism' which emphasised the interests of longer term corporate/management interests. Other member states came in somewhere between these two distinct approaches. These differences prevented the EU agreeing on framework norms for financial markets in the way it had for goods markets. Unlike in the goods market, member states effectively still pursued policies aimed at maintaining their own model of capitalism and promoting national financial sectors.

Deepening Integration in Financial Markets from 1998

At the end of the 1990s, various factors came together to give the integration of the EU financial markets more impetus. There was the introduction of the Euro that removed a major barrier to capital market integration and strengthened the argument in favour of the creation of an integrated EU financial market in order to reap the full benefits of the Euro. The creation of a genuine single European financial market was also promoted as enhancing the competitiveness of European business by providing access to a larger and more efficient capital market. This was important given, for example, the lower cost of capital for firms drawing on the New York financial market. The argument was also made that a continued fragmentation of the EU financial markets along national lines would undermine the competitiveness of EU financial and investment services companies, just as the fragmentation of the EU market in goods had undermined the competitiveness of EU manufacturers in the 1970s and 1980s. Against this background the Commission put forward proposals for a single financial market in its 1998 Financial Services Action Plan (FSAP) for the period 1999–2005. The Commission initiative was adopted by the Council in December 1998 and sought the completion of a single market, while maintaining effective prudential regulation (European Commission, 1998). Prudential control was high on the agenda in the late 1990s because of the recent experience with the Asian Financial crisis.

The approach adopted by the Commission was analogous to that of the Cockfield White paper for goods launched slightly more than 10 years earlier. The FSAP listed 42 measures that were considered necessary to harmonise EU regulatory standards in the financial sector (European Commission, 1999). These measures covered banking, securities, insurance, mortgages and pensions and were intended to help bring about broad equivalence in the national regulatory regimes that was necessary for home country control to function properly. Despite this agreement to work on a list of specific standards/norms, underlying differences remained. As noted above, there were differences between the regulatory 'cultures' in the member states. There was also the question of how EU regulatory standards should relate to international regulation. If the EU could develop common EU regulatory standards, it could be expected to have a major influence on international standards (Becht and Correia da Silva, 2007). But some member states, such as Britain, and some interests preferred the international level and feared EU standards would be more restrictive and thus undermine the competitive position of the City of London as a financial market. The approach to financial markets was also shaped by the prevailing mood of the late 1990s, which was one of fatigue with EU level legislation. The sentiment of the member state governments at the time of the Cardiff European Council in 1998 when the Single Financial Market Action plan was adopted, was generally sceptical of the need for greater centralisation and favoured more flexibility.

Before very long however, there was recognition that the institutional arrangements for EU decision-making in financial market regulation were not fit for purpose. Financial markets were developing, and new 'products' were being introduced that Commission officials could not easily follow. EU legislation on financial regulatory standards was being adopted, but these tended to lag behind the implementation of international agreements by the member states. Thus, new standards would be agreed in the various international bodies such as the BCBS and adopted at the national level before the EU endorsed the same international standard in an EU directive. So the role of the EU in international financial regulatory standards-making was one of a follower rather than a leader. In an attempt to improve and speed up the EU decision-making process as well as bring more clarity into the complex decision-making procedures within the EU, the Commission set up a Committee of Wise Men under the chairmanship of Baron Alexandre Lamfalussy.

The resultant Lamfalussy Report, which was devised initially for the dynamic securities sector, found widespread support and was adopted by the Council in 2001(Lamfalussy, 2001). In 2003 the approach was extended to the banking, insurance and pensions sectors. The Lamfalussy approach was intended to streamline decision-making and promote greater cooperation between member state regulatory bodies and the EU institutions (especially the Commission).

Lamfalussy favoured a structured cooperation between national regulatory bodies rather than the loose *ad hoc* cooperation that existed before.

After five years, there were a number of reports on the progress towards the Single Financial Market and the Lamfalussy process.[2] The general conclusion from these was that although most of the 42 pieces of legislation on specific norms had been agreed (39 had been adopted by 2004 and 41 by 2006), there was still no consistent implementation in the member states. The stress was therefore on the level-three and level-four implementation and enforcement provisions of the Lamfalussy process; see Figure 4.1 below. As noted above, the directives adopted left scope for differing national implementations with the result that divergences remained (Casey, 2006). Common regulatory standards were a necessary step towards equivalence of national regulation to create a single market, but were not sufficient. The Lamfalussy process had made improvements in the procedures for adopting implementing legislation at the EU level and established the means of greater co-operation between the national bodies, but there had been limited convergence on how these national bodies went about their supervisory functions (Larosiere, 2009).

The idea of a single EU-level supervisory agency was proposed by – among others – the French finance minister at the time of the debate on the Constitutional Treaty, and Germany was seen as being favourable towards the idea (Stichele, 2008).[3] A number of commentators suggested that a move towards a single EU regulator might be necessary if cooperation between national regulatory bodies did not improve. Indeed, even the Lamfalussy Report envisaged that an EU-level supervisory body might be required if less binding cooperation failed (Lastra, 2003). But this ran counter to the general trend away from more centralisation and EU-level regulation and was opposed by member states which feared that EU-level supervision would be heavy-handed. Even closer co-operation between the various national regulatory bodies does not appear to have been considered necessary or desirable by the member state governments. With no agreement on the issue the Commission accepted that cooperation between the national regulatory authorities would continue to be of a predominantly voluntary nature. The general sentiment was that there was a need for a 'regulatory pause'. The EU therefore

---

[2]   See the speech by Alexander Schaub, DG internal Market and Services, 8 December 2004, available at http://ec.europa.eu/internal_market/speeches/2004/2004-12-08-schaub; A. Murray, 'Over but far from finished – the EU's financial Services action plan' Policy Brief Centre for European Reform 2004 available at http://www.cer.org.uk; and for a view from the financial institutions, 'Working Document of DG Internal Market Services, 'Review of Financial Services Action Plan: publication of report of four independent expert groups for comment', 7 May 2004.

[3]   The relevance of the debate on the Constitutional Treaty is that any body at an EU level exercising discretionary powers must be provided for in the treaty. Those favouring such a centralized regulatory agency therefore needed to ensure there was provision for it in the revised treaty.

renewed efforts to bring about a genuine single European financial market, whilst eschewing binding regulatory co-operation.

In 2005 the Commission produced a white paper on financial services policy 2005–2010 (Commission, 2005). The White Paper argued for a redoubling of efforts to complete the legislative programme set out in the Financial Services Action Plan and to implement the provisions fully, stating that implementation by the member states had been poor. The white paper also stressed the need for better EU regulatory and supervisory structures. The proposals included delegation of tasks and responsibilities between supervisors and efforts to develop a common supervisory culture through exchange programmes between member state supervisory bodies. This can be seen as recognition of the continued lack of agreement on 'framework norms' for financial markets. There was also a call for, but no clear proposals on, a clarification of the role and responsibilities of home and host state regulators, such as in the event of a failure of a group that operates on a pan-EU basis. But the Commission still favoured an 'evolutionary approach' given that closer cooperation would 'raise [...] difficult issues of political and financial accountability, especially when support from the public purse might be called upon' (European Commission, 2005, p. 10). On the external front, the white paper argued for a 'strengthened European influence' in global financial market regulation and for Commission participation in the Financial Stability Forum. The Commission also proposed a continuation of bilateral Financial Market Regulatory Dialogue (FMRD) with the US and other leading economies. These FMRDs had been set up as part of the wider bilateral cooperation with the US on regulation and are conducted in parallel to discussions in various international financial bodies such as the BCBS. This was in the Commission's interest, since it led on these.

It has been argued that the system of 'structured' co-operation of national regulators was not up to the task of supervising the increasingly pan-EU operations of financial companies (Véron, 2007; Lannoo, 2008). The early 2000s had finally seen a significant increase in the cross border activities of European financial institutions. These pan-European activities posed challenges to member state supervisory agencies. How were these to be supervised if there were divergences between the approaches to supervision among the national regulatory authorities? The approach adopted was again one of co-operation between the national authorities in that colleges of regulators were to be set up to supervise each cross-border group. But there remained limitations to this. The nature of financial market operations, with the increased use of innovative products such as derivatives and more opaque market practices, made it very difficult for supervisory bodies everywhere to have a clear view of what was going on in the markets and thus the scale of risk exposure of banks and other financial institutions. This was true for all financial markets, but the burgeoning cross-border nature of the financial markets in Europe made this all the more difficult. Co-operation within the colleges began in the mid-2000s, but one might argue that the colleges of supervisors were still feeling their way when the sub-prime driven financial crisis began to unwind in 2007.

The member states in the Council (ECOFIN) produced road maps in October 2007 and May 2008 to guide the EU towards strengthened regulatory standards and cooperation in supervision. In terms of supervision the roadmaps urged better cooperation between supervisors and in crisis management as well as improvements in the supervision of cross-border bank and insurance companies (European Commission, 2007). The road maps called for a clarification of the EU's rules on state aid in the event of a need for a member state government to support a bank or insurance company in difficulties.[4] Finally, the ECOFIN road maps included provision for a simulation exercise to test the cooperation machinery in the event of a financial crisis. This was clearly in response to the growing threat of a crisis in 2007. A number of simulations of a financial crisis were run. One was initiated by the Commission in 2007, and other similar exercises were run by national authorities, such as the British FSA. There were no detailed reports of these simulations, but it has been reported that some of the findings were not very reassuring (Pauly, 2007). In 2007 the ECOFIN called for the adoption of a Memorandum of Understanding (MoU) on the management of a systemic crises. One has to question whether a voluntary MoU was a sufficient response. It was already clear that in the event of a crisis there would be a need for public funds to support banks in difficulties. But the MoU had only an indirect reference to the need for such funding. There was no *ex anti* agreement on what arrangements there would be for burden-sharing in the event of governments stepping in the support a pan-European bank. In a crisis uncertainty about funding or delays in deciding who pays what could be expected to make things worse.

When the financial crisis hit the EU in September 2008, therefore, the *acquis* was not complete. Legislative measures were in place to create a single financial services market, but implementation was not really satisfactory. More importantly, from the point of view of dealing with the crisis, the EU was still pursuing an evolutionary – that is, voluntary approach – to cooperation between member state supervisory bodies. National interests, a lack of agreement on financial burden-sharing (Goodhart and Schoenmaker, 2006), vested sector interests[5] and a divergence in supervisory approaches combined to block the reforms that were

---

[4]   The treaty prohibits state subsidies and thus by extension support to bail out financial institutions, but it provides for exceptions including in cases when there is a 'serious disturbance for the economy', which could clearly be argued were a major bank to collapse.

[5]   These vested interests consisted of offensive interests of the larger banking and financial institutions in expansion based on relatively high leverage and ease of access to markets and defensive interests of banks in smaller EU member states which feared the domination of larger groups supervised by home regulators in other member states that were not sensitive to the potential implications of financial difficulties for bank operations in other markets. An example which came to light in the crisis was the withdrawal of assets from the new member states by the large banking groups based in the established financial centres in the old member states once the crisis threatened their stability.

needed to strengthen the EU regulatory machinery and ensure that it was fully prepared for a crisis.

EU Decision-Making and Negotiation in International Financial Market Regulation

This section considers EU decision-making in financial market regulation and in particular the interplay between decision-making on EU financial market regulation and the engagement of the EU and member states in international negotiations on the subject. As noted above, decision-making in the field of finance is especially complex, with various EU and member state bodies engaging in different forums. This is especially true when it comes to considering the EU response to the financial crisis, the specific case study in this chapter. This section provides a description of decision-making in the core area of financial market regulation, but also covers decision-making in the ECB and coordination of member state governments in the Council on fiscal policy, as these were important elements of the EU response.

In financial market regulation, the EU has competence for drafting and introducing EU legislation on regulatory standards. It is the European Commission that drafts proposals that are then adopted by the Council and the European Parliament using the OLP. Member state regulatory agencies are integrated into the process as part of the four-tier Lamfalussy procedure. In response to the weakness of cooperation on regulation exposed during the financial crisis, the Lamfalussy process has subsequently been strengthened by the establishment in January 2011 of the European System of Financial Supervision (ESFS).

Because of the nature of international financial markets one cannot easily delineate between the EU-level financial market regulation and what happens at the international level. At the international level, one is faced with an equally complex picture, with European Commission, member state regulatory agencies and ministries/senior officials all engaging in negotiations. The ECB also plays a role. These various EU actors are engaged in financial diplomacy in the G20, the IMF, the Financial Stability Board (FSB) and the specialist regulatory bodies such as the BCBS, IOSCO, and so forth. Access to EU financial markets is also negotiated in the WTO within the framework of the General Agreement on Trade in Services (GATS), in which the decision-making procedures set out for external trade in the previous chapter apply.

Shared Competence for Financial Market Regulation

The EU is competent for the European financial market. Art. 63 (TFEU) prohibits all restrictions on the movement of capital and payments between the member states and between member states and *third countries*, and Art. 64 (TFEU) stipulates that the OLP is to be used in this policy area (see Figure 2.4 for a summary of the OLP). It is noteworthy that Art. 63 prohibits restrictions on capital flows between EU member states and third countries. The special legislative procedure (SLP)

– that is, unanimity within the Council – is required to place any restrictions on capital flows or reverse liberalisation under Art. 63 (TFEU), thus making a policy reversal to more restrictive policies harder than liberalisation. Financial services are to be liberalised in line with the liberalisation of capital movements (Art. 58 TFEU). This applies to regulation – in other words, to the adoption of EU legislation setting out regulatory standards for the EU market.[6]

As noted above, there has been debate about the need for EU-level supervision to replace the various member state supervisory bodies. Under EU law (in actual fact the case law of the ECJ), however, it is not possible to delegate discretionary powers to any body that is not provided for in the treaty. An EU-level supervisory body would need to exercise discretionary powers and neither the TEC nor the TFEU provides for such an EU level agency.[7] The need for a treaty change considerably strengthens the position of those member states that argue against centralised EU level supervision.[8] One potential legal route to an EU-level supervisory body would be through the ECB and the use of Art. 127(6) (TFEU), which allows the Council to grant powers to the ECB. But this would also require unanimity and as a number of member states have been opposed to the ECB acquiring regulatory powers, not least those that are not in the Euro, it has been and probably remains a political non-starter.

The Lamfalussy Report led to the introduction of a four-level decision-making structure with the Council and European Parliament acting on a Commission proposal on level one to set out the principles of EU legislation. See Figure 4.1. Level two consists of the Commission working with functional committees composed of senior national officials to adopt implementing legislation. Committees at ministerial or deputy ministerial level and including central bank participants from each member state, have been established for this purpose. These are the European Banking Committee (EBC), the European Insurance and Occupational Pension Committee (EIOPC) and the European Securities Committee (ESC); see Figure 4.2. The Commission then exercises the right of initiative, guided by dialogue and advice from the level-three committees consisting of member state regulatory/ supervisory bodies. These have subsequently been developed into authorities; see discussion of the EU response to the crisis below. At this level, the expertise of the member state bodies, who in turn draw on the input from market practitioners, is

---

[6] The European Parliament only has co-decision powers for EU legislation under OLP; it has no competence with regard to the positions which the EU institutions – such as the presidency, the Commission or the European Central Bank – take in international organizations (see Stichele, 2008).

[7] The Commission has not challenged this position, but makes the case that Art. 114 (TFEU) (the approximation of policies) might be used as the legal basis for delegating such powers to an EU-level authority.

[8] In the debate on the Constitutional Convention France proposed including provision for EU-level supervision, but this was before the financial crisis and member states and regulators were more sanguine about the ability of a voluntary approach to cooperation. Other member states such as Britain opposed this centralization of regulation.

Level 1	Legislation setting out broad objectives	Council and European Parliament legislate on the bases of Commission proposals
Level 2	Implementation	Ministerial level committees; EBC; ESC; EIOPC
Level 3	Transposition and cooperation at the level of financial institutions	CEIOPS, CESR, CEBR (member state supervisory agencies)
Level 4	Enforcement	European Commission

EBC	European Banking Committee
ESC	European Securities Committee
EIOPC	European Insurance and Occupational Pension Committee
CESR	Committee of European Securities Regulators
CEIOPS	Committee of European Insurance and Occupational Pensions Supervisors
CEBR	Committee of European Banking Regulators

Fig. 4.1   The Lamfalussy Process

intended to inform the Commission on technical aspects of regulation. Level four then concerns enforcement with the Commission assuming responsibility. This approach was first adopted for securities then for banking and pensions.

As the following section will show, the financial crisis has brought about a strengthening of EU internal decision-making. The De Larosiere Report of March 2009, which considered the EU response to the financial crisis with particular regard to financial market regulation, proposed the establishment of the ESFS in which the various EU-level committees became the European Banking Authority (EBA) based in London, the European Securities and Market Authority (ESMA) in Paris and the European Insurance and Occupational Pensions Authority (EIOPA) in Frankfurt with powers to oblige greater coordination between the member state bodies.

The EU Role in International Financial Regulation

The overall coordination for internal EU policy on financial market regulation takes the form of 'roadmaps' proposed by the Commission and adopted by the ECOFIN Council. These include proposals for legislative action on regulatory standards or cooperation, such as the Roadmap of October 2007 or that of May 2008. Proposals for legislation setting out broad objectives is then dealt with at level one of the Lamfalussy process with the Commission initiating the process with a proposal, based on advice and assistance from respective authority in the European System of Financial Supervision. This then goes to the member states for consideration. The proposals go to the Economic and Finance Committee,

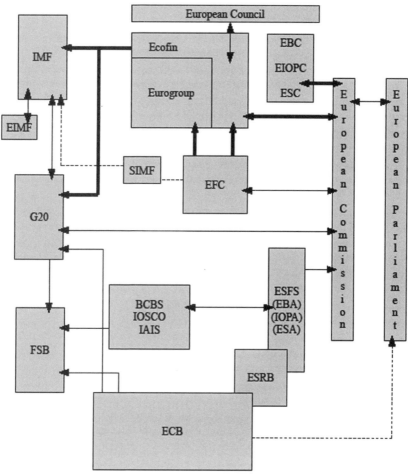

IMF   International Monetary Fund
EIMF   European coordination group in Washington
FSB   Financial Stability Board
BCBS   Basel Committee for Banking Supervision
IOSCO   International Organization of Securities Commissioners
IAIS   International Association of Insurance Supervisors
ESFS   European System of Financial Supervision
ESRB   European Systemic Risk Board
EFC   Economic and Finance Committee
SIMF   SubCommittee on the IMF
ESC   European Securities Committee
EBC   European Banking Committee
EIOPC   European Insurance and Occupational Pension Committee

Fig. 4.2   Decision-Making in EU Financial Market Regulation

which, with the assistance of its Sub-Committee on Financial Services, considers proposals before they go to the ECOFIN Council. Legislation setting out the broad aims of EU policy is then adopted by the Council and the European Parliament using the OLP.

More detailed provisions are then dealt with in the respective committee – that is, the European Banking, Insurance and Occupational Pensions or Securities Committee– before the transposition in terms of application by financial institutions across the EU is ensured by the various member state supervisory bodies coordinated within, for example, the European Banking Authority. Figure 4.2 provides a diagrammatic overview of decision-making.

The impetus for new or revised regulatory standards or practice can also come from the international level. Indeed in financial services this has tended to be the case to date. Initiatives for new regulations come from the specialist bodies or, as in the response to the international financial crisis of 2008, from the G20 summit meetings. The job of coordinating international work on financial regulatory standards falls to the FSB. When the impetus for new regulation comes from the international level, these agreed international regulatory standards are then adopted in EU legislation using the procedure described above.

The EU input into the international level of regulatory standards-making is fragmented. The EU input into the G20 summits is through some member state governments (France, Germany, Italy, the Netherlands and Britain) as well as the ECB and the European Commission. The president of the European Council has also participated in the recent G20 summits. Member states represent themselves in the G20. As in the case of the G7 finance ministers or the G8 summits, there is some informal coordination before G20 summits, usually on the fringes of ECOFIN meetings and ultimately in the European Council. For example, in preparation for the London G20 summit in April 2009, preparation included informal coordination in the Economic and Finance Committee (EFC), the Eurogroup and ECOFIN, as well as an informal meeting of heads of state and government in Berlin in late February 2009. But the member states represented by their ministers of finance are not obliged to hold to any agreed position and may well cooperate as much with other non-EU members of the G20 as with EU partners.

The Economic and Finance Committee (EFC)

The Economic and Finance Committee is the key coordinating committee for financial policy including the regulation of financial markets. Established in January 1999, it replaced the former Monetary Policy Committee one of the oldest working committees of the EU dating back to 1958. The EFC is recognised in the treaty under Art. 134 (TFEU). The EFC prepares ECOFIN Councils as well as Eurogroup meetings (carried out in the Eurogroup sub-committee of the EFC). It covers key issues relevant to EU financial diplomacy, namely monitoring financial stability, reviewing the policies of member states and preparing for international meetings. There are two representatives from each member state on the EFC, one from a ministry (finance) and one from the central bank. There are also two

EU member	G8	G10	G20	FSB	BCBS	IASB	IAIS	IOSCO	CPSS	CFFS
Austria							x	x		
Belgium		x			x		x	x		
France	x	x	x	x	x	x	x	x	x	x
Germany	x	x	x	x	x	x	x	x	x	x
Italy	x	x	x	x	x		x	x	x	x
Luxembourg					x		x	x		
The Netherlands		x	x	x	x	x	x	x	x	x
Spain			x		x	x	x	x		
Sweden		x			x		x	x	x	x
United Kingdom	x	x	x	x	x	x	x	x	x	x
Commission			x	x	x		x			
ECB				x						

Fig. 4.3   **Representation of the EU in International Financial Institutions. Source: Based on Becht and Correia da Silva (2007) updated by the author. The remaining member states are only represented in the IAIS and IOSCO.**

representatives from the ECB. The chair (president) of the EFC is elected by the members of the committee for two year terms, so there is no rotating presidency. Coordination with the Commission is facilitated by the fact that the Commission (DG EcoFin) provides the Secretariat. The EFC maintains links with the Economic and Monetary Affairs Committee of the EP by attending meetings and hearings. The full EFC meets once a month for two days. Restricted meetings are held with ministers only when member state economic policies are discussed. Twice a year the EFC meets as a 'Financial Stability Table' when it is enlarged to include the presidencies of the three authorities responsible for banking, securities and insurance under the ESFS. Decisions in the EFC are as in most EU bodies taken by consensus. Should there be recourse to a vote however, there is no weighted voting but one member one vote. The Commission has no vote. The EFC rather like the Trade Policy Committee has sought to promote active dialogue, which means no public minutes of meetings. There are various sub-committees dealing with the IMF (the SCIMF), the Eurogroup and a working group on sovereign debt.

EU participation in the FSB is similar to that in the G20. See Figure 4.3 for a summary of EU participation in the various international financial institutions. The member states in the FSB are essentially the same as those in the G20 and are represented by finance ministries, central banks and member state supervisory bodies. The European Commission and ECB are also present, but not the president of the European Council. As the focus of the FSB work is regulatory standards, the international level standards-making bodies such as the Basel Committee on Banking Supervision (BCBS), the International Association of Insurance Supervisors (IAIS), the International Organisation of Securities Commissioners (IOSCO) and the International Accounting Standards Board (IASB) are also included.

The International Monetary Fund (IMF) plays a fairly limited role in setting regulatory standards. Its role has been more in assessing the stability of its members' economies under the so-called Art. IV procedures. The IMF played a role in the response to the financial crisis by providing loans, and the IMF's capital was increased after the crisis to enable it to provide more support. After the 2008 financial crisis, the IMF is also expected to assume a more active role in assessing systemic risk. The IMF has also played a role in providing loans to some Eurogroup member states in the aftermath of the financial crisis. EU representation in the IMF has been the subject of a good deal of debate, much of it pointing out the EU's over-representation but limited influence.[9]

EU Representation in the IMF

The member states provide the EU presence in the IMF's Executive Board and Governing Council. There has been informal coordination in the EFC's sub-committee (SIMF) since 2001 and more formally since 2003. The chair of the EFC attends ECOFIN meetings. Any agreed position is however, not binding on member states. The EUIMF group brings together EU representatives on the IMF's Executive Board, the Commission, which provides the secretariat, and the ECB in Washington, D.C. EUIMF meets once a week, but with 50 or so participants, it is more a means of exchanging information than coordinating EU positions. On the Executive Board of the IMF Germany, France and Britain hold permanent seats, and six member states have seats as constituency chairs (some rotating with other members of the respective constituency). In the debate on the EU constitutional treaty, France and Germany proposed a consolidation of the EU representation in the IMF, but this ran into opposition from member states reluctant to give up their 'national' seats (Eurodad, 2008).[10] As part of the 2010–2011 reform debate on IMF quotas, which increased the role of the emerging markets such as China, the EU agreed to reduce the number of seats it holds on the Executive Board by two from 2014 (Pickford and Joicey, 2011).[11] The ECB also has observer status,

---

[9]   See for example, Gstoehl, 2008 and Bini Smaghi, 2006.

[10]   Art. 138 TFEU provides that the Eurozone member states may, on a proposal from the Commission, 'adopt appropriate measures to ensure unified representation within the international financial institutions and conferences'.

[11]   For a discussion of the options see Bini Smaghi, 2006 and Eurodad, 2008.

and when the Euro is subject to an Art. IV surveillance the EU is represented by the ECB, the EU presidency and the chair of the Eurogroup.[12]

Work developing international regulatory standards takes place in the various specialist bodies; the BCBS for banks, IOSCO for securities, the IAIS for insurance and the IASB for accounting standards. The work in these organisations, like that in the FSB, IMF and to a lesser extent the G20, is mostly done by the leading OECD countries. Again it is the member states rather than the EU that are represented in these bodies, and then not all member states. There are only a few EU member states in the BCBS and even fewer in the IASB, but all member states are represented in IOSCO and IAIS.[13] As in the case of all the international financial institutions, representation is shaped by the relative importance of national financial markets. Hence Luxembourg is included in the BCBS, but not larger states such as Poland. The European Commission also sits in the BCBS and the IAIS. This may facilitate some coordination of input, but the key coordinating role would seem to fall to the ESFS authorities that sit at both the international and EU negotiating tables on regulatory standards and are therefore decisive in determining whether the EU leads, follows or maintains the same speed as international regulatory standards-making. To date, cooperation in the ESFS's predecessor committees has been weak.

The European Central Bank (ECB) plays an important role in EU financial diplomacy through its autonomous decisions as well as through its presence in many international financial institutions. Within the EU, the ECB has no competence for the regulation of financial markets, although through its role in promoting cooperation between member state central banks it has had something of an oversight function. But as noted above, the ECB is represented in all key EU decision-making bodies, the EFC, the Eurogroup, informal ECOFIN meetings, as well as international bodies such as the FSB and IMF. The financial crisis highlighted the need for more effective monitoring of systemic risk and within the EU a European Systemic Risk Board (ESRB) was established in January 2011. See the section below on the EU response to the crisis for a discussion of the ESRB. The ECB provides the secretariat for the ESRB and is likely to play an important part in the work of Board.

---

[12] The impact of the Euro in the IMF was discussed in the Executive Board in 1998 with the conclusion that the IMF was a country-based organisation and that membership of the Euro did not affected the rights and obligations of member countries (Kiekens, 2003). The debate on whether the IMF could have the EU as a member (Smets, 2009) provided a means of deflecting discussion of any rationalisation of EU seats on the Executive Board. For many years this was a taboo subject among the member states.

[13] It is of interest to note that the private standards-making body of the IASB has recently been drawn more into public policy-making with the establishment of a Monitoring Board in 2009 that have as members a number of regulatory agencies including the European Commission. The purpose of the Monitoring Board is to ensure that the IASB meets the needs of public policy in terms of accounting standards.

The European Central Bank

The ECB has three levels of decision-making. The General Council that includes all the central banks in the European System of Central Banks (ESCB) – in other words, all member state central banks. The Governing Council, which meets twice a month and includes all the central banks of member states in the Euro. The Governing Council takes decisions on Euro monetary policy. Recommendations and regulations adopted by the Governing Council are implemented by the Executive Board led by a president appointed for eight years, a vice president appointed for four years, and four board members. Decisions of the Governing Council can be taken by votes. There is a maximum of 21 votes of which the Executive Board has and will retain six votes, regardless of how many countries join the Euro, large members states currently have four votes between them, medium-sized member states have in total eight votes and smaller member states three.

Financial markets are also shaped by other policies in which there is EU exclusive competence. Access to EU financial markets is determined by EU trade and competition policy. In trade policy, as discussed in Chapter 3, the Commission negotiates for the EU in GATS or bilateral negotiations. Since the adoption of the TFEU all trade negotiations on financial services are now EU exclusive competence. European competition policy is also relevant to financial market regulation. For example, the EU's response to the financial crisis included an easing of competition rules to enable member state governments to provide financial assistance to banks. The Commission has full delegated power in competition.

Factors Shaping EU Financial Diplomacy

This section applies the analytical framework from Chapter 2 to the case of financial market regulation. The general position appears to be that the EU's role in this policy area is as one level or forum in a multilevel process of negotiation. But why is this case? How does the relative importance of the various factors identified in the analytical framework differ in the case of financial market regulation from that of trade in which the EU's role is more that of a distinct actor?

Economic/Market Power

By virtue of the importance of its financial markets, the EU has considerable potential in terms of economic power. The EU market is more important than the US and Japan and other major financial markets in numerous core areas. In contrast to international trade, there is as yet still only a limited challenge from the major emerging markets. Asian economies hold the bulk of foreign currency reserves and therefore has considerable influence over exchange rate policies, but neither China nor other Asian countries yet play much of a role in setting financial market regulation. In terms of bank assets, insurance premiums, bond markets,

Market	Bank assets	Insurance premiums	Stock market capitalization	Debt securities
EU	50	38	25	35
US	13	32	36	35
Japan	10	16	10	12
Others	27	15	19	15

Fig. 4.4   EU Contribution to World Financial Activity (2008/2009). Source IMF, Bank for International Settlements and SwissRe.

debt insurance and payments, the EU is more important than the US, with Japan a distant third. Although New York and other US markets are more important in equity and above all in the derivatives that were at the centre of the recent financial crisis, it is not a great deal larger than the EU; see Figure 4.4.

But EU market power also depends on the degree of integration of its financial markets and the ability and willingness of the EU to use the leverage such market power provides to shape outcomes. European financial market integration is incomplete.

The future of financial market integration in the EU remains uncertain. The crisis has shown the weakness in the voluntary cooperation approach to supervision. When the crisis came, market integration had outstripped the ability of the nationally based supervisory bodies to cope. In these circumstances, the policy options were broadly to strengthen EU (and international) cooperation in supervision or to consolidate national supervision at the cost of some of the benefits of market integration.[14] The predominant policy response has been to strengthen EU-level regulatory cooperation (see discussion below), but it remains to be seen whether this response will continue once the immediate pressure of the crisis has passed. Continued integration would enhance the EU's market power. Indeed, one could argue that the EU's potential relative market power in financial markets could be as great as in trade, where it plays a leading role in international negotiations. The effects of the 2008 financial crisis can be expected to result in a shift towards a greater relative importance of the financial markets in major emerging markets, but it will be some time before this erodes the EU's position.[15] Potential market power does not by itself mean an ability to shape agendas or outcomes. This depends on whether the EU is recognised as an actor in financial diplomacy, how developed the domestic *acquis* is and how cohesive the EU is in decision-making and negotiation.

---

[14]   For the case for some national consolidation see, for example, Charles Goodhart in evidence to the House of Lords (2009). For the alternative argument, see the evidence of the British Bankers Association given to the House of Lords (2009) Select Committee on Europe. More generally, on the transatlantic debate on this point see Posner, 2009.

[15]   See European Commission, Commission Staff Working Document, Europe's Financial Integration Report 2009 SEC(2009)1702, 11 December 2009.

Recognition

Looking first at *de facto* recognition there can be little doubt that it is the member states that are generally recognised as the negotiating partners in many international financial negotiations. This has long been the case in the G7 finance ministers and remains the case for the G20. The only time the Commission is recognised is when there is discussion of a topic that is EU exclusive competence. Member states are also recognised in the IMF where the only recognition for the EU is for the ECB and for the chair of the Eurogroup when the Euro is being discussed. In the international bodies that shape financial regulatory standards, it is the national supervisory authorities or central banks that are recognised.

Representation of the EU member states in the various international organisations is also hierarchical. Some member states have permanent chairs on the IMF Executive Board others do not, some are members of the G20, others are not, some are on the FSB, and others are not. This hierarchical representation creates difficulties coordinating EU policies. The hierarchical representation of member states in international organisations also contributes to poor policy coordination within the EU.

A consequence of the recognition of member state governments or agencies is that negotiation and coordination takes place with third countries at the same time or sometimes in advance of coordination within the EU. This enables member states with a privileged representation to have a direct input into the international debate, rather than having to fight for their position in the EU first. This is clearly relevant in financial market regulation where the British, for example, have (at least to date) held positions closer to those of the US than some of their EU partners. When member state governments coordinate with third parties, the focus of negotiation clearly becomes the international level rather than the EU level. This has been the case in the G7 finance ministers meetings or G8 summits and is likely to be the case in the G20.

Systemic Factors and External Drivers

There appear to have been three main external drivers in the case of EU financial diplomacy. As in goods and services markets there is the need to compete. This has been discussed above and need not be rehearsed here. The analytical framework suggests that demands on the EU to negotiate can be also seen as a second external driver. This exists in the sense that some EU member states, the presidency of the Council and the Commission participate in G7/8 meetings and in IMF discussions. But these negotiations are about broad policy aims. They have promoted a degree of coordination between EU member states and efforts to develop common positions, but these positions are not binding on member states. EU coordination has also been in response to developments in the G7 rather than proactive attempts by the EU to shape G7 discussions. The third external driver is financial crises, and in particular the crisis that broke in the EU in September 2008. The effects of these can be observed in the increased efforts to coordinate EU policies during the 2009–2010 period. By definition, a crisis requires immediate action so in the absence of well-established procedures *ad hoc* coordination and cooperation has been necessary. As shown above the EU was working on what to do in the case of a financial crisis, but only in 2008. Once the immediate crisis has passed the incentive for action – and often the willingness to make any sacrifices needed to reach common positions – may decline. In other words when the external driver is intermittent EU decision-making may not be strengthened. If anything the need for immediate action has favoured *ad hoc* intergovernmental coordination.

Normative Power and the Acquis

EU normative power in financial market regulation is weak because there is no agreement on framework norms. This is due to a divergence between the Anglo-Saxon approach to financial markets favouring a large and open capital market able to compete internationally with other capital markets and thus favouring 'light touch' regulation, and the other major EU member states that have placed less emphasis on the competitiveness of financial market and more on the role of finance in funding economic development. It remains to be seen how the experience of the 2008 financial crisis will affect these two views, but without major structural changes in the scale and nature of the various European capital markets, differences are likely to persist, even if there is a general move towards more regulation. This difference of views has never been fully reconciled within the EU, which for many years during the 1990s opted for a form of competition between the different member state approaches. German initiatives in 2000 and 2007 that tried to include hedge funds in tighter regulation were blocked by Britain and the US and the recent crisis has strengthen the position of the critics of the Anglo-Saxon shareholder value model. The underlying normative position in France has also been that 'the job of banks is to finance economic development not to engage in speculation'.[16]

Despite a lack of agreement on the framework norms governing financial markets the EU has sought, with the Single Financial Market (SFM) initiative of 1998, to achieve broad equivalence of regulatory standards. But the lack of consensus on framework norms was accommodated by flexibility in the many of the Directives which left scope for a continued variation in national approaches and standards. For example the Directive on guarantees of bank deposits set only a minimum level of guarantee, but left scope for 'competition' between member states in offering higher guarantees.[17] Member state discretion on implementation of EU provisions is not unusual. One key difference however, is that in financial markets the EU has tended to adopt specific norms or regulatory standards that

---

[16]   See, for example, the speech by President Sarkozy to the 63rd session of the UN General Assembly, 23 September 2008, quoted in Helleiner and Pagliari, 2008.

[17]   This scope for national variations meant that when the financial crisis hit in October 2008, member states could still opt to act unilaterally without coordinating with others.

have been developed at the international level. Generally, the EU does not develop distinctive, EU-specific norms because of the need to compete in international financial markets. The EU follows international standards rather than lead in shaping them as would perhaps be expected of a body with normative power (Posner and Veron, 2010).

There are numerous examples of the EU following rather than leading in the adoption of international standards. The Capital Requirements Directive of 2006 adopted the Basel II rules developed in the BCBS in 2004. When Basel II was judged to be inadequate because its capital requirements worked pro-cyclically, the Commission proposed amendments, but only after these had been agreed in principle in the G20.[18] With regard to guarantees for depositors, the European Commission had for some time sought to introduce uniform rules, but member states watered down Commission proposals and insisted on retaining flexibility on the guarantees they provided. When the crisis struck and depositors threatened to shift funds to banks whose governments offered higher guarantees, the member states agreed to more harmonisation, but again the EU action came only after this policy had been agreed internationally in the G20.

When the EU gets close to leading in the application of rules, such as in the case of regulation of hedge and other alternative funds, the debate gets heated. Thus, when the Commission's proposed Alternative Investment Fund Directive (AIFD) was tabled to ensure inclusion of such funds in regulatory oversight, there were protests from the US on the grounds that the proposals were protectionist.[19] The British hedge funds sector, which accounts for the bulk of all hedge funds in the EU, mounted a campaign to stop the directive and the British government intervened. The issue was not so much protectionism as the EU getting ahead of the international level in setting regulatory norms. There had even been an international agreement at the Washington G20 summit on the need to ensure that all financial institutions were adequately covered by prudential regulation. But there was resistance to the EU leading in shaping specific regulatory norms for fear that these would differ from the international standard.

EU adherence to international norms is not dissimilar to what has happened in other policy areas. For example, as Chapter 3 showed the EU *acquis* in the shape of the SEM Directives owed a good deal to work conducted in the OECD and similar forums during the 1970s and 1980s. In the field of environmental policy, the EU has also adopted ideas developed elsewhere. The difference between financial

---

[18] The revised Commission proposals followed international norms by limiting bank exposure to any one party, establishing colleges of supervisors, including clear definitions of quality of capital and including rules on securitised debt (one of the instruments that had been at the centre of the financial crisis) which required the originators of securitised debt to retain a proportion (5 per cent) of the risk.

[19] The proposed regulation included a provision requiring fund managers to meet regulatory standards equivalent to those applicable in the EU if they are to have access to investors in the EU.

regulation and these other policy areas, however, appears to be that in finance the EU has been reluctant or unable to be the first to apply the international standards. In the case of goods markets and the environment the EU has pressed ahead with the adoption of international standards ahead of its main competitors. In trade and in issues relating to the environment, this has been supported by those who wish to see the EU provide leadership, but also by those whose saw a competitive advantage in adopting the norms first. In the case of financial regulation the absence of a consensus on framework norms appears to also mean no support for taking a 'lead' in the application of norms in order to shape their use.

Member and Sector Interests

Member state interests are closely associated with sector interests and are to a very significant extent the key variables that have determined the pace of progress and scope of the *acquis*. Sector interests vary from issue to issue and a detailed analysis across all sub-sectors of financial markets is not within the scope of this volume. As the framework in Chapter 2 suggests, however, there may be general issues relating to the member state positions that are worth mentioning. First is the issue of the defence of national fiscal sovereignty. This has limited the scope for EU-level coordination in international financial institutions because of a concern that coordination will lead to greater integration. The effects of this can be seen in the member state approaches to the supervision of financial markets. By blocking an *ex anti* agreement on financial burden sharing, the member state insistence on fiscal sovereignty represents a check on effective EU-level supervision of cross border financial institutions. The other general issue concerns the different national views on framework norms.

Sector interests need to be assessed on a sub-sector by sub-sector basis, but broadly speaking Britain-based financial institutions have tended to favour market-based solutions and have opposed (and continue to oppose) EU-level regulatory standards or attempts at EU-level supervision out of concern that this will undermine the ability of the London based companies to compete internationally.

The Institutional Cohesion

The issue of EU competence in the field of financial diplomacy varies between the areas of monetary policy, access and competition (full EU/ECB competence), fiscal policy (member states) and financial regulation (shared competence). This makes for a complexity when it comes to policy coordination. The initiative to revamp decision-making on financial market regulation that led to the Lamfalussy proposals illustrated the general weakness of decision-making regimes prior to Lamfalussy. The reforms that the Lamfalussy process introduced are also of fairly recent vintage, and even then cooperation was only voluntary. By the time the financial crisis hit in 2008, the decision-making regime could not be said to have been well established. Delays in decision-making during a crisis simply fuelled the crisis, so member states stepped in, in a more or less coordinated fashion. In other words the decision-making regimes in the EU for financial diplomacy are either based on voluntary cooperation or in the case of the ESFS are not well established.

The EU Response to the Crisis

This chapter has focused on financial market regulation. The EU response to the crisis also included monetary policy responses from the ECB and other central banks in the form of increased liquidity and lower interest rates as well as fiscal policy measures by the member states. There were also some small measures taken in the form of EU expenditure and investment by the European Investment Bank (EIB). The immediate need in late 2008 was to address short-term issues such as the 'credit crunch' or the drying up of interbank lending and the consequences for the real economy of the financial crisis. There were medium-term measures required in terms of restoring confidence in financial market regulation, such as action to address the weaknesses in the Basel II framework for risk assessment, which had clearly failed to ensure systemic stability. But only once the immediate anti-crisis responses had been taken, was there then time to consider the medium to long term issue of how to improve financial market regulation, although general principles concerning regulation, such as the aim to ensure that all financial instruments were covered, were included in early statements of the EU and G20.

In a sense, the EU response to the crisis could be said to have started in October 2007 and May 2008 when the ECOFIN Council adopted it's Road Maps for the EU financial market policies. These decisions reflected a recognition of the need to strengthen EU cooperation in regulation and supervision. The Road Maps included proposals for (i) enhanced deposit guarantee schemes, (ii) better co-operation between supervisors, (iii) measures to strengthen supervision of intra-EU bank and insurance groups, (iv) improved cooperation in crisis management, and (v) EU-wide simulation of the arrangements for crisis management of cross-border groups. A Memorandum of Understanding (MoU) on cooperation between financial supervisory authorities, central banks and ministries of finance of the EU was also adopted in June 2008 and signed by 118 institutions in 27 member states, a number which says something more about the scale of the challenge of coordination than its efficiency.

The Immediate Measures

The first EU response to the crisis came in the form of a meeting of the heads of state and government of the four EU members of the G8 in Paris on 6 October 2008. These were joined by the president of the ECB, the president of the European Commission and the chair of the Eurogroup. This meeting was followed the day after by a meeting of ECOFIN. The ECOFIN Conclusions stressed the need for cooperation, but also that public intervention would take place at the member state level in a coordinated fashion. There was agreement to recapitalise vulnerable, systemically relevant financial institutions and a strong signal that the pro-cyclical mark-to-market valuation of assets should be used more flexibly. In order to enable member state support for banks, there was agreement that EU state aid controls would be relaxed and that the Growth and Stability Pact would be applied to reflect the exceptional circumstances of the crisis. Finally there was agreement to adopt common standards for deposit guarantees. The immediate focus was therefore not on regulatory issues except those that had an immediate effect, and there was only a general statement favouring cooperation on supervision.

Other meetings followed that broadly endorsed this approach. There was a summit meeting of the Eurogroup in Paris on 14 October 2008, the first meeting of the Eurogroup at head of state and government level. This was followed by a meeting of the European Council on 16 October which endorsed the approach developed in the ECOFIN and Eurogroup meetings. The European Council also stressed the need for international cooperation and two days later President Sarkozy as president of the Council and Commission President Barosso met with President Bush to propose what was to be the first G20 summit meeting, which then took place in Washington on 15 November 2008. At the EU level, an informal European Council meeting took place on 7 November to agree on the EU approach to the G20 meeting. The EU aims that emerged from these meetings included rather more on the regulatory issues. There was a policy of including all market segments in regulation in the future, an aim for greater transparency, reform of accounting standards, the introduction of colleges of supervisors (at the international level), and improved surveillance to prevent destabilising imbalances. The EU favoured IMF coordination of the FSB and greater resources for the IMF. These aims were broadly reflected in the G20 conclusions, but the G20 also called for fiscal stimulus and on this point there was a divide within the EU between Britain and France that favoured significant fiscal stimulus and Germany that was more cautious.

On the EU-wide regulatory framework the Commission moved on 8 October 2008 to establish a High Level Group chaired by M. De Larosiere to discuss the causes of the crisis and propose how the EU should respond. The Commission also moved to accelerate certain elements of the Road Map including proposals to harmonise deposit guarantees, setting minimum levels of guarantee at Euro 100,000 and adjustments to the use of mark-to-market evaluation methods. The deposit guarantee case shows how delays in fully implementing genuinely common regulatory standards made the EU vulnerable in the crisis.

Perhaps the best illustration of how common EU action was finally brought about after much foot dragging and opposition by member states was with regard to coordination of financial market supervision. Early in the French presidency in July 2008 there had been proposals to strengthen supervisory cooperation backed by strong demands from the European Parliament for more effective action. But these were opposed by member states concerned about more regulatory control at the EU level and the lack of any agreement on financial burden sharing in the case of any bailout.[20] The De Larosiere report published in March 2009 was critical of the voluntary co-operation between supervisory bodies within the EU, arguing that this was not functioning adequately. De Larosiere made two proposals on institutions. First, that there should be a European Systemic Risk Council (ESRC) chaired by the ECB and including the Commission, CEBS, CESR, CEIOPS to address the macro prudential risk, which had been largely overlooked in regulatory practice leading up to the crisis. The focus on micro supervision of specific banks had failed to see the broad systemic problems that were building up in financial markets. The second proposal was for the creation of the European System of Financial Supervision (ESFS) with three authorities that would have binding powers to ensure coordination and common supervisory practices across the EU. De Larosiere proposed the introduction of the ESRC in 2009–2010 and the ESFS in 2010–2011. In April 2009 a special informal meeting of finance ministers and central bankers endorsed the need for an ESRC, but stopped short of endorsing the ESFS. Again, differences of interest over the form of supervision seem to have got in the way of agreement. A number of member states had reservations concerning the stronger powers for the new authorities and Britain remained opposed to any powers that might impinge on fiscal sovereignty. On the other hand, there were member states pushing for stronger powers for the authorities and these were backed by the European Parliament.

In September 2009 a compromise was reached that provided for a so called 'triple lock' on decisions taken by the new authorities. This was in effect a right to seek three reviews of any decision taken by one of the authorities. The first review is possible in the ECOFIN Council. If the member state concerned gets no satisfaction there, it could then seek a simple majority of the member states in ECOFIN to overturn the decision. If this failed there can be a final appeal to the European Council. There were also issues relating to the establishment of the ESRB and in particular to the proposal that it be chaired by the ECB. Here the compromise was that the chair would be appointed by the General Council of the European System of Central Banks (in other words including a vote by all EU central banks).

The ESFS with its three new authorities for banking, securities and insurance supervision was finally agreed by the European Parliament in September 2010, and the new authorities started work in January 2011. The case of the new supervisory arrangements illustrated that member state interests in the form of sensitivity to any encroachment on fiscal sovereignty remained a key factor in shaping EU policy. These member state interests also reflected sector interests, especially those in the City of London which were concerned about EU level regulation affecting their international competitiveness.

---

[20]   Where fiscal commitments were not concerned, there was less resistance to EU-level regulation, as in the case of rating agencies where a significant consensus had already emerged before October 2008.

Effectiveness

Conventional wisdom is that the EU has not been effective in financial diplomacy. This appears to be born out by the discussion above and also seems to be the case for financial market regulation. In other words, there is a confused picture in terms of formal competence for the EU and reluctance to adopt pragmatic approaches to international negotiations. Other key reasons for the poor performance of the EU in financial diplomacy are the fragmented and hierarchical representation of the EU and member states in international financial institutions and the lack of any agreement on framework norms for financial markets.

Preparation for international negotiations is also poor. The Commission could provide a lead here in the same way it does in international environmental negotiations by pushing the domestic agenda and proposing strategic aims for international negotiations, but this has not happened. The main reasons for this appear to be a reluctance or inability of the Commission to overcome the underlying differences between member states and the timing of the efforts to establish a single financial market which coincided with a desire for more voluntarist approaches after 2000. During the first Barroso Commission, the Commission was willing to accept a gradualist, progressive approach, which meant that EU-level coordination on financial market regulation fell behind market developments.

The EU has not been effective in shaping agendas and, as noted above, has tended to follow rather than seek to shape agendas. The main reason for this seems to be the lack of a consensus on framework norms. During the crisis in late 2008 the EU (or rather the member states that were also members of the G7/8 and G20) does appear to have been able to shape the international agenda, for example in the agenda for the first series of G20 meetings. But this was during a lame duck US Administration.

In terms of the effectiveness of the EU in negotiations, there is no delegation to a single EU negotiator as in the case of trade, or environmental diplomacy. Coordination is the order of the day. The coordination also tends to be *ex post* in response to the international initiatives coming from bodies such as the G20 and the FSB in which EU member states shape policy in coordination with other third countries. Coordination at the EU level comes in the shape of the EFC and ECOFIN or on occasions the European Council. In most cases there is no medium- to long-term strategic approach to negotiations. In the case of financial market regulation the Commission has sought to provide a strategic direction through Action Programmes on domestic regulation. But for the most part, the EU has not been able to lead in international negotiations on financial regulation because of a desire on the part of key interests to avoid any lead for fear that the EU would get out of line with regulatory standards set elsewhere. This policy has been strongly influenced by member state and sector interests that wish EU financial markets to remain internationally competitive. Any suggestion that the EU is getting ahead of international standards and thus providing a lead has tended to lead to strong opposition, as in the case of the Alternative Investment Funds Directive (AIFD).

If one defines EU financial diplomacy as including the ability of the EU to regulate financial markets effectively, then the EU has clearly not been effective in the implementing phase. The lack of effective EU-level coordination of supervision contributed to the damage caused by the financial crisis in 2008. Had EU-level supervision kept up with developments in financial markets, the EU might have contained some of the impact of the financial crisis.

Conclusions

The EU role in international financial market regulation has been as one level or forum in what is in effect a multilevel process of negotiations. The EU has been an important forum for discussion rather than a distinctive actor. It has been the member states that have led in negotiations in the IMF, FSB and G20. In these international level negotiations the member states have coordinated their positions, but have done so through voluntary means, which has meant member state interests have often prevailed over any general EU-level preference. The EU does not therefore appear as a distinctive actor in these negotiations in the same way it does in international trade or environmental negotiations. The EU does, however, possess important market power so that international financial standards will only be effective if the EU implements them. It is possible, therefore, to argue that the EU has normative power in international financial market regulation, but its recognition as an actor is limited by the important role that EU member states play in their own right in international negotiations. But if, as argued in Chapter 2, the exercise of normative power requires the EU to take a lead the implementation and thus interpretation of internationally agreed principles or norms, this chapter suggests that the EU has limited normative power in international financial market regulation.

The analytical framework developed in Chapter 2 offers a number of explanations for the role of the EU in international financial markets. The EU is not recognised as the actor representing the member states, because it remains the member states that are recognised through their representation in the international organisations that deal with financial market regulation. This representation is also hierarchic, which appears to confirm the view that such representation in international institutions undermines EU level cooperation.

The EU's role has also been affected by the delayed and incomplete nature of the EU *acquis* on financial markets. Efforts to realise a genuine single financial market in the EU came late after the SEM for goods. This helps explain why the EU has a less cohesive position in external negotiations on financial markets. Some progress was possible on the detail of the *acquis* and thus towards developing specific norms, but there remained no consensus on framework norms for financial markets in the EU. There remained (and remain) fundamental differences between member states on the role that financial markets should play and in particular on the regulatory framework for financial markets. This lack of consensus on framework norms meant that specific standards were often watered down by exceptions. The retention of member state competence for supervision also meant that the implementation of specific standards/norms was not uniform. The lack of a consensus on framework norms then worked against the EU exercising any leadership in financial market regulation.

The EU comes under pressure to improve policy coordination when there are tensions or crises in the international financial system. This was of course the case during the 2008–2009 financial crisis. But such external drivers, though exerting significant pressure for the short term, have been only intermittent. The financial crisis thus offers an opportunity for greater cooperation and for making advances in common EU regulation, but once the immediate pressure of the crisis has passed there is a tendency of the member states to revert to their previously held positions that had held back stronger EU-level regulation. The 2008 crisis led to a redoubling of efforts to strengthen EU financial standards and supervisory cooperation, and the European Commission has assumed a more active role. But at the time of writing it remains unclear whether this will lead to a permanent shift towards greater EU-level cooperation.

Structural differences between the member states go a long way to explaining the different member state interests. The size of the London capital market and the concentration of financial services in Britain meant that British interests were significantly shaped by a desire to retain the competitive position of the British financial services sector. A strong financial sector was then seen as a means of ensuring low-cost finance for the rest of the economy. In other member states the balance was different with the competitiveness of industry and the general economy given greater emphasis and less focus on the competitiveness of financial markets.

EU decision-making in the field of financial market regulation was still in the process of being strengthened when the financial crisis struck. The evolutionary approach to cooperation in regulation and especially supervision meant that there was no established decision-making regime (or *de facto* competence) in place. This may have been due to the use of the voluntary approach adopted, but equally important was the fact that the efforts at greater cooperation were still relatively recent.

Finally, coherence in EU financial policy was an issue in the sense that greater cooperation in financial market regulation was significantly inhibited by member states jealously guarding fiscal sovereignty.

Chapter 5
EU External Environmental Policy

Introduction

International environmental policy is a field in which the role of the EU has evolved progressively over a period of a little over 30 years. When international environment policy first emerged in the 1970s, the EC's role was insignificant, and the member states showed limited coherence in negotiations. During the 1980s, there was more of a common EU position in the negotiations on the Montreal Protocol on Ozone Depleting Substances. But since the 1990s, the EU has assumed a more important – indeed a leadership – role in international environmental diplomacy. The EU has developed this role despite the absence of any reference to the environment in the Treaty of Rome. The European Community was granted express powers to negotiate on international environment topics only in the Single European Act (SEA) in 1986 and more specifically in the Treaty on European Union (Maastricht). The EU has competence for domestic environmental policy, but it has been shared between the member states and the EU when it comes to conducting international environmental negotiations. The adoption of the TFEU has led to differing interpretations in terms of external competence, with the Commission arguing that it effectively extends competence to the EU.

Although policy coordination within the EU has at times been laborious and slow, shared competence has not prevented the EU developing common policies and positions in international environmental negotiations. Convergence between the positions of key sector interests over time, together with fairly consistent public support for environmental policies, means the EU has come to support common framework norms and built a strong internal *acquis* in the field of the environment. Agreement on framework norms together with strategic direction from the Commission has facilitated joint action in international fora. The need for action, such as on climate change and demands on the EU to adopt common positions in advance of key international negotiations, has provided more or less consistent pressure on the EU to develop its positions on international environmental policy. But the EU has assumed a leading role in international environmental policy in part because the US opted not to provide any leadership during the 2000s. International environmental diplomacy, like the case of trade diplomacy, is, however, now becoming more and more multi-polar in that solutions to challenges such as climate change require cooperation among all major economies. As the case study on climate change discussed in this chapter shows, EU leadership based on normative power has not been very effective. But in terms of the debate on EU economic diplomacy, there seems little doubt that the EU (as opposed to the member states) will continue to play a major role in international environmental diplomacy.

Following the pattern of the previous chapters, the next section provides a summary of the historical evolution of the EU role in international environmental negotiations as background for the following sections. The chapter then describes how the EU goes about decision-making and negotiation in this policy area. This is followed by a discussion of the relative importance of factors identified in the analytical framework in chapter two. A more detailed case study of climate change is then provided to help to bring out the specific challenges facing the EU during negotiations and to illustrate of how the effectiveness of EU policy in this field could be assessed. It should be noted, however, that although climate change in the most high profile case in EU international environmental policy, it is not typical. Precisely because of the high profile of the issue member state ministers (and heads of government) wish to play a more active and visible role than in lower profile issues. As a result, the role of member states especially in the big environmental conferences is greater than in most environmental negotiations.

The Evolution of EU Environmental Policy

The Treaty of Rome contained no reference to the environment. Thus, unlike trade or other policy areas such as competition or agriculture, there was no express EEC competence in the field. Engagement of the EEC began in the 1970s when member state responses to international environmental challenges and negotiations, such as those following the UN Conference on the Human Environment in Stockholm in 1972, led to a concern in the Commission that actions taken by the member states in pursuit of international agreements could pose a threat to the common market for goods. This led to the production of the first European Programme of Action on the Environment in 1973. In the absence of any explicit treaty provisions the Commission used Art. 100 (EEC), which was intended for measures to tackle barriers to trade within the common market, to support proposals on environmental policy. At the time Art. 100 (EEC) required unanimity, so progress on environmental issues, as on all Art. 100 provisions was slow.

In the 1960s and 1970s, the US led when it came to framing the debate on environmental policy. In international negotiations, such as on the 1979 Convention Long Range Transborder Air Pollution (LRTAP), the member states were represented by the presidency of the Council of Ministers and the Commission, with the Commission speaking on issues, such as trade, that were Community competence. The Community gained some formal recognition in that provisions were added to the LRTAP agreement on the participation of Regional Integration Organisations (REIO) to facilitate the participation of the Community. But this had to be negotiated in the face of opposition from some of the Community's negotiating partners. At this stage, however, the Community was not recognised as an actor, as shown by the case of the negotiations of the CITES (Convention on International Trade in Endangered Species) agreement that was negotiated by the member states and only subsequently implemented in Community legislation.

During the 1980s the Community began to develop a more common, cohesive approach with the presidency negotiating on issues of national competence and the Commission on issues of Community competence. In the negotiations on the Montreal Protocol on Ozone Depleting Substances, the Community's negotiating partners again questioned the role of the Community, with the US expressing doubts about the ability of the Community to ensure proper implementation of commitments by all EC member states. The USSR was opposed to the Community becoming a signatory because it did not wish to grant the EC political recognition. Initially divided on the issue of controlling ozone depleting substances, the Community's position evolved during the negotiations thanks in part by a consensus among business interests and public opinion in favour of measures to ban the production of the main ozone depleting substances. The Community agreed to the Montreal Protocol, but member states also had to sign the agreement, because the financial assistance for developing countries clearly fell under member state competence. In the SEA of 1987, the Community was given express competence to negotiate international environment agreements, something that was further strengthened in the Treaty on European Union (Maastricht) in 1991. Since the early 1990s, the EU's role in international environmental policy has grown stronger.

The framing of the climate change negotiations was influenced by international epistemic communities building on work in the scientific community. The International Metrological Institute (IMI) in Stockholm conducted a five-year research programme with the support of the World Metrological Organisation and the United Nations Environment Programme (UNEP) on the causes and consequences of greenhouse gases, the results of which were presented in 1985. These findings led to the establishment of the Advisor Group on Greenhouse Gases (AGGG) consisting of scientists, again with the active support of the UNEP. This was followed by the Intergovernmental Panel on Climate Change (IPCC) in November 1988. These two bodies provided the link between the scientific community and policy-making. By the late 1980s the work of such epistemic communities, combined with pressure from NGOs and public opinion in general, forced more and more governments to take climate change seriously. Governments moved to regain control over the process and thus the framing of the issues by creating the INC (International Negotiating Committee) in February 1990.

At the end of the 1980s there was a shift in the respective positions of the US and the European Community. The US, which had made much of the running in international environmental policy up to that time, began to shift to a more sceptical position on climate change. Europe was moving in the opposite direction due to the pressure of public opinion for action to contain global warming and to growing support among business especially in member states such as Germany, the Netherlands and Denmark, which recognised the case for – and opportunities in – investment in low carbon and low or alternative energy products. At an EC level, much of the initial response came, as one would expect, from ministries of the environment, but without there being a great deal of horizontal coherence between the environmental policy objectives and other ministries. For example, the EC environment ministers set a target of a 20 per cent reduction of EC carbon emissions over the period 1986–1995, but this was not supported by the decisions of other often more weighty government departments, such as finance and energy. Commission proposals for a carbon tax, seen by environmental interests as an important plank of EC policy in the run up to the Rio UN Conference on Environment and Development in 1992, required unanimity and were opposed by a number of EC member states.

At the beginning of the 1990s, the EU moved to adopt a more proactive position in climate change negotiations by setting the target of stabilising emissions of greenhouse gases. The Commission drove this policy forward and framed the debate by producing Communications on climate change in 1988 and 1989 (Wettestad, 2000). This proactive position was made possible by initiatives taken at the member state level and some fortuitous developments. Countries such as Germany, the Netherlands and Denmark set the pace by setting targets for reductions in emissions, in the case of Germany 25 per cent reductions by 2005. Germany was considerably helped in this by the fact that German unification meant it could credit large reductions in carbon emissions due to the replacement of very polluting plant in the former German Democratic Republic (GDR) and the collapse in industrial output after unification. In the case of Britain, the switch to gas for power generation also enabled significant reductions of emissions compared to the more carbon intensive coal-fired power generation. The EU's position was, however, also driven by external factors and a desire to provide leadership in the international debate on climate change.

In 1991 the European Commission proposed a package of measures including a carbon tax, a SAVE programme on energy efficiency measures, an ALTENER programme to promote the use of renewable sources of energy and an EU Monitoring Mechanism to gather information on member state programmes and carbon emission levels. The impact of the package was limited. Member states opposed tax measures for reasons of fiscal sovereignty and differing energy supply structures. France favoured a carbon tax because it produced most of its electricity by low carbon nuclear power, member states which used less nuclear power favoured an energy tax, and Britain was opposed to any tax measure adopted at an EU level. The SAVE and ALTENER programmes were very modest with only Euro 45m and Euro 40m, respectively, set aside for multi-annual programmes. The EU Monitoring Mechanism was more successful and established the basis for future EU commitments on carbon emissions. But it also focused on policy development at the member state level (Wettestad, 2000). A further factor at work in the early 1990s was the backlash against further EU legislation and regulation among member state governments following the intense activity of the SEM programme. In this respect, EU climate change policy appears to have been affected in a similar fashion to financial regulation.

The efforts of EU environment ministers helped ensure that the EU set the pace in the run up to the negotiation in 1992 of the Framework Convention on

Climate Change (UNFCCC), at least in terms of setting targets. But the EU arrived at the Rio conference without a very cohesive position. As noted above, much of the initiative came form individual member states, and in the pre-negotiation phase member state governments were also recognised as negotiating partners rather than the EU. One example of bilateral negotiation was President George H.W. Bush's effort to persuade Chancellor Kohl of Germany to drop the idea of specific targets for green house gas emissions in the run up to the conference. The lack of a well-developed EU position left scope for individual member states to engage the US directly in negotiations. As a result, it was a modest compromise worked out between the British and the Americans that shaped the final outcome of the negotiations. One could argue therefore that the EU exhibited (rather weak) normative power or directional leadership, but was unable to bring any instrumental power to bear in order to shape the actual negotiations (Andresen and Agrawala, 2002). The US, by threatening not to participate and thus using its economic power in a negative sense, brought pressure on other parties to give way on key issues. The use of such leverage was not something the EU seemed capable of, in part because there was no consensus on such a step and in part because the withdrawal of the EU would have left the stage clear for individual member states to conclude agreements. This was something the Commission and integration minded member states wished to avoid because of the threat this posed to EU leadership in climate change policy.

At the time of the Berlin Committee of the Parties (COP) 1 meeting to discuss implementation of the UNFCCC, the EU was able to form a coalition with the non-oil-producing developing countries and thus isolate the group of countries more sceptical of the need for international targets on carbon emissions in the JUSCANZ group (Japan, USA, Canada, Australia and New Zealand). But at that time the EU was preoccupied with its internal negotiations on a burden sharing arrangement among EU member states within the EU 'bubble' (i.e., an overall EU commitment carbon emission reductions) in advance of COP 3 in Kyoto. For some time it had been clear that in order to be effective in international negotiations the EU needed binding obligations on each member state. This meant coming to terms with the different member state interests resulting from the different energy supply structures. Initial efforts to agree on a set of reduction targets based on 5 per cent reductions for the 'greenest' member states (Germany, the Netherlands and Denmark), stabilisation for the mid-range of member states (Britain, Italy and France) and increases in carbon emissions for the new member states, failed. It was not until more objective measures based on a breakdown according to energy supply and emitting industries were developed during the Dutch presidency in late 1996 that progress could be made on the internal EU approach. These objective measures were developed in a specialist Ad Hoc Group on Climate Change, but the success also owed much to the determination of the Dutch presidency to push the agreement through.

The agreement on the internal distribution of emission reductions was therefore driven by a desire to lead in international negotiations in the COP 3 at Kyoto

(Yamin, 2000; Ringius, 1997; and Falkner, 2007.) Agreement on the 'bubble' enabled the EU set an overall target for reductions in greenhouse gases (GHGs) of 15 per cent by 2010. Once again then the EU appeared to be providing directional leadership in a form that did not suit the US. In the US there remained a resistance to targets because of higher adjustment costs resulting from structural features of the US economy, and the fact that the US had done little to contain emissions during the period of relatively rapid economic growth during the 1990s. During the Kyoto negotiations of COP 3, the US pursued alternative, more market-based approaches, such as Joint Implementation, the Clean Development Mechanism (CDM) and quota trading. Some of these US proposals were presented only during the course of the negotiations in Kyoto. The CDM idea was developed overnight during the negotiations (Yamin, 2000, p. 61). The EU found it difficult to respond flexibly to such alternative proposals. Discussions within the Council in location were seen to be 'cumbersome and long-winded' (Grubb, 1999, p. 112). Indeed, EU Ministers were still trying to agree on a common response to the CDM while key decisions were taken in the plenary (Vogler, 2005). Here, then, was another case of the EU finding instrumental leadership (the use of leverage and trade-offs during negotiations) to shape outcomes far harder than directional leadership (in other words the use of normative power through EU level policies). As a result of these weaknesses in the EU decision-making capabilities, or perhaps because the US had a stronger negotiating position thanks to the domestic constraints it was under,[1] it was the US which shaped the outcome of the negotiations not the EU. It can therefore be argued that the Kyoto Protocol, in the shape of the inclusion of the CDM and market-based approaches, owes more to the US instrumental effectiveness in shaping outcomes than the EU directional leadership (or normative power) in the run-up to the negotiation.

The story post-Kyoto will be taken up later in the chapter. But this account of negotiations up to and including the negotiation of the Kyoto Protocol suggests that the ability to provide directional leadership or the possession of normative power may not be sufficient to ensure the effectiveness of EU environmental diplomacy. The EU needs perhaps both a greater willingness to use market power and/or an ability to shape negotiations or exercise instrumental power. It is therefore necessary to understand how the EU goes about decision-making and negotiation in international environmental negotiations.

---

[1]   The Byrd-Hagel Resolution of 1997 in the US Senate requiring developing countries to make commitments on carbon reductions before it would ratify any treaty could be seen as strengthening the US hand in negotiations.

Decision-Making and Negotiation

Domestic Decision-Making

As in nation states, the domestic policies of the EU affect its international position, and vice versa. This is especially the case for EU environment policy where the *acquis* has a direct bearing on its external policies. In the last decade, the EU efforts in pollution abatement in general and its desire to provide leadership in international environmental policy have led it to press ahead with internal EU policies as a means of 'showing the way' to the rest of the world. Whilst there is always a link between domestic and international levels in economic diplomacy, the balance or sequencing can vary. In environmental diplomacy, the EU has actively sought to 'get ahead' of other countries in terms of, in particular, carbon emissions reduction and the reduction of other GHGs. In the previous chapter we saw how EU domestic policy on financial market regulation has followed international regulatory standards-making. In Chapter 3, in the case of international trade, we saw how the *acquis* in the form of the SEM shaped the EU negotiating aims and positions in multilateral trade negotiations. Internal decision-making is therefore a factor in external policies.

In internal decision-making in environment, as in other policy areas in which the EU has competence, the community/EU method applies and the Commission has the right of initiative. Commission proposals are based on work in comitology, in other words the various advisory committees made up of member state representatives. In climate change this is the Climate Change Committee (CCC). Inter-service consultation is undertaken within the Commission in which the Directorates General (DGs) of the Commission seek to balance their sometimes competing interests. This means balancing the positions of DG Environment, or since 2010 the DG Climate Action and those of DGs Enterprise, Energy, Trade, and so on, which will be concerned to ensure the interests of EU industry, energy supply and markets are respected. The European External Action Service (EEAS) which has replaced most of DG Relex (external relations) with the implementation of the Lisbon Treaty may also have an important input. Any disagreements between Directorates General will then be resolved through the cabinets of Commissioners concerned or ultimately in the Commission College. The Commission's proposals are also discussed in the Working Group on the Environment, the main technical level Working Party on environment policy, which brings together representatives of the member states with the Commission. This Working Group meets very regularly, up to two or three times a week on different environmental topics.

The formal Commission proposal then goes to the Council for consideration, first to COREPER I and eventually to the Council of Environment Ministers. The formal decision-making procedure in the Council is qualified majority voting (QMV) on topics that are EU exclusive competence, or unanimity if the topic is mixed competence. Art. 192 (2) (a –c) (TFEU) (see discussion of treaty rules below) specifies when a policy is EU or mixed competence. If it is exclusive EU competence, then OLP applies and the European Parliament will have co-decision-making powers. If mixed or shared competence then the Special Legislative Procedure (SLP) will apply which means unanimity and only consultation with the EP. The Treaty of Lisbon provides flexibility, however, in the sense that the Council may decide unanimously to opt for the use of OLP. Given the member states positions in the past it would seem unlikely that this option will find much if any use.

Competence

EU decision-making in external environmental policy is influenced by whether formal competence is shared or exclusive. In most international environment policy there has been shared or mixed competence. But in environmental as in trade diplomacy, member state governments have been pragmatic about shared competence and have to date opted to nominate a single negotiator or team of negotiators to represent the EU. In international environmental policy, a form of supervised delegation has been used, but rather than the Commission alone, as in the case of trade, the job of conducting negotiations had been shared between the Commission on issues of EU competence and in the case of climate change a 'troika' made up of the current presidency and incoming presidencies and the Commission for political level negotiations and 'negotiation leaders' for technical issues. Who negotiates for the EU has therefore varied between issues within environmental diplomacy. In negotiations on the Montreal Protocol on ozone-depleting substances, the member states delegated the task to the Commission as sole negotiator. This was also the case for much of the Biosafety Convention. Delegation of *de facto* competence to the Commission occurred because the issues were directly related to trade, an area of exclusive EU competence. But in climate change negotiations it has been the Troika that has negotiated.

This decision-making regime has been shaped by a number of factors. First, the determination of the member states to retain powers to engage directly in international environmental negotiations and not cede full competence to either the Commission or a troika. This is in contrast with trade where member states were ready to cede *de facto* competence to the Commission even for issues that were of mixed competence (see Chapter 3). The treaty in Art. 191 (2) (TFEU) refers to member state governments engagement in negotiations. Another important factor is that, due to the nature of the issues in external environmental policy, negotiations have a significant impact on policy areas in which the national governments have resisted any function integration process that threatens national sovereignty. One such issue is energy policy and the choice of sources of energy where Art. 192 (2) (c) (TFEU) explicitly protects member states powers. The willingness to delegate *de facto* competence to the Commission for the negotiations on the Montreal Protocol could therefore be seen as due to the relative absence of spillovers into sensitive policy areas apart from trade. Finally, there is the question of path dependency. EU environment policy is still relatively recent compared to external trade. Member state willingness to delegate *de facto* competence to the Commission on trade was progressive and occurred once there was mutual agreement between the Commission and Council on the ground rules. It therefore seems to be the case that it took time for member state governments to develop confidence in any EU decision-making regime for EU environmental diplomacy. It is also necessary to distinguish between environmental negotiations that have a high political impact, such as the big climate change negotiations and the more technical work that goes on all the time. Given the political resonance of the climate change issue in national and EU politics, ministers and heads of state and government have wanted to be seen to be tackling the problem. This means member state governments have wished to retain a role in the high profile events.

Treaty provisions

The Treaty of Rome provided no powers for the EEC to engage in external environmental negotiations. Implied powers in external environmental policies were confirmed in a number of European Court of Justice (ECJ) cases following the AETR case, such as the Rhine Navigation case (1/1976). Implied powers are when external competence is based on EU internal competence. In the case of the Rhine Navigation case the ECJ argued that this is the case even when the internal powers have not yet been applied, which was broadly the case during the 1970s when the EEC's internal policies were not well developed.

Express powers were not granted to the EC until the adoption of the SEA which entered into force in July 1987. The Treaty on European Union (TEU) (Maastricht) in Art. 130r elevated cooperation in environmental policy to a core objective of the EU on a par with economic integration *per se* and these provisions were carried over into Art. 174 and Art. 175 of the Treaty Establishing the European Community (TEC). Art. 174 (TEC) made internal environment policy EC competence so that for decision-making the Community/EU method applied – in other words, Commission right of initiative – a qualified majority vote in the Council and co-decision-making with the European Parliament. But this was subject to the derogations in Art. 175 (TEC), which effectively made external environmental policy an area of shared competence. Art. 174 (TEC) also made clear that both the EC and the member states could negotiate in their respective spheres of competence and that EC powers to negotiate were without prejudice to member state competence (Delreux, 2006, p 236).

The Debate on the Constitutional Treaty and the Impact of the TFEU

An important aim of the debate in the Constitutional Treaty was to make the EU more effective and to strengthen the EU's role in the world. The debate focused on the Common Foreign and Security Policy, but it also had a bearing on other aspects of EU external policy including external environmental policy. There had been criticism of the performance of EU environmental diplomacy on a number of grounds, and it was hoped that treaty changes geared to improving the external representation of the EU would rectify these. The criticism was that

EC environmental diplomacy lacked consistency and a clear strategy, due to the central role played by the six monthly rotation of the presidency and thus lead EU negotiator (Engelhofer and Van Schaik, 2003). There was also criticism of a lack of horizontal coherence between international environmental and other policy areas, such as trade, external competitiveness, foreign relations, development, and so on. Criticism of the EU was particularly marked following The Hague COP of the UN FCCC in December 2000, at which the EU was seen to be preoccupied with internal discussions on what the common EU line should be and not able to play a constructive role in international level negotiations. The EU experience in The Hague and other negotiations including those in 2009 in Copenhagen are discussed in the case study in below. A number of suggestions were proposed to address these perceived shortcomings including the delegation of all (*de facto*) competence to the Commission, in order to gain more consistency, enable the EU to be more flexible and to avoid 'interminable' discussions among EU member states during negotiations (Grubb and Yamin, 2001). It was also hoped that more general changes under discussion in the Constitutional Convention, such as ending the rotating presidencies and establishing a single representative for the EU in external policies, would help by reducing the inconsistency in policy due to changes in the presidency and strengthen horizontal cohesion across policy areas.

The TFEU has led to a dispute over the interpretation concerning the competence for negotiation of international environment agreements due to the co-existence of Art. 218 TFEU and Art. 3 TFEU. Prior to the Lisbon Treaty there was a distinction between the treaty basis for EC environmental diplomacy in areas of exclusive competence (where the issues were predominantly trade in nature), and those of mixed competence. In the case of the former Art. 300 (TEC) in combination with Art. 175 TEC was the treaty basis. Under Art. 300 TEC the Commission made recommendations to the Council on the agenda and negotiating aims. The Council then authorised the Commission to negotiate in consultation with a special committee. This Art. 300 (TEC) approach was essentially derived from the experience of the EC in trade. As in external trade, the Council also had the option of giving the Commission negotiating directives during the course of negotiations. Any final agreement resulting from a negotiation was then adopted by the Council either by QMV, when this was the basis for decision-making on internal policy, or unanimity for cases in which member states retained competence. The European Parliament was only involved through consultation and had no power to grant assent.

For environmental diplomacy in which there was mixed competence, the treaties provided no guidance apart from the general obligation upon the member states to cooperate. The member states were thus free to devise whatever form of representation they wished for external environmental policies.

The ratification of the Treaty of Lisbon has in theory established in Art. 218 (TFEU) one treaty framework covering all EU economic diplomacy. In the case of international environmental negotiations Art. 218 would need to be used in conjunction with Art. 192 TFEU (formerly Art. 175 TEC) to provide the legal basis for EU participation in negotiations. Article 218 (3) states that 'The Commission, or High Representative of the Union for Foreign Affairs and Security Policy where the agreement envisaged relates exclusively or principally to the common foreign and security policy, shall submit recommendations to the Council, which shall adopt a decision authorising the opening of negotiations and, depending on the subject of the agreement envisaged, nominating the Union negotiator or the head of the Union's negotiating team' (Art. 218 (3)).

The Council then designates a special committee to work in consultation with the EU's agent and can give negotiating directives. The Council must authorise the signing and conclusion of agreements. The Council, or at least a number of member states, such as Britain and Denmark, appear to interpret this article as meaning that the Council can either nominate the Commission or anyone else to conduct negotiations. In the case of climate change negotiations this interpretation would mean the Council could continue with the practice of choosing the Commission to negotiate in those cases when the policy areas are predominantly exclusive EU competence, or the troika. An alternative Commission interpretation argues that the Council can authorise either the Commission or the High Representative, but the latter on foreign policy issues. This interpretation then means that only the Commission can be authorised to negotiate on non-foreign policy issues.

Art. 191 (TFEU), like Art. 174 (TEC) sets out the policy objectives for EU environmental policy and Art. 192 (TFEU) provides the legal basis for adopting international environmental agreements. This is important because although Art. 191 TFEU envisages the adoption of environmental provisions using the OLP, Art. 192 (TFEU) retains the clear derogation from the use of OLP when the provision concerned is 'primarily of a fiscal nature' or significantly affects 'a member state's choice between energy sources and the general structure of energy supply' (Art. 192 (2) (a) and (c) TFEU). There are also criteria concerning waste, water resources management, and town and country planning. Measures primarily of a fiscal nature clearly cover any kind of a carbon or energy tax, and most climate change provisions can probably be interpreted as significantly affecting member state choice of energy sources and supply. The member state governments have in any case insisted that this is the case. When any of these criteria are satisfied in an international environmental negotiation, Art. 192 (TFEU) provides for the use of the Special Legislative Procedure (SLP) (unanimity in the Council and limits the European Parliament to consultation).

The European Commission argues that there should be EU competence for external environmental negotiations. In doing this, it draws on Art. 3 (TFEU) which comes under the principles section of the treaty and states that 'The Union shall also have exclusive competence for the conclusion of an international agreement when its conclusion is provided for in a legislative act of the Union or is necessary to enable the Union to exercise its internal competence, or in so far as its conclusion may affect common rules or alter their scope'. This appears to draw on AETA case law to the effect that the EU has implied external competence in environmental policy.[2] The Commission also argues that Art. 17.1 TEU (Treaty of European Union) envisages external representation only by the Commission or the High Representative. The main thrust of the Commission's argument appears to be that there should be only one representative of the EU in any future international environmental negotiations, so that even if a representative from a member state were to be nominated they would speak only for the EU. This would preclude any future direct involvement of member states in negotiations.

The TFEU of course provides for a president of the European Council, but the role of the European Council in EU environmental diplomacy has been to set overall targets or at the most resolve major problems of policy coherence. It remains to be seen whether the president of the Council assumes a more active role, say in G20 summit–level meetings on the environment. The TFEU has introduced the position of High Representative of the Union for Foreign and Security Policy (HRFSP) and the European External Action Service (EEAS). There is therefore the potential for the HRFSP and EEAS to play a role in promoting greater coherence in policy. In terms of the organisational structure neither DG Environment nor DG Climate Change are to be integrated into the EEAS. This does not of course preclude more effective policy coordination between the EEAS and the DGs responsible for international environmental policy.

Much will depend on how the treaty provisions are interpreted. In 2010 there was an early indication of the inter-institution debate on who should lead in EU environmental diplomacy in the fight over who should represent the EU in negotiations on a UN International Agreement on the Control of Mercury. The Commission argued that it did not need to share the negotiating role with the Council and withdrew the EU negotiating position when the Council insisted on a shared role.[3] This dispute was widely interpreted as a proxy for the issue of who would negotiate on climate change, the more high profile issue. The member states were clearly concerned about setting a precedent for climate change where they were not ready to cede *de facto* competence to the EU for future negotiations.[4]

The EU Decision-making Process in Each Phase of Negotiations

Given the nature of the EU and the shared competence (at least to date) in environmental diplomacy the decision-making processes in the EU are complex. To simplify, it is helpful to distinguish between different phases of the negotiation process. In this we shall draw on the phases of negotiation identified in Chapter 2. Figure 5.1 also provides a diagrammatic overview of the decision-making process. This section also draws on practice in climate change. Decision-making in other

---

[2]   Judgment of the Court of Justice, AETR, Case 22/70 (31 March 1971).

[3]   The Commission argued that a failure on the part of the Council to nominate the Commission to negotiate under Art. 218 TFEU meant that the Council had in effect rejected the Commission's proposed negotiating position.

[4]   http://www.euractiv.com/en/sustainability/eu-struggles-find-voice-environment-issues-news-494446.

environment policy areas diverges in that the Commission tends to play a more consistent steering role.

When it comes to *framing negotiations* and agenda setting – that is, identifying the problem and issues to be addressed – the European Commission fulfils an important role in that it produces the drafts of Action Plans, such the EU's Climate Change Action Plans and the February 2010 Climate and Energy Package that clearly represent an EU contribution to issue framing. The Commission does not do this in isolation, of course. It receives guidance and general orientation from the European Council on broad EU aims. For example, the European Council has identified global warming as an urgent issue and set the aim of containing global warming to less than 2 per cent of the pre-industrialisation level. There are many interests within the EU and beyond that seek to frame the international environmental debate, including in particular epistemic communities, which as noted above have played a central role in the climate change debate by focusing attention on the need to act on global warming. Environmental interest groups and civil society NGOs in general have also been active in trying to frame the debate as have the more conservative interests of the energy consuming sectors of the economy. EU Action Plans are adopted by the Council and European Parliament using OLP, so that both member states and EP have a formal role in setting overall targets for EU policy and thus legitimise the EU level input into framing the international debate.

Preparation is a vital and often underestimated phase in any negotiation and one in which policy-making and administrative capacity is a key factor. Within the EU the detailed preparatory work takes place in expert working groups that bring together Commission officials and experts from the member states. Probably the most important working group is the Working Group on International Environmental Issues WGIEI; see Figure 5.1. This is chaired by the rotating presidency and includes member states as well as the Commission as a non-voting member. The WGIEI fulfils a similar function to that of the Trade Policy Committee (TPC) in trade policy. Like the TPC the WGIEI also meets in different formats to cover the various topics including climate change, global environmental aspects of sustainable development, bio-safety, biodiversity and chemicals. The meetings on climate change have been the most frequent, between once and twice a month, with regular monthly meetings on the other topics. In climate change there are also expert groups working in specific topics, such as the Clean Development Mechanism (CDM), carbon trading schemes (CTS) and carbon sinks that serve the WGIEI. The EU's position on detailed aspects of any negotiation is developed in these expert groups. Decision-making in the WGIEI follows EU competence – in other words, QMV for EU competence questions and unanimity for shared competence issues – but as in most EU working groups decision-making is in practice based on consensus. The WGIEI reports formally to the Working Group on the Environment, which covers both internal and external environmental issues and meets as often as once or twice a week. The Working Group on the Environment in turn reports to COREPER I and thus to the Council (of Environment Ministers). The EU position prior to any negotiation is adopted

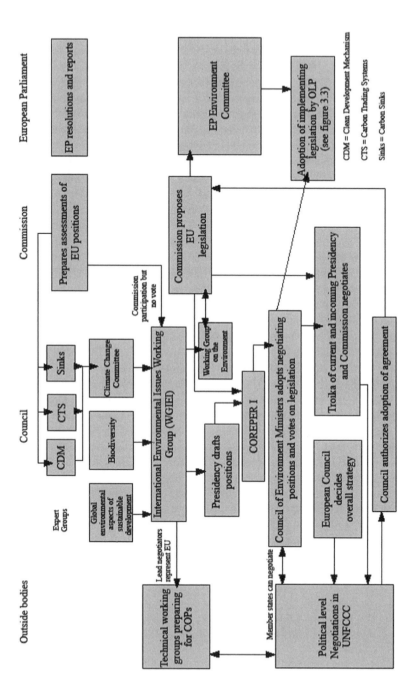

Fig. 5.1   EU Decision-Making in Climate Change Policy

by the Council of Environment Ministers acting by QMV on EU competence issues or unanimity on issues of shared competence.

As for the *negotiations proper*, it is helpful to differentiate between the technical and political level negotiations.[5] In practice, the two levels are of course inextricably linked. Given the nature of most economic diplomacy topics, the substance is in the detail. This means that ministers must negotiate on detail provisions on the basis of briefs from officials that work on the detail most of the time. When it comes to heads of state and government, the tolerance for dealing with the detail is, however, generally lower. The ability of the EU to manage this transition from technical to political level negotiation is a factor in its effectiveness during the negotiation process. In Copenhagen in December 2010 technical work preceded the arrival of environment ministers, who in turn preceded the arrival of heads of state and government. For nation states it is not easy to coordinate these different levels, but for the EU the challenge is that much greater.

The EU input into technical level work is controlled by the WGIEI that appoints a 'negotiation leader' to represent the EU. Negotiation leaders are experts in the particular policy area under discussion and can be either national or Commission experts. In this pragmatic approach the EU selects the person with the best skills and expertise, rather than follow competence or the rotating presidency. On occasion, an expert from a member state that has held the presidency may stay on for some time after the term of the presidency is over in order to make full use of the substantive technical knowledge gained and the relationship he or she has built up with their opposite numbers in the EU's negotiating partners. The use of such 'negotiation leaders' therefore facilitates continuity in the EU's approach to negotiations. Policy consistency is also helped by the functional nature of the working group structure and the presence of the Commission in the working groups as a store of institutional memory. The WGIEI makes direct submissions to the technical working groups in any given negotiation.

At a political level, the formal EU position is generally drafted by the presidency, drawing of course on the work of the WGIEI. In this the presidency may be assisted by the Council Secretariat, especially when the member state holding the presidency is relatively small and may lack the capacity to cover all policy areas. This presidency draft goes to COREPER I and thus on to the Council of Environment Ministers. The presidency therefore retains an important role in coordinating decision-making within the EU, both between the technical and political levels as well as between member states. Activist member states, keen to push the international debate, have frequently given the EU the impetus to overcome internal difficulties and establish the EU as a leader in international negotiations, with the member state itself taking an active role in shaping the EU's negotiating stance. Despite the troika changes in the EU negotiating team

---

[5] The description in this section is based on the EU procedures as of 2010. In 2010 the debate on the implications of the TFEU on the *de jure* competence with respect to EU environmental diplomacy began. As this debate was unresolved at the time of writing the existing procedure is described.

can undermine mutual confidence between negotiators over the course of a long negotiation, such as those leading up to a COP, and thus have an adverse effect.

The position of the EU is further complicated by the fact that the member state governments have retained the right to negotiate themselves. This has given those member states that wish to get involved in negotiations the ability to do so. As noted above, Britain engaged in bilateral negotiations with the US at the Rio negotiations on the UNFCCC. In the dying hours of The Hague COP meeting in 2000, Britain again sought, but in this case failed, to find a compromise between the EU and US positions. The challenge of coordinating policy becomes even greater when the member states are represented by heads of state or government who want to be able to make decisions themselves.

Another challenge identified is how to ensure the EU can respond flexibly during negotiations. Good preparation and EU common policies based on the EU's internal environmental regime may enable the EU to provide directional leadership or normative power in international negotiations. But negotiators also have to be able to respond to proposals tabled by their negotiating partners. Issue linkage or the additions of new proposals are regularly used in the final stages, sometimes in the final hours, of negotiations. The mechanism the EU uses to enable flexibility are the Council meetings in location during the crucial days or hours of a negotiation in order to adjust the EU position as negotiations develop. A similar approach is used in high-level trade negotiations such as at WTO ministerial meetings. Typically there will be a meeting before negotiations start and then the Commission or negotiating troika, or negotiation leader, will report back to the member states on developments at the end of the day. When the EU is criticised for spending more time negotiating among its members than with other countries, it is because these Councils in location are working to find an agreed EU response to a development in negotiations.

The effectiveness of a negotiator can also be influenced by his or her ability to *implement* the results of an agreement. In the case of the EU, it is the Council of Ministers that authorises acceptance of any negotiated agreement (Art. 218 TFEU). The formal rules for decision-making are that the Council will authorise adoption of the agreement by a qualified majority vote or unanimity depending on formal competence. One can expect disagreements between the member states and the Commission on the legal basis for authorising adoption of an agreement. In the case of the Kyoto Convention, there was a dispute over whether QMV could be used to adopt the agreement. In the end, QMV was used, which may perhaps be seen as a precedent for future agreements. The results of environmental negotiations also have to be implemented in EU legislation. Again, depending on the legal basis either OLP or SLP will be used. Whilst there may be disputes over who has the competence to conclude an agreement or the procedures for implementation, the EU has never failed to implement an important international environment agreement in EU law.[6]

---

[6]   There are more instances of the EU failing to enforce or comply with the details of an agreement, but not of the EU failing to implement legislation.

Factors Shaping EU Environmental Diplomacy

All the factors discussed in the analytical framework are relevant to EU international environmental policy. The relative importance of these factors will vary from case to case and over time, so it will be important to qualify any general conclusions made here for environmental diplomacy in terms of the specifics of the case in hand. The following section provides a more detailed discussion of the EU decision-making and negotiation in the climate change negotiations between 2000 and 2010, and thus a better opportunity to discuss the relative importance of different factors and to assess the effectiveness of EU environmental diplomacy.

The summary of the evolution of EU environmental diplomacy above suggested that the interaction between a desire to provide international leadership and the EU's internal policy development has been central. Internal EU policy development has in turn been significantly shaped by member state and sector interests. The ability of the EU to project normative power and thus provide 'directional leadership', a topic widely discussed in the context of EU environmental diplomacy, also seems to turn on the ability of the member states and various interests to reach agreement on framework norms for which the development of internal policies provides a proxy. The success or otherwise of the EU in international negotiations, what could be seen as instrumental leadership, appears to be influenced more by institutional questions including who negotiates for the EU, how they are supervised and questions of *de jure* and *de facto* competence. Compared to EU trade diplomacy, the institutional arrangements and practice in environmental diplomacy are of more recent origin. The hypothesis put forward in Chapter 2 that it is the existence of established decision-making regimes or *de facto* competence which counts suggests that EU environmental diplomacy should become more effective with time. This does indeed appear to be the case if one compares the position in the late 1980s with that in the late 1990s (Vogler, 2006; Oberthur and Kelly, 2008; Ott 2001).

Relative Economic Power

There are a number of ways in which the EU could be said to exercise economic power in environmental diplomacy. First, there is the importance of the EU as an emitter of greenhouse gases. The EU produced 3787 million tonnes of CO2 in 2008. This is significant, but the EU share is declining due to the economic growth of China and other major emerging economies and the success of the EU in checking and slightly reducing its emissions.[7] Its position in environmental diplomacy could therefore be compared to that in trade, in the sense that its relative importance is declining. While no international agreement is possible without the EU's participation, the EU must get the support of other major economies/

---

7   In 1999 the EU produced 3809 m tones of CO2 compared to 5506 for the USA and 3091 for China. By 2008 EU CO2 emissions had dropped slightly to the 3787 m tonnes while US emissions had increased to 5596 and Chinese to 6550 m tones. http://epp.eurostat. ec.europa.eu/cache/ITY_O.

polluters or emitters of greenhouse gases if it is to address the challenges posed by global warming.

Second, as in trade or finance, there is the question of how the EU can make use of this economic or market power to further environmental policies. This it does to a degree by setting high environmental standards that imported products must meet if they are to gain access to the EU market. But most pollution and carbon emission occurs during the production process and to date existing GATT national treatment rules for 'like products' have been interpreted as precluding discrimination between products in terms of how they are produced. The only differentiation possible is between products that have different product characteristics.[8]

Lack of progress in climate change negotiations has led to a debate within the EU on the merits of border measures such as border tax adjustment measures (BAMs), with some member states supported by environmental interests favouring BAMs if only as a means of providing leverage in negotiations. But there remains insufficient support within the Council for wielding such a big stick. European business has also opposed their use on the grounds that they would undermine the non-discrimination principle of rules-based multilateral trading system that the EU supports. There is also a risk of retaliation if other countries seek to extend their regulatory norms extraterritorially. In the debate on coherence, the views of DG Trade have also tended to prevail over those in DG Environment or climate change who might be more supportive of enhancing the EU's leverage.

By leading in implementing carbon reduction targets and carbon trading, the EU has in effect adopted a policy with strong unilateralist elements, even though it has sought to persuade others to follow its lead. The reluctance to use potential market power by threatening to close the EU market to countries that do not make sufficient effort to reduce GHGs tends to confirm the unilateralist nature of EU policy. This contrasts with the US position, for example, which has been based on fairly strict reciprocity in the sense that it will only participate in international efforts to set targets for reduced GHG emissions if others do the same. As the US and China are the world's largest emitters of GHGs, this provides them with considerable leverage as an agreement without them makes little sense. The EU is, on the other hand, able and willing to use financial inducements to promote its environmental diplomacy in an effort to buy developing country support.

Recognition

Despite these limits on the use of its economic or market power, the EU has progressively gained recognition as an actor in international environment negotiations. As noted above, this started from a low base in the 1970s, but around the end of the 1980s and the beginning of the 1990s there appears to have been a shift towards greater *de facto* recognition of the EU. Similar to the position

---

[8] For some time environmental interests have argued that there is scope under the GATT rules to apply environmental regulations to production processes and methods. In the context of carbon emissions this debate is likely to become more important. (See WTO and UNEP, 2009.)

in financial diplomacy but unlike trade, the member states could still engage in negotiations in their own right and were consequently on occasions recognised as negotiating partners. The British interventions to broker compromises with the US during the Rio negotiations on the FCCC and in Kyoto in the COP 3 are examples of this, but other member states have also engaged directly in negotiations. Formal recognition was granted to the EC as a Regional Integration Organisation (REIO) during the negotiation of the LRTBP and the EC/EU is also a signatory of 60 multilateral environment agreements, such as the Convention on Biodiversity, UNFCCC, and so on, alongside the member states. In this sense there is no major difference between trade agreements and environment agreements. As Chapter 3 showed, most trade agreements negotiated by the EC were mixed agreements requiring signature of both the EC and the member states. It is also worth noting that the member states have equal, non-hierarchic status in international environmental organisations. Again this is similar to the case for trade, but different from the hierarchical representation of member states in international financial institutions.

Normative power

The literature on EU environmental diplomacy has tended to stress the role of the EU as a directional leader in shaping international environmental policy. Such directional leadership would then constitute a form of normative power. But does the EU really have such power? In the analytical framework a distinction was made between general norms, framework norms and specific norms or standards. In the field of environment, general norms would be support for broad concepts such as sustainable development or low carbon growth. Framework norms can be seen the balance between the competing 'regulatory' and 'market-based' approaches to environmental policy. Detailed norms would then be the specific provisions set out in EU directives or regulations, such as emission standards for cars or similar provisions.

It can be argued that the EU moved towards the acceptance of common framework norms during the late 1980s and 1990s when the more sceptical or reluctant member states and interest groups moved to accept sustainable development and ecological growth. This was the result of public opinion, shaped by environmental NGOs, which drew on the work of environmental scientists and epistemic communities such as the IPCC. Environmental objectives were also integrated into the political systems of many EU member states through the growth of green parties and the responses to such green politics by the major political parties. Business opinion in general also shifted towards an acceptance of the need for ecological growth and began to see the benefits to be gained from leading in developing environmental technologies. This is analogous to the compromise between '*laisez-faire*' and '*dirigist*' approaches to market regulation for goods in the 1980s.

In specific policy areas, there were moves towards a compromise positions in which the environmental lobbies accepted more market-based approaches and moved away from a rigid regulatory approach in order to make progress, and opponents of tight environmental regulation accepted the need to act. This was, for example, the case in climate change with the move towards acceptance of carbon emissions trading by both the mainstream environmental NGOs and moderate business interests. Agreement on these framework norms enabled the EU to develop its internal policies and to deepen the EU *acquis* and thus strengthen the EU's specific norms. The development of such common norms then provided the EU with its lead in international environmental/climate change policy.

Member State and Sector Interests

Even when there is an agreement on general and framework norms, specific policies, norms and standards can still be shaped by member state and sector interests. Again the more general member state interests have taken the form of a desire to hold the line on fiscal sovereignty, which has meant member states have blocked any form of EU-level energy or carbon tax and argued for a looser coordination of national energy taxes instead. This precluded the use of an energy/carbon tax that would have strengthened the EU's ability to provide leadership at the time of the Rio conference in 1992. There are similarities here with financial regulation, where an evolution towards more *de facto* competence for the EU has also been checked by member state concern about policy spill-over or creeping integration.

Member state interests also diverge between France, which supplies most of its electricity by nuclear energy and Germany, the Netherlands and Denmark, which use fossil fuels and have been reducing their nuclear capacity. France with significant nuclear capacity favours carbon taxes, because its producers would pay less and thus become more competitive vis-à-vis producers in member states that rely on fossil fuels to generate power. Structural differences also posed a considerable, although not insurmountable challenge in the debate over burden sharing. Similarly sector interests between the major energy consuming sectors and those that stand to gain from reduced emissions also have to be factored into the EU debate.

The Acquis

Specific EU norms and standards are also shaped by member state and sector interests. Indeed, the scope of the *acquis* can be seen as an indicator of the degree to which such differences can be reconciled through debate and dialogue within the EU. During the 1980s and especially during the 1990s Commission-led initiatives within the context of agreement on framework norms produced a progressively more extensive domestic *acquis* in environmental protection. Interestingly the Commission was motivated by a desire promote EU leadership in international environmental policy. Thus, before the Rio conference as well as in the run up to the COP 3 meeting in Kyoto and the COP 15 in Copenhagen, the Commission came forward with proposals on internal policies in order to strengthen the EU's credibility and ability to lead in the international negotiations.

The External Drivers

The EU's desire to lead therefore helped drive internal EU policies and the *acquis* on the environment. But why would this be the case? There are a number of possible explanations. First, there was recognition that leadership was needed if international efforts were to make progress. As US leadership was fading or not forthcoming, progress on global challenges such as climate change required the EU to play a role. In order to lead the EU had to show that it could overcome the challenges of internal policy coordination. This would explain why environmental interests favoured EU leadership. For EU industry and business in general there was and remains an interest in ensuring that the EU is not alone in carrying the costs of pollution abatement, which meant ensuring that its international competitors faced similar controls. Business interests in environmental technology have also favoured EU leadership because commitment to pollution abatement helps to maintain the incentives for investment in environmental technologies.

For those interested in EU integration, such as the Commission and more integration-minded member states, EU leadership on the environmental also offered a means of legitimising the broader European project, especially during the 1990s when support for European integration was not very strong. By definition many environmental issues cannot be resolved by national governments due to global externalities. With growing public demand for action on a number of environmental challenges, if the EU could succeed in addressing the issues it could provide legitimacy – and create public support – for the EU. If the EU could also assume a leadership role in international environmental negotiations, this could enhance the standing of the EU in international relations. For those who favoured the EU becoming a stronger actor in international relations, the environment therefore offered a policy area in which it could establish itself more easily than some other fields such as foreign or security policy.

Quite apart from the desire to lead in international negotiations, the challenge to find a common EU position in response to developments in international negotiations also constituted an external driver for EU environmental diplomacy. This pressure has been fairly consistent for the best part of 30 years, making the external drivers of EU environmental policy similar to those driving EU trade diplomacy.

Institutional Factors

With no EC competence from the start, EU environmental policy has developed differently to trade. Environmental diplomacy has been an area of shared or mixed competence and one in which the member states have retained their rights to negotiate. The form of delegated supervision used has therefore included the member states. The role of the presidencies raises questions about consistency, and there are also issues concerning the coordination between technical level negotiations and those at the political level. *De facto* competence has therefore differed somewhat but not dramatically from the position in trade. In the field environmental policy, the internal EU decision-making regimes and procedures are of relatively recent origin. As the summary of the evolution of policy shows, the EU had difficulties reaching a common position in the 1980s, for example, at the beginning of the negotiations on the Montreal Protocol, but things have improved with time. A comparison of the Rio negotiations with those in Kyoto on climate change also suggests that EU decision-making cohesion has improved with time. This would seem to be related to the progressive acceptance of a *de facto* EU competence for external environmental negotiation, even if *de jure* competence remained shared. This is in line with the hypothesis that cohesion in EU policy is more likely the more established the decision-making regimes and procedures become.

Coherence

The need for policy coherence in the environmental field has been important, but not decisive, for EU environmental diplomacy. Certainly links with other policies such as energy policy have been crucial in shaping the EU's positions on some issues including climate change. Links with fiscal policy have, as noted above, also shaped EU policy in the sense that a lack of agreement on an energy tax had an important and broadly negative impact on the coherence of EU policy.

The issue of coherence with external trade policy has been much discussed, but until recently trade and environment policies have been kept largely separate. Environmental and trade policy-making were on different tracks until the 1990s, and subsequently there was considerable resistance to any effort to 'integrate' the two such as through the use of trade instruments as a means of enforcing environmental agreements. Although trade provisions have been included in many multilateral environment agreements they have seldom been used. The international trade policy community, including the EU trade policy community in the member states and DG Trade, also opposed linkages between the two policy areas for fear of green protectionism. The question of coherence with trade policy is, however, likely to become more important in the future especially if there is no progress on international cooperation in climate change. In such a case there will be mounting pressure to use trade instruments to further EU climate change objectives and prevent carbon leakage.

Finally, there is the question of coherence with EU foreign policy. EU environment policy has at times assumed a central role in EU foreign policy, thanks to the level of recognition of the EU and the developed EU norms. In future there may be more pressure to have EU foreign policy serve the interests of EU environment policy in the sense of using it to persuade more countries to support EU policy initiatives. In the Copenhagen COP, for example, many developing countries failed to support the EU even though they receive significant levels of EU aid. This raises the question of coherence with EU development policy, but also the much broader question of whether the EU can combine coherence and effectiveness across all external policies.

The Case of Climate Change from The Hague to Copenhagen

This section picks up the account of the EU's role in climate change negotiations after COP 3 in Kyoto. After the adoption of the Kyoto Protocol in 1997, the EU continued to provide leadership in terms of pressing for completion of the negotiations at COP 6 in The Hague in November 2000. When the US repudiated Kyoto, the EU led by first ratifying the Protocol itself and then used environmental diplomacy to persuade Japan and Russia to do so. The EU subsequently adopted internal carbon reduction policies and led efforts to negotiate the post-Kyoto arrangements by proposing significant emissions targets and setting the agenda on other issues such as adaptation, technology transfer and finance. But this generally impressive performance in directional leadership was not matched by the EU's performance during negotiations themselves, as The Hague COP6 and Copenhagen COP 9 have shown.

The Kyoto Protocol set overall reduction target of 5.2 per cent for GHG by 2008–2012 with differentiated commitments by the various parties. The EU had the target of 8 per cent below the 1990 base, and the US 7 per cent. Developing countries were not committed to specific targets. But Kyoto left many details to be settled in terms of how these reductions were to be achieved. It is not the purpose of this chapter to provide a detailed discussion of the issues in COP 6.[9] Among the issues to be resolved were provisions on carbon sinks carbon sequestration in forestry, the scope for carbon trading and funding for the Clean Development Mechanism (CDM), which was mostly destined for developing countries. There were important transatlantic differences over the first two issues in particular, and demands from developing countries for finance under the third. The US approached the COP 6 under severe domestic constraints. Rapid economic growth during the 1990s and no real action to contain CO_2 emissions meant it could only achieve the 7 per cent target at considerable cost. The Byrd-Hagel Resolution of 1997 specified that the US Congress would not ratify any agreement which did not include the major GHG emitters in the emerging markets. Finally, there was a lame duck administration and it was not clear what positions the incoming George W. Bush Administration would adopt. Faced with these constraints, the US negotiators sought to ease the pressure on the US by seeking an agreement that would allow extensive use of carbon sinks as well as freedom to trade carbon permits with countries such as Russia and other transition economies. For its part, the EU, with support from developing countries, saw these efforts as a US attempt to reinterpret Kyoto in such a fashion that it could continue with business as usual. The US had support from other members of the so called umbrella group which included OECD countries like Japan and Australia.

There were high expectations of The Hague COP 6 on the part of the environment movement, and the meeting had been widely discussed in the media. There was therefore pressure on politicians to produce a result. This was one of the big events of the environment diplomacy calendar with 10,000 delegates participating. But

---

[9]   For a summary see for example, Buchner (2001) or Grubb and Yamin (2001).

the preparation was arguably poor. The text produced for the conference was complex and ran to hundreds of pages. There was also a lack of urgency in the preparation for the conference, possibly because the participants believed that a deal would be done in the final hours of the negotiations as it had been in Kyoto. There was therefore limited progress in technical negotiations during the first week of negotiations, which meant a great deal was left for ministers to do when they arrived for the second week.

The EU was represented by the troika, led by the French presidency, which adopted an aggressive position vis-à-vis the US arguing that the US with 4 per cent of world population accounted for 25 per cent of global GHG emissions and that it had to do more to curb emissions. This assertive approach by the French presidency was an illustration of how the negotiating style can vary between presidencies and member states. It contrasted, for example, with the sort of value-creating or less assertive approach a British presidency would take. The EU position was to ensure that the use of carbon sinks and trading was limited so that they could not be used as a means of avoiding real reductions in emissions. But in the final stages of the negotiations EU ministers, like all the politicians present were struggling to get to grips with the complexity of the negotiations.

When there was only 24 hours left, the chairman of the UNFCCC, Jan Pronk of the Netherlands, tabled a long-anticipated chair's text. This sought to resolve a number of key political issues, but in doing so set aside the existing texts that had been the focus of the more technical negotiations up to that point. The negotiators therefore had to respond to this change of tack within a matter of hours. The US did so by introducing new ideas, such as the use of farmland as carbon sinks. This again looked like an attempt to avoid new commitments and continue with business as usual, although the US did show some flexibility by moving from a target of 310 m tons of CO_2 to 125 m tons for such sinks. The EU found it difficult to respond to the new text and new proposals from the US. It took the environment ministers meeting in location a long time to agree on a new position and when it did it held to a position that the original aims of the Kyoto Protocol should not be watered down. This meant no agreement with the US.

Facing deadlock, Britain followed the precedent set in Rio and Kyoto and sought to negotiate a deal with the US; something, as discussed above, it was legally able to do at the time. A form of agreement was reached, apparently during a long telephone conversation between Prime Minister Tony Blair of Britain and President Bill Clinton (Ott, 2001; Grubb and Yamin, 2001). This included a further concession by the US on the figure for carbon sinks, but many issues were not included and it is not clear that both sides had the same understanding of what had been agreed. The British–US deal was then presented to the troika by the British Deputy Prime Minister John Prescott. There was some uncertainly as to whether the troika agreed with the proposed deal or not. In any case the agreement was presented to the Council meeting in location in the early hours of the morning. The Council rejected the British–US negotiated deal as being too soft on the US, and Mr Prescott famously stormed out of the meeting suggesting that the proposal had not been seriously considered (Grubb and Yamin, 2001).

Once again, then the EU failed to retain a cohesive position in the heat of a negotiation. It is not clear whether it was more the intervention of member states ministers, general disorganisation or inflexibility in the EU decision-making that led to the collapse of the negotiations. As noted above, the negotiations were poorly prepared and arguably could have been better chaired. There were also major substantive differences between key participants, with the US facing very tight domestic constraints. Many commentators and environmental groups applauded the EU for standing up to the US and preventing what they saw as a US attempt to water down the Kyoto Protocol.

Continued Leadership

Although the EU position during the Hague negotiations was not flexible, the EU subsequently shifted from a tough position favouring regulation as a means of reducing emissions to a more 'moderate' position favouring the use of market based instruments. This constituted a move towards the US position, even if the EU retained its support for binding targets. In 2003 the EU adopted the EU emission trading directive (ETD) as part of its European Climate Change Programme, again a case of the EU seeking to show the way forward and project 'normative power' (Oberthuer and Kelly, 2008). In 2004 the EU also adopted the so called Linking Directive, which was intended to link the EU emissions trading scheme with that provided in the Kyoto Convention. This shift towards 'market-based' approaches was a result of pressure from some member states and a willingness of the Commission to move towards a compromise position from the one it had held in favour of regulation. The shift towards such a compromise position was possible because it fell within the EU framework norms for climate change. Business recognised the continued need to act on climate change and environmental NGOs recognised that compromises were needed if real action was to be taken. In short, there was a broad convergence of interests on the issue of climate change due in no small part to a socialisation process in which key actors moved to accept the need for action.

In the mid-2000s there were also broader political factors that favoured a proactive EU position on the environment in general and climate change in particular. Within the EU, the French and Danish no votes on the Constitutional Treaty suggested a weakening in public support for European integration. To counter this disaffection, the Commission and pro-integration forces favoured strong EU policies on climate change as a means of promoting support for the EU and legitimising the European project. Internationally, the absence of US leadership in climate change that was even more pronounced under the two Bush administrations provided an opportunity for the EU to assume a leadership role.

With consensus on framework norms within the EU, it was possible for the EU to press ahead with a domestic *acquis* that then enabled it to retain its directional leadership, or normative power in the debate concerning the post-2012 provisions on climate change. In these negotiations which began in 2005 in Montreal, but in earnest with the adoption of the Bahli Roadmap in December 2007, the EU's aims were to establish a legal regime with set targets to ensure that emission reductions were sufficient to ensure that global warming peaked at 2 degree centigrade above the pre-industrial level. The EU approach was again characterised by a dynamic link between domestic EU policy, and the EU's aims in international negotiations. Again driven by Commission proposals, the EU adopted a climate change and energy package that became law in June 2009.[10] The EU also moved to strengthen its post-Kyoto emissions trading scheme. In January 2009 the Commission then produced a paper setting out the EU negotiating objectives for climate change (European Commission, 2010). This included the objective of targets for emissions reductions, financing low carbon development and adaptation, and proposals to build a global carbon market. The Council of Ministers and the European Council endorsed these proposals and reaffirmed the 20: 20: 20 target (a 20 per cent reduction in GHGs from the 1990 base by 2020, to be increased to 30 per cent if other countries make significant commitments; 20 per cent energy saving; and 20 per cent of power generation by renewable energy sources also by 2020. The 20 per cent target for reduced GHGs was unilateral and neither dependent on other countries' commitments nor on the use of offsetting land use measures.[11]

In comparison the US commitment was equivalent to just 4 per cent on the 1990 base, which looks more like business as usual. Japan set a target of 25 per cent reduction of carbon emissions, but this was dependent on reciprocal reductions by others. Although there was some concern among European business that the EU commitments were not being met by others, there was generally broad support for these unilateral measures.[12] The EU *acquis* was also extended to include binding emissions targets for cars, after voluntary measures had failed to produce rapid enough results. These issues were of course not uncontested, with industry and environmental NGOs adopting opposing positions. There were also questions as to whether the EU measures went far enough and whether the EU would be able to live up to its own commitments.[13] But the broad consensus on climate change combined with EU competence and the drive of the Commission facilitated progress at the EU level. Finally, in the run up to Copenhagen, the European Council endorsed the financial envelope for funding low carbon growth and adaptation that was seen as a means of persuading the developing countries to support a comprehensive post-2012 regime. The EU no doubt did so in the hope of showing the developing countries that it was not just making vague promises of aid. The European Council even agreed to provide Euro 2.4 bn in immediate

---

[10]   http://ec.europa.eu/environment/climat/climate_action.htm. Accessed 20 December 2010.

[11]   In July 2010 proposals were tabled for the EU to commit unilaterally to a 30 per cent reduction in emissions in order to maintain incentives for investment in energy saving, alternative energy production and low carbon growth.

[12]   In the revised emissions trading scheme there was provision for some free carbon permits to EU producers faced with higher costs and increased competition due to the lack of a 'level playing field'.

[13]   Without getting into a detailed debate on the substance the defence against the ineffectiveness of the EU scheme to reduce emissions is that the framework rules have been established within which the EU can in future tighten up on the granting of permits.

funding to help developing countries already affected by climate change. Here then was the EU providing directional leadership, showing the way forward exercising normative power and using economic or financial incentives to promote its policy.

As at the time of The Hague negotiations, US negotiators were again constrained by domestic pressures. The Obama Administration still needed to get Congressional (Senate) support for cap-and-trade legislation if it was to have a chance of achieving even modest targets for reductions in carbon emissions and funding developing country adaptation. In order to get Congressional support, the US negotiators still had to ensure that China and India were included in any process. Concerned about its ability to make commitments, the US sought to play down expectations of a comprehensive agreement.

The negotiations were as before complex and ambitious in scope. Work in the various technical working groups such as the Ad Hoc Group on the Kyoto Protocol and on Long-Term Cooperative Action made progress, but not fast enough. In these the EU was represented by the Commission or negotiation leaders. During 2009 climate change again also became high politics with the topic being considered by heads of state and government at the G8 summit in Italy in July, the G20 summit in Pittsburgh in November and the special UN Summit on Climate Change in September in New York. The Copenhagen conference like that in The Hague 10 years before was a massive affair and there were various coordination and logistic problems.[14] As is often the case with large conferences, there was criticism of the Danish chair, especially as the chair was changed halfway through the conference when the Danish Prime Minister took over from the minister for climate change. A 'Danish text' was leaked and upset developing country participants, who thought it was biased in favour of the developed countries. But there was little progress made on the draft negotiating text tabled before the conference or on the 'Danish text' by the time the heads of state and government from 120 countries arrived towards the end of the negotiations. This was an unprecedented number of heads of state and government for an international environmental conference. Negotiations were then taken up at the highest political level. Whilst this offered an opportunity to overcome impasses at the technical level, it also created difficulties in coordination within delegations including in particular within the EU delegation. In Copenhagen the EU was represented by the negotiation leaders in the technical working groups, by the troika led by the Swedish presidency and ministers of environment meeting in location in Copenhagen at ministerial level. But then the heads of state and government arrived in the closing days with less knowledge of the detail but a desire to be seen to be reaching an agreement because of the high public profile of the negotiations. Although the EU was speaking with these different voices, there were not the same tensions that arose in The Hague. But then the EU negotiating machinery was never really tested, because the EU was not directly involved in the crucial negotiations.

---

[14]   For a discussion and description of preparation and course of the Copenhagen COP, see, for example, Christiansen, 2011.

The Copenhagen Accord, so named because a number of countries refused to endorse an 'agreement', was negotiated at the last minute by the United States and the BASIC countries (Brazil, South Africa, India and China). In these negotiations India, Brazil and South Africa (IBSA) spoke more or less with one voice, a development which has led some to argue that the major lesson from the conference was the rise of the emerging powers. This was a lesson that EU trade negotiators had arguably already learned in 2003 at the Cancun WTO Ministerial meeting. Close coordination between IBSA supported by China meant the US had to negotiate with them if it was to get an outcome that included China and India. In terms of national preferences, an outcome that did not bind anyone to specific targets suited the US and the BASICs. At the same time, heads of state and government could avoid being seen to have presided over a failure. The Copenhagen Accord recognised the scientific case for a peak of 2 degrees over pre-industrial levels, but made no commitment to achieve this goal. The Accord included no limits on emissions, only voluntary targets, to be submitted by the end of January 2010, for developed countries. Developing countries were to set objectives for domestic measures. Funding was envisaged for developing countries, but there were no specific commitments. There was agreement on a Monitoring, Review and Verification procedure which the US insisted upon to ensure developing countries implement their domestic measures, but even this was watered down due to opposition from China, which generally sought to avoid any binding obligations. The Copenhagen Accord was not at odds with EU policy, but simply fell far short of EU ambition.

The EU, along with Japan and other countries, was largely sidelined and left to rubber stamp a deal struck between the US and the IBSA countries and China (Egenhofer and Georgiev, 2010). The EU was not called upon to make any difficult decisions during the negotiation because it had already committed to do far more than required by the Accord. The only real decision it had to take was whether to endorse the Accord even though it fell far short of EU aims. This it did because something was better than nothing.

What lessons can be drawn from the Copenhagen negotiations? First, one can make a fairly strong case that the EU was effective in keeping climate change on the agenda, just as it had succeeded in getting the Kyoto Protocol ratified (Egenhofer and Georgiev, 2010). It has been suggested that the EU will inevitably lose influence as the power relationship in the international economy shifts in favour of the emerging countries. It is also interesting to note that the IBSA countries, like the G20 group of developing countries in trade negotiations, was able to form an effective coalition and speak with one voice during the negotiations. There is no evidence of the EU suffering from a lack of preparedness or inflexibility in responding to the negotiations themselves, nor had there been a lack of leadership on the part of the EU during the period leading up to the negotiations. The EU showed the way, but the others chose not to follow. If the EU failed to shape the outcome it would appear to be due to a lack of any real leverage in the negotiations. As the EU had already done much of what was needed to reduce its carbon emissions, subject of course to implementing the commitments, it had no negotiating coinage. The US and China as the major emitters of carbon and other GHGs had made no commitments, they had the negotiating coinage to shape the outcome.

Effectiveness

Turning to the question of the effectiveness of the EU in the case study considered above of the negotiations leading up to Copenhagen, there would seem to be a fair amount of evidence that the EU is effective in preparation. In key negotiations it has agreed negotiating positions in advance, both in negotiations during the 1990s and in the run-up to Copenhagen. The EU was also able to agree on negotiating objectives and set these out months before Copenhagen. The one area where the EU was perhaps less well prepared was in its assessment of the positions of its negotiating partners. It has been argued that in The Hague negotiations the EU was too focused on its own objectives and failed to take adequate account of those of its negotiating partners. The same could be said of the EU in its preparation for the Copenhagen COP in 2009.

In terms of framing climate change negotiations, the EU can take credit for keeping the danger of global warming on the agenda. Whilst there were of course, many organisations making this case, the EU was the only major economic power to take a lead. Also with regard to agenda setting the EU was reasonably effective. The issues of targets, carbon trading and funding that were on the agenda in the run up to the Copenhagen COP were actively promoted by the EU. In general the EU, through its normative power, could be said to have had a significant impact on the agenda. Even if the norms promoted by the EU were not necessarily distinctive, as in the case of carbon trading, it has been the EU that has led in applying them. This effectiveness in framing negotiations and shaping agendas is in line with the finding that the EU provides directional leadership; that is has normative power.

The area in which the EU appears to have been less effective is in negotiations proper, or in providing instrumental leadership in international environmental and climate change negotiations. This is true in the case of the COP 3 in Kyoto and COP 6 in The Hague. In the heat of negotiations, the EU has found it difficult to respond to competing proposals from its negotiating partners.

In Copenhagen in 2009 the EU was widely seen as having been marginalised. There are a number of possible reasons for this. The first, which is related to the EU's economic or market power, stems from the fact that unilateral measures taken by the EU had reduced its leverage in negotiations. This is important when international negotiations are still characterised by implicit or explicit expectations of reciprocity, as is the case in climate change. Having taken the lead on climate change, the EU had already done everything it was asking others to do. Compared to the US or the BASICs, it had nothing to offer apart from funding for clean development. A related point is the tendency of the EU to eschew aggressive value-claiming positions. This is due to a lack of consensus among EU member states on the desirability of such policies as threatening to adopt border adjustment measures. These would enable to EU to make use of its market power. In contrast to other major emitters of carbon which have shown themselves willing to reject binding commitments on carbon reduction unless others do the same, the EU therefore had little negotiating leverage. Whilst leading in the adoption of carbon reduction gives the EU normative power, it also denies the EU the ability to use its market power in more value-claiming or mixed negotiating strategies.

Another reason why the EU has been ineffective in negotiations is simply because it has faced coordination problems during the course of negotiations. These are part due to the need for the EU negotiators to get approval from the member states for any positions or concessions during the negotiations. But here the structure of the principal–agent relationship is not much different in environment from that in trade, where the EU has been more effective. Both take the form of supervised delegation. In trade the Commission also needs to get the support of the Council meeting in location before it can conclude any agreement. What differs is the fact that the EU negotiator in climate change negotiations has been a troika led by the presidency. This creates communication or coordination problems because of the rotating nature of the EU presidency or when heads of state and government seek to get involved. As the Copenhagen COP showed, the EU also faces greater coordination problems between the levels (technical, ministerial and heads of state and government levels) than for other state actors.

The EU has a good record in terms of ratification of international agreements and their implementation in EU law. This is in many respects the flipside of the difficulties getting agreement in the Council in location. Once ministers have signed up to an agreement, there is little risk of involuntary defection (Putnam, 1988). This may become more of an issue in the future with the growing influence of the European Parliament. Finally, the EU is on somewhat weaker ground when it comes to actually ensuring the implementation of policies. It has struggled to meet some of the targets it has set itself for reductions in carbon emissions, although the economic downturn following the financial crisis in 2008 has meant that the EU is currently on target.

Conclusions

The EU has emerged as an actor in international environmental negotiations and in particular in climate change. Indeed, the EU has provided leadership in the international debate and negotiations on climate change for some time. The analytical framework developed in Chapter 2 helps to explain why the EU has led in climate change, but lagged in financial market regulation. Two key factors have been exclusive EU competence for internal EU policy and a burgeoning consensus on framework norms for climate change among the member state governments and interest groups. These have enabled the European Commission to drive forward common EU policy on climate change policies that have then provided the basis for the EU approach to international negotiations.

Over the course of the last 20 years or so, the EU has also established a regime of de facto competence for international environmental policy. Although the formal competence for external EU environmental policy remains mixed or shared (or at least contested), this appears to pose less and less of a problem as the EU decision-making regime has come to be accepted. In this respect, environment is similar to external trade, although the decision-making regime for the latter has been established for even longer. One important difference of course is that there remains scope for member states to get involved in negotiations. This can cause coordination or continuity problems even when the Commission is present.

The assessment of effectiveness shows that the EU has been relatively effective in most stages of negotiation with the exception of the negotiations themselves. Whilst this has generally been put down to the cumbersome EU decision-making process during negotiations, these are not much different in the environment to those in trade, where there have been less problems, at least in recent years. Whilst coordination issues have caused difficulties in climate change negotiations, the case study suggests that the EU's lack of effectiveness is also due to its success in pushing through EU level climate change policies. This has meant the EU has lead in adopting active policies, but has done so unilaterally. The success of EU external trade policy in the past has been thanks to a combination of a strong EU policy which deepened integration and thus enhanced EU market power, and an established decision-making regime and strategic leadership by the Commission in shaping the EU's negotiating agenda. In climate change the EU has little market power due to its unilateral policies.

Chapter 6

EU Development Policy

Introduction

Europe is of considerable importance for development. Europe's input is particularly vital for Africa and sub-Saharan African, which has been largely left behind in the process of globalisation and has failed to make the progress in economic development and poverty reduction which a number of Asian countries have over the past decade or so. Europe is the main trading partner for Africa and its main provider of development assistance.

The EU's role in development has evolved over a period of 50 years. Taken together, EU and member state aid accounts for some 55 per cent of total official development aid (ODA). The EU has also committed itself to reach the target of 0.7 per cent of GNP for ODA by 2015. In terms of trade, the EU is the largest importer of products from developing countries. The EU, led by a number of member state governments, has also played a leading role in pushing for developing country debt relief.

EU development policy is however, embedded in a multilateral process that includes both member state, as well as the policies and initiatives taken by other multilateral organisations, such as the World Bank, UNIDO, WTO, and so on. Debt reduction negotiations have taken place in the G8, in which the four EU members of the G8 have led as much as the EU presidency or the Commission. Competence for development policy is shared between the EU and the member states, something the Lisbon Treaty confirms. Member state governments have pursued development policies and initiatives both bilaterally and through these multilateral organisations as well as through the EU, so that EU development policy could be said to be more part of a wider multilateral approach than in the case of trade or environmental policy.

A clearly defined EU development policy, which would give the EU a clearly distinct identity in the field, has been slow in the making. There are various reasons for this. A solid treaty base for development policy did not exist before the Maastricht Treaty (TEU), even though there had of course been cooperation between member states and the Commission before 1991. Member state governments have been reluctant to cede competence to the EU in development aid, which is of central importance to foreign policy vis-à-vis the majority of countries in the international system. National governments therefore resisted Commission efforts to drive forward initiatives for fear that this would lead to an erosion of national sovereignty. In the early years, national vested interests resisted the opening up of aid budgets to competition from contractors from other member states. EU development policy has been viewed as inefficient, so some national development bodies have opposed shifting scarce resources to the EU level. Finally, there has also been a belief that cooperation at a wider multilateral level is a better means of delivering development.

With development policy shared between the EU and the member states and limited EU level funding, there has been a premium on ensuring vertical coherence (between the EU and national level policies and actions) and horizontal coherence (between the various EU policies that affect development such as trade, agricultural and fisheries policy). While years of experience may have eased, but by no means resolved, the challenge of achieving vertical coherence, the task of bringing about coherence between different EU policies has become arguably more difficult. The EU has been seeking to promote greater horizontal coherence in various Policy Coherence for Development (PCD) initiatives, and some key policy areas such as agriculture are beginning to become more development conscious. The EU is also seeking to incorporate foreign policy along with other external policies including development cooperation, trade and humanitarian assistance within a single framework in the European External Action Service (EEAS) following the application of the Lisbon Treaty.

The Evolution of EU Development Policy

The negotiations on the Treaty of Rome only came to relations with developing countries at the very end. At the insistence of France and Belgium, countries which retained colonies at the time, and in the face of opposition from Germany and the Netherlands, which sought a more global approach to developing countries, Part IV of the Treaty of Rome was added to address the question of 'associated countries' as they were called. This offered reciprocal access to markets on a most-favoured nation basis. In other words, all EEC countries would have access to the French and Belgian colonies in Africa, and the latter would have access to the EEC market. In return, all EEC countries were to share in the provision of financial support for development. The independence of the African colonies shortly after the signature of the Treaty of Rome meant that Part IV of the Treaty became largely redundant, although it remained relevant for the dependent territories.

In 1963, the Yaounde I agreement was signed between the EEC and the 18 now-independent states of West Africa. This provided for reciprocal access to markets, with scope for both sides to restrict imports in sensitive products. Funding for development, largely in the form of infrastructure projects, was provided via the 2nd European Development Fund (EDF). Funding for the EDF came from the EEC Member States not from any common EEC budget, although member state contributions to the EDF were geared to member state contributions to the EU budget. Even at this time there was awareness of the need for horizontal coherence, and there was provision for the EEC to 'take account of the interests of the associated states when drawing up the CAP' (Art. 11 Yaounde I) (Frish, 2008). Yaounde I was followed by Yaounde II in 1969, and in response to pressure to include other African countries, the Arusha agreement was also signed with the states of the East African Community (EAC). The main components of Yaounde II and Arusha agreements were market access and development funding. Humanitarian assistance in the form of food aid was also provided by the EEC from late 1968 and accounted for about a quarter of aid.

With the 1973 enlargement of the EC, a new agreement was signed in Lome in 1975 which included 46 developing countries, many of which had been former British colonies. Lome I reflected the nature of the development debate at the time, which was strongly influenced by the more assertive position of developing countries as expressed in their demands for a New International Economic Order (NIEO). Led by the G77, the developing countries were pressing for improved terms of trade, more access to developed country markets, debt relief, increased development assistance and a bigger say in international economic institutions. Lome I provided for preferential access for developing countries. Here the EC followed the precedent set in the GATT, which had already moved to provide such favourable treatment for developing countries in 1964 with the introduction of Part IV of the GATT and the subsequent enabling clause. But the GATT Generalised System of Preferences (GSP) scheme was intended to be based on MFN – in other words, to provide preferences for all developing economies.

Lome I also went some way towards meeting the demands of the developing countries for improved terms of trade by establishing the commodity stabilisation programme STABEX covering 12 – mostly agricultural – commodities. This was aimed at stabilising commodity prices rather than addressing the terms of trade concerns of developing countries at the time, which were that the manufactured exports of the developed countries were favoured over the raw materials and agricultural commodity exports of the developing exporters. Development aid was provided by the EDF that now rose to Ecu 3 bn. The various Lome agreements that followed provided the focus of EU development policy through to 2000. These became more wide ranging through the inclusion of political aims such as human rights, in line with the general trend towards making development assistance more conditional upon good governance in the recipient countries. Again in line with the general trend in development policy, the later Lome agreements began to move away from project support, towards general budgetary support. EDF funding rose to Ecu 10.8 bn for Lome IV with additional funding from the European Investment Bank (EIB). But most support for development still came in the form of bilateral funding from the EC member states with funding under the EU budget accounting for about 20 per cent over the period of the Lome agreements.

During the life of the Lome agreements, a period of 20 years or more, EC development policy evolved pragmatically, as there was no formal treaty base for policy. The first legal basis came in the Maastricht Treaty. In addition to some general policy aims (see the next section), this introduced the requirements of complementarity (of EU with member state policies), coherence (between different EU policies such as development and trade policy) and coordination (of policy within and between the various EU institutions). On the one hand, this requirement to ensure policy coherence was an opportunity to more fully integrate development into all EU policies. On the other hand, Maastricht also set out aims for more common foreign and security policy. As development policy constitutes an important part of relations with developing countries, this posed a potential threat for development policy in the sense that foreign policy might trump development aims.

In fact it took the EU some time to act on the objective of developing the greater coherence required by the Maastricht Treaty. It was not until into the 2000s that real efforts were made to make EU development policy more coherent. This delay was due to the same kind of factors mention above that had hindered efforts to promote a more cohesive approach in the past.

The Cotonou Agreement of 2000, signed by the EU and its member states with the 78 ACP states, reflected EU and general trends in development policy thinking at the time. One notable and controversial addition was that of 'good governance'. The ACP states feared that the inclusion of good governance would make the provision development assistance conditional upon the EU's definition of good governance. This was a break from previous more neutral policy under the Lome agreements and shook the ACP belief that aid under the EDF and EU funding was secure. The conditionality element of EU aid was strengthened by the inclusion of Euro 3 bn that was explicitly conditional upon good governance. Funding was however, further increased to Euro 22 bn over eight years (2000–2007), with most funding still channelled through the EDF, the 'EU' funding still controlled by the member states meaning that it does not come under the EU budget, or through bilateral funding directly from the member state governments.

In trade between the ACP and the EU, the Cotonou Agreement envisaged the negotiation of region-to-region Economic Partnership Agreements (EPAs) with the ACP regions which would be compatible with the WTO provisions under Art. XXIV of the GATT on preferential trade agreements (and Art. V of GATS for the services provisions). This meant the end to the non-reciprocal treatment for the ACP states which, from the mid-1990s, had been sanctioned by a WTO waiver from the MFN obligations of the EU and ACP states under the GATT 1994, although there remained in practice scope for some asymmetry favouring the ACP partners. Such a shift to the reciprocal EPAs had a number of causes. First, the EU had lost the first banana case in 1993 brought under Art. XXIV of the GATT against the preferences it provided under Lome on the grounds that these discriminated against non-ACP developing countries. The existing EU preference policy therefore became subject to challenge under the strengthened dispute settlement provisions of the WTO. Although the EU, with support from the ACP states, had obtained a waiver that allowed a continuation of ACP preferences, first under Lome IV and then, following a two-year hiatus, under the Cotonou Agreement until 2007, there was a concern that waivers would become increasingly costly in terms of concessions the EU would be required to make in order to get the support required in the WTO General Council. At the time the EU was also pressing for a new round of multilateral negotiations and so did not wish to damage its credibility by seeking exceptions from existing multilateral commitments. Nor was the EU ready to continue indefinitely with the existing regime in the hope that it would not be challenged. In a move that favoured all least-developing countries (LDCs), the EU unilaterally agreed to remove tariffs on all exports from LDCs, with temporary exceptions for three sensitive products: rice, sugar and bananas. This was the everything-but-arms (EBA) policy of 2001, so-called because there was to be free trade in everything but arms. New GSP and GSP plus policies were also introduced which were designed to be in line with GATT (1994) obligations. There was probably also an expectation that a new round of trade negotiations would lead to a further erosion of ACP preferences. Negotiating EPAs that removed preferences for the ACP but offered little in return was, however, always going to face opposition from the ACP.

Other external factors also shaped the EU position on development. The UN Conference on Finance and Development in Monterey in 2002 provided a major external driver for the EU member states to support a common approach. Thanks to the lead by the EU Council of Development Ministers and the Commission, the EU was able to fulfil a leading role by pledging to meet the target of 0.7 per cent of GNP for development aid. EU member states carried this objective into the G8 negotiations leading up to Gleneagles in 2005 and offered further debt relief.

During the 2000s, the EU also finally moved to enhance policy coherence. In 2005 the Commission felt able to propose the adoption of an EU development policy. While this finally emerged as the European Consensus on Development, rather less definite than a common policy, it was the first time EU aims on development cooperation had been agreed in a formal statement. The Consensus included agreement to press ahead with the aim of the 3Cs policy coherence set out in the Maastricht Treaty. The Consensus was then followed up by a Commission initiative on a Code of Conduct on Complementarity and Division of Labour between the EU and Member States on development policy in 2007.

Decision-Making in EU Development Policy

The decision-making on development policy has been significantly affected by the Lisbon Treaty because many of the functions carried out in development were absorbed by the newly created EEAS in 2010. This section describes decision-making procedures and practices prior to the reorganisation in 2010. Past practice is important because it has shaped the path dependence of decision-making on development, which has been identified as a factor in shaping the EU's role in this policy area. Past practice is also likely to shape the decision-making practice that emerges from the new arrangements. The section also introduces a discussion of the changes that will be brought about as a result of the Lisbon Treaty. As the establishment of the EEAS only took place towards the end of 2010, at the time of writing it was too early to say how these latest changes in the arrangements for decision-making in development policy would work in practice.

As mentioned above, Part IV of the Treaty of Rome was added at the last minute to cover the African colonies of France and Belgium. These provisions in Art. 131-6 of the EEC set out the aim of promoting development in all colonies or overseas territories of the EEC member states. There was to be reciprocal market access, most-favoured-nation status (among the signatories), national treatment and right of establishment. Free movement was mentioned, but was subject to a public policy exception and was in effect controlled by EEC member states. Implementation was to be via unanimous Council decisions following a Commission proposal. These provisions were carried over into the Treaty establishing the European Community (TEC) Art. 182 and the Treaty of Lisbon (Arts 198–203) for the few remaining dependent territories of the EU member states.

With decolonisation, there was no treaty basis for negotiating agreements with developing countries, so the EEC used the alternative instrument of Art. 228 TEU (ex Art. 130 TEC and now Art. 217 TFEU) to conclude association agreements. This was not without some controversy, as Art. 228 TEU was intended for agreements with reciprocal rights and obligations, which was not the case for the Lome agreements. Agreements negotiated under Art. 228 TEU were mixed agreements, and the procedure used was for the Council to provide a negotiating mandate following a Commission proposal. The Commission then negotiated with the assistance of a special (Council) committee. Any agreement was adopted by unanimity within the Council. The trade provisions in the treaty Art. 113 EEC (Art. 133 TEU and Art. 207 TFEU) were used to negotiate and conclude agreements that had significant development implications, such as the Kennedy and Tokyo Rounds of the GATT, the GATT/UNCTAD GSP scheme and commodity agreements within the UN. As discussed in Chapter 3, Art. 133 TEU used the Community method similar to that of Art. 228 above, but with the formal Council decision-making based on a qualified majority voting.

The Single European Act (SEA) of 1986 added very little to the provisions on development. There was an indirect reference to development cooperation in the context of external relations in Art. 30.2, which called on the EC to be 'a cohesive force in international relations'. But it was not until the Treaty on European Union (TEU) (Maastricht) that development cooperation was given a firm treaty basis. Art. 3 (r) listing the aims of the EU included reference to 'a policy in the sphere of development cooperation'. There was also reference to the general aim of 'sustainable development' Art. 6 TEC (Art. 11 TFEU). The main innovation in the Maastricht Treaty was the inclusion for the first time of a section on development cooperation (Title XVII). This set out for the objectives of sustainable economic and social development especially for the most disadvantaged (i.e., LDCs); a smooth and gradual integration of developing countries into the world economy; a campaign against poverty; developing and consolidating democracy and the rule of law and respect for human rights and fundamental freedoms (Art. 130u). As noted above, the Maastricht Treatt (TEU) also established the so-called three 'Cs': complementarity (Art. 130 (u) TEU), coherence (Art. 130 (v) TEU) and cooperation (Art. 130 (x) TEU).

Otherwise, Maastricht reaffirmed the existing procedures that had been used since the 1960s covering budgetary matters and the conclusion of agreements with third parties on development cooperation. Art. 130 (v) specified that decisions on EU funding for development would be taken by co-decision under Art. 189 (c) of the treaty. This did not apply to funds provided by the member states under the EDF. Art. 228 (TEU) (Art. 300 TEC) remained the provision used for negotiating agreements between the Community and third parties which covered development cooperation. In other words the Commission negotiated with the help of a special Council committee, the Council adopted any agreement by unanimity and the Parliament only had to give its assent if there were budgetary or institutional implications, which there generally have been in all association agreements the EU has negotiated.

The Treaty of Lisbon (TFEU) brings development cooperation within the single heading of external relations of the EU along with foreign and security policy, trade and humanitarian aid. The EU's actions on the international scene are guided by the general aims set out in the Chapter 1 of Title V of the Treaty on European Union. These include human rights, respect of human dignity, the principles of equality and solidarity and the principles of the UN Charter. Art. 21 TEU also lists some general aims including (i) security, (ii) support for democracy and the rules of law, (iii) peace and conflict prevention, (iv) the sustainable economic, social and environmental development of developing countries, with the *primary aim of eradicating poverty*, (v) the integration of all countries into the world economy, including through the progressive abolition of restrictions on trade, (vi) support for measures to preserve global nature resources in order to ensure sustainable development, (vii) assistance in natural and man-made disasters, and (viii) good global governance.

Title III of the TFEU sets out the provisions on development cooperation and largely confirms the approach adopted in the Maastricht Treaty. The EU's development cooperation policy is to complement that of the member states, but adds that these 'reinforce each other' (Art. 208 (1) TFEU). This seems to be more balanced than the provisions in the Maastricht Treaty. On horizontal coherence, the TFEU again stresses that the Union shall 'take account of the objectives of development cooperation in the policies it implements'. Art. 209 reaffirms that the European Parliament and Council shall agree on the EU development budget on the basis of the OLP. Art. 210 also provides somewhat stronger provisions on cooperation between the Union and the member states on development policy.

Decision-making in EU development policy therefore continues to face the challenge of the three Cs if it is to be effective and enhance the EU's external role as is the aim of the Lisbon Treaty. There is the need to ensure vertical coherence between the member state development policies and EU policy. This is due to the continuation of shared competence, but more importantly the fact that member states continue to provide aid in addition to that provided through the EU. Then there is the challenge of ensuring effective co-ordination between the various bodies and institutions that decide on EU policy and administer it. The adoption of the Lisbon Treaty has if anything accentuated these tensions, at least in the short term, because it brings development policy into European External Action Service (EEAS) and provokes yet another reorganisation of development policy-making in the EU. In the debate on how the Lisbon Treaty provisions should be implemented there are differing views. One argues in favour of the integration of development policy with these other policies because this would provide an opportunity of achieving the long sought after goal of policy coherence. This view seems to be supported by the majority of member state governments and is reflected in the Council proposals on the EEAS. At the other end of the debate is the sense that development policy, with its emphasis on long-term poverty reduction, risks becoming subservient to short term foreign or security policy issues (Bond, 2009). This view is supported by some development NGOs and by at least some members of the Development Committee of the European Parliament.

Decision-making in most aspects of EU economic diplomacy is complex. This is especially the case in development cooperation because of the increased desire for coherence. The following section sets the scene by describing the role the various institutions have played to date, before attention is turned to the impact of the Lisbon Treaty. Figure 6.1 provides a simplified diagrammatic presentation of EU decision-making in development policy.

The European Commission

Within the European Commission there are different levels of decision-making. The college of Commissioners brings together Commissioners with responsibility for a range of policy areas that can have a significant bearing on development policy. Central among these are the Commissioners and Directorates General (DGs) covering the policy areas of an external nature (external relations, trade, development), but also those with responsibilities which are predominantly 'domestic' in character, but which have significant external implications (environment, agriculture and fisheries, food safety and consumer affairs). Each Commission DG is also supported by a number of Committees (chaired by the Commission, but including member state participants, such as the EDF (ACP states), ALA (Asian and Latin American states), MED (Mediterranean partners) and Food Security Committees which advise the Commission when it is developing proposals. There is also a network of expert groups that are likewise chaired by the Commission.

The Directorate General for Development (DG Dev) is responsible for promoting coherence and developing EU policy, but its role has in the past been eroded due to the relative increase in the importance of other DGs for EU relations with developing countries and by repeated reorganisations within the Commission. Prior to the 1990s, DG Dev was responsible for EU Official Development Assistance (ODA), the main plank of EU policy and also negotiated association agreements such as Lome. In the Delors' Commissions 1985–1995, a

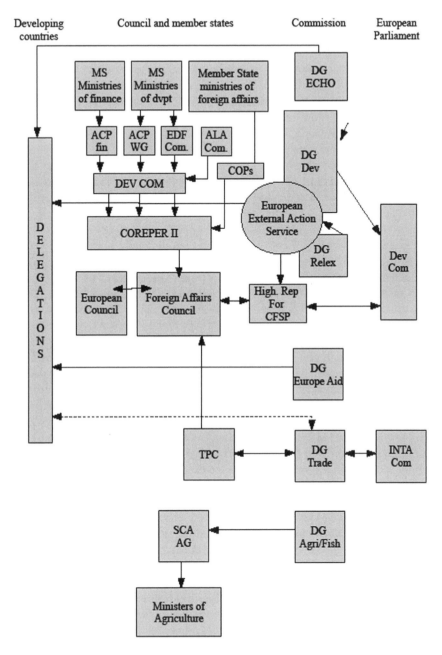

Fig. 6.1   Overview of EU Decision-Making in Development Cooperation

regional division was introduced with one Commissioner responsible for the ACP and one for Asia and Latin America. This led a weakening of development policy. The Prodi Commission introduced further changes with the aim of strengthening the Commission in external relations. At the time, the Commission's strategy was said to have been influenced by a desire to prevent the encroachment of intergovernmental decision-making due to the strengthening of pillar two CFSP and partly in order to improve what was generally recognised as the poor performance of the Commission in delivering ODA. The first change was to give the DG External Affairs (DG Relex) a greater role. The DG for Trade (DG Trade) was created and took responsibility for all trade policy, including trade relations with developing countries. Before 2000, most trade had been dealt with by DG I, which covered multilateral trade issues and some regional issues, such as transatlantic relations, but not trade with the ACP states. EuropeAid was created to improve the implementation of EU aid programmes. This effectively left DG Dev with development policy, but with a reduced means to implement it, as well as the challenging task of promoting policy coherence for development (PCD).

Other DGs therefore lead on external policies of importance to development, such as DG Trade in the DDA and the negotiation of the EPAs and DG Maritime Affairs and Fisheries in bilateral fisheries agreements with developing countries. The former DG Justice, Freedom and Security, now DG Home Affairs, dealt with migration issues. On some topics the lead has been shared. For example, on the reform of the sugar regime which was of considerable importance to a number of ACP and other developing states, DG Agriculture led on compensation/subsidies for the EU producers and DG Development on assistance for the ACP countries.

The DG which leads in the Commission has also tended to determine which Council Working Group has dealt with an issue. Established Council Working Groups then tended to be dominated by existing, domestic interests which have not always been open to the interests of developing countries (CEPS, 2008, 29). Similarly, expert working groups which advised the Commission have tended to be filled with technical experts who have not always had the wider view. For example, sanitary and phytosanitary (SPS) measures are drawn up with a view to public health in the EU based on the latest technical knowledge, but there has not always been much thought given to the difficulties that developing countries might have in meeting them. SPS measures taken by the EU have become a more important barrier to market access as CAP reform has eased some of the tariff and quota barriers to access for developing countries (Mathews, 2009).

As in all policy areas interservice consultations take place between Commission DGs before any new policy is adopted. This does provide scope for DG Development to feed into policies led by other DGs. Some of the interservice consultations also take place through semi-permanent structures to speed up the process. Prior to the creation of the EEAS there was already concern about the depletion in the size of DG Development (with only about 200 officials) compared to DG Relex (with about 1000 officials) and doubts had been raised about DG Dev's ability to provide much of a development input into inter-service consultations or the Impact Assessments of policies that provide another channel through which it is possible to ensure the development angle is incorporated into all EU policies. (CEPS, 2008, 31)

The Council

Within the Council, the Development Council had struggled to match the importance of some other Councils. Meetings only took place twice a year, and not all member states were represented at ministerial level. The Development Council also tended to produce policy statements rather than legislate, as other Councils did. This was inevitable given that in development policy there were no internal legislative measures required. There was a Development Council until 2002, when, as part of the reorganisation of the EU to ease decision-making before the 2004 enlargement, a consolidation reduced the number of Councils to nine. The Development Council was subsumed into the General Affairs and External Relations Council (GAERC), which was to cover foreign and security policy, trade, development and humanitarian assistance. Although this was presented as more of an organisational simplification, subsuming the development council into GAERC immediately raised fears in the development community that more immediate foreign policy interests would crowd out longer-term development policies. As shown in the discussion of trade in Chapter 3, it was easier for trade to hold its own in GAERC given that most trade issues are exclusive competence, compared to development that remained firmly mixed, and the strength of the lead by DG Trade and the seniority of the 133 Committee. Subsuming development into GAERC did not mean development ministers stopped meeting, as there remained scope for GAERC to meet in a development format. GAERC also offered the opportunity of promoting coherence in the EU's external relations in all key policy areas thanks to the more frequent meetings of GAERC. The GAERC also prepared the European Council so that it provided an opportunity to feed development related issues into decisions at the level of heads of state and government.

If foreign ministers were preoccupied with foreign policy issues and neglecting development, one remedy lay in COREPER, which is well placed to retain a broad overview of EU policies and thus promote horizontal coherence before issues reach the council level. But COREPER is handicapped in this task by the fact that it is split between COREPER II, which deals with external relations issues including development, trade and foreign policy as well as topics such as economic and financial affairs, and COREPER I, which deals with the more 'internal' topics of agriculture, fisheries, internal market, and so on. Horizontal coherence is equally important with regard to these 'internal' EU policies. Studies of the policy coordination for development (PCD) in the Council have suggested that COREPER has not been very active in this form of coordination (CEPS, 2008, p. 22).

Beneath COREPER are the various senior council preparatory committees. As in the other policy areas discussed in the previous chapters, these committees can play a major role in policy formulation. Many issues are in effect resolved at the senior preparatory committee level, with few issues going to the Council. The SCA (agriculture and fish) submits 'A points' directly to the Council for Agriculture without going through COREPER and the TPC has also largely sidelined COREPER for more run of the mill issues. The Development Committee (DevCom) functions at this level and has played an important role in pushing for a coordination of policies within the Commission and horizontal coherence within EU policy, but domestic vested interest groups are often well established in comitology and Commission advisory groups. The use of consensus in most decision-making also means that member states can defend existing positions and veto reform as, for example, member states with important fishery interests have done in the SCA on fisheries agreements with developing countries. Some committees may also have developed normative positions over the years which do not always meet the needs of development policy. For example, the TPC has tended to support progressive trade liberalisation based on reciprocity which may not always be easily reconciled with the approach favoured by the development committee. At the level below the senior council preparatory committees, there are a number of important Council Working Groups, such as the ACP working party, the ACP Finance Working Party and the EDF Committee. There is coordination among these as well as between these and the Development Committee at the level of the member states. In other words, member state representatives on the various committees coordinate their input into EU-level policy, to a greater or lesser degree. Thus, at the national government level there is also an issue of coherence, and in some cases there are problems. Participants in the ACP finance group tend to be from ministries of finance, while those in the ACP working group come from development ministries, and there is not always good communication between them. At the same time some member state governments have led in integrating development cooperation into various policy areas as well as pushed for increases in ODA funding and a more 'development friendly' EU-trade policy. As will be discussed in the following section some Council presidencies in the 2000s have pushed to introduce PCD at an EU level.

The European Parliament

In comparison with the Commission and the Council, the European Parliament has a very simple structure for dealing with development cooperation. The Development Cooperation Committee deals with policy formulation as well as implementation and budgeting in so far as the EU development budget is concerned. The Development Cooperation Committee is a fairly senior EP committee, compared even to the INTA Committee. The Development Committee has sought to increase its powers by making the case for bringing EDF funding within the EU budget, which would give it scrutiny powers over EDF spending. But despite repeated efforts, with Commission support, EDF funding remains outside the EU budget and not subject to EP co-decision-making

(Ordinary Legislative Procedure). The Development Committee also scrutinises agricultural, fisheries and trade agreements, including the EPAs and as such has established a position as one of the major protagonists of a stronger and more coherent EU development policy. The other major protagonists are DG Dev, the development ministries in the Member States, especially the northern member states and the development NGOs.

The Phases of Programme Management and Allocation of Functions

The division of labour between the various EU institutions and within them between the various DGs and Councils or council committees has an impact upon the decision-making process and how the EU negotiates with developing countries. This will continue to be the case with the introduction of the changes resulting from the TFEU. In order to understand the EU decision-making and negotiation process in development policy, it is helpful to go into a little more detail on the procedures and existing division of tasks.

Decisions on development priorities are divided into five phases. The first covers a five-to-seven-year period for the overall country or regional strategies (country strategy programmes or regional strategy programmes CSP/RSP) and includes development, trade, political dialogue and governance issues. The regional dimension is important when the ACP partners are pursuing regional integration objectives or when there is funding regional infrastructure or energy projects. This is followed by the allocation of funds for the country or regional for the programming period. The third phase consists of shorter term national or regional indicative programmes (NIPs and RIPs) which deal with specific activities and projects designed to achieve the country or regional programmes. Phase four concerns the annual programmes for each country and region, and phase five concerns implementation.

Until the end of the first Barroso Commission in 2009, there was a division by regions. DG Relex led on phases 1–3 for the neighbourhood countries, the Mediterranean, Asia and Latin America, thus deciding on the disbursement of funds under the SI (Stability instrument) of Euro 2.1 bn, the ENPI (European Neighbourhood Programme) of Euro 11.2bn and the DCI (Development Cooperation Instrument) for Asian and Latin American developing countries of Euro 16.9 bn. All the figures here are as agreed for the budget period 2007–2013 (Gavas and Maxwell, 2009). DG Enlargement dealt with the Western Balkans and the allocation of funds under the IPA (Instrument for Pre-Accession countries) of Euro 11.5 bn over the same period. DG Development was responsible for phases 1–3 for the ACP states disbursing Euro 22.7 bn under the European Development Fund (EDF). DG Echo, which deals with humanitarian aid, also reported to the Commissioner for Development and ran the EU's Euro 5.6 bn programme of humanitarian aid.

In line with the aim of enhancing the allocation and implementation of programmes, DG EuropeAid was responsible for phases 4 and 5 (annual programmes and implementation) for all funds except IPA, which was run by DG Enlargement, and the humanitarian aid run by DG ECHO. It must be stressed of course that all the country and regional programmes run by the EU are decided upon together with the recipient country or region, so EU development diplomacy in terms of providing funding really takes place at this time. In this process, the EU delegations in the countries and regions concerned play a key role and are also responsible for ensuring the programmes are carried out effectively. Before the establishment of the EEAS, the delegations reported to DG Relex and in an effort to ensure effective implementation, DG EuropeAid reported to the Commissioner for External Affairs, giving Relex an important coordinating role.

The issue of country desks should also be noted. The various Commission DGs had geographic desks. In other words, they had country or regional expertise which could be used to help define the objectives of programmes and promote coherence. The Council Secretariat also had country desks to help administer the Common Foreign and Security Policy of the EU, for which funding allocation was based on EU policy objectives, not on joint decisions with the recipient countries. So there was a duplication of geographic desks.

The Implications of the Lisbon Treaty for Decision-Making

As noted above, the adoption of the TFEU has brought EU development policy together with other external policies. Art. 205 TFEU (Part V, External Action) refers to the general aims of the Union's external action in Art. 21 of the Treaty of European Union. Art. 27 TFEU establishes the High Representative of the Union for Common Foreign and Security policy (HRCFSP), who shall represent the Union and will be assisted by the European External Action Service (EEAS) made up of Council, Commission and member state staff. In March 2010 the HR Ashton tabled a Proposal for a Council decision establishing the organisation and functioning of the EEAS.[1] This was agreed by the Council in April 2010. Within the EP Development Committee, there is fairly strong support for retaining some autonomy for EU development policy in order to reduce the risk of development aims being subordinated to foreign policy objectives. But this view does not seem to have prevailed and the Council approved arrangements for the EEAS on 27 July 2010. After subsequent discussions on the budget and in particular EP scrutiny of the EEAS budget, the EEAS was formally established on 1 December 2010.

With the new arrangements, elements of EU development policy will be integrated into the EEAS (see Figure 6.1). First of all, some of the DG Dev directorates – including Directorate D responsible for relations with the ACP states and Directorate E responsible for relations with other states in East and Southern Africa, the Indian Ocean and the Pacific – will be moved to the EEAS, along with

---

[1]   See Council Decision Establishing the Organisation and Functioning of the European External Action Service, 8724/10 April 2010.

some programming functions. The regional units in DG Relex have also been transferred to the EEAS.[2] Overall responsibility for development policy will be shared between the HRCFSP and the Commissioner responsible for development policy in DG Dev. The EEAS will share with the Commission responsibility for the first three phases of programming cycle. The EEAS shall give 'strategic political guidance' and 'shall contribute to the programming and management cycle for all the geographic funds' (Art. 8(1) of Council Decision on the EEAS). This will apply in particular to country allocations, CSPs/RSPs, NIPs and RIPs. EuropeAid will come under the responsibility of the Commissioner for Development again, so that in principle development policy and the implementation of aid programmes will come under DG Development. Any changes to the basic regulations for funding programmes will be submitted jointly by the EEAS and the Commissioner responsible for the ACP or for the European neighbourhood countries. The European Neighbourhood Programme and the enlargement functions and funding are brought together under one Commissioner.

The delegations of the EU in all countries and international organisations will report to the EEAS, and therefore ultimately to the HRCFSP. The EEAS will have geographic desks for all countries and regions as well as for horizontal themes such as multilateral topics. There will be no duplication of the EEAS country desks in DG Relex or DG Dev. This appears to mean that the EEAS will gather up much of the institutional capacity/memory of the EU, both from the Commission and Council Secretariat. But there are some exceptions. As noted in Chapter 3, DG Trade will remain outside the EEAS and will retain its country desks, which means a measure of autonomy for trade policy that could affect coherence with development policy.

The decision-making procedures for development are therefore again in something of a state of flux. This time due to fundamental changes in the way the EU organises its external policies. It seems likely that development will be more integrated into general EU external policy than trade or the environment. As discussed above, this provides opportunities for the EU to become more coherent in its approach to developing countries and dangers in the sense that development policy could be undermined should the new arrangements mean a greater focus on short-term foreign policy objectives. Only time will tell how the EEAS will function and therefore which of these proves to be the case. The final outcome depends in part on what sort of officials take over the various responsibilities. For example, will there be a preponderance of general foreign policy staff, or will there be staff with experience in development? Will staff with development expertise be rotated into posts in the EEAS? But it seems clear that the creation of the EEAS means a further period of uncertainty surrounding decision-making in development policy. In Chapter 2, it was argued that EU decision-making and

---

[2]   The EEAS will have six divisions, budget and personnel, global affairs (including for example, climate change); multilateral issues (such as the UN and G20); accession and neighbouring countries; industrialised countries; and developing countries.

negotiation will be more effective when there are well-established regimes. This seems certain not to be the case in development for some time yet.

Factors Shaping EU Development Policy

This section applies the analytical framework from chapter two in order to assess the factors that have shaped the role of the EU in development policy. It also draws on the discussion of the evolution of EU policy above.

The EU has *economic power* or leverage it can bring to bear in the service of development policy. The EU as a whole – in other words, EU budget funds, EDF and the ODA of the member states – accounts for more than half of all ODA worldwide. The effectiveness of such support therefore depends crucially on how well EU-controlled funds are coordinated with the various member state programmes. Where EU funds are complementary to member state funding programmes, one can expect more effective delivery of development assistance. For one thing, the capacity of some least developed countries to absorb major funding is limited. Such vertical coherence has not always worked very well, so that the potential for EU policy effectiveness has been reduced.

The EU also has significant market leverage it can bring to bear in the service of development. The EU is also one of the largest importers of exports from developing countries and particularly from LDCs. Access to the EU market in agricultural products, fish and manufactured products is important for developing countries. Just how such market access is used to promote development depends on horizontal coherence between EU policies. In this respect, there have been some clear cases of incoherence between policies. Often cited are the cases of agriculture and fisheries, in which the EU continues to protect EU producers in ways that are at odds with the interests of developing countries in some sectors. Although there has been reform of EU agricultural support, as discussed in the case study in Chapter 3, and some efforts to sensitise agricultural policy to the interests of developing countries.

The EU is *recognised* as an actor by developing countries. Indeed, there is an extensive network of bilateral and regional programmes developed between the EU and developing countries. The EU's role has been consolidated by the consecutive multi-annual programmes, such as the Lome agreements. More recently, there have been the EPAs negotiated between the EU and ACP states. But member states are also recognised as actors by developing country governments, as they provide both ODA and other forms of assistance. Developing countries therefore negotiate with both the EU and the individual member states, thus diluting the degree of recognition for the EU, compared for example to trade or international environmental policy.

The *external drivers* of EU development policy take the form of the need to develop common positions for major international negotiations, such as the International Conference on Financing for Development in Monterey in 2002, or more regular meetings of the G8 or now the G20 which discuss development-related topics. More important perhaps are the expectations of developing countries in terms of development assistance and support. In recent years, there has also been a securitisation of development due to a growing awareness of the link between collective security and development. In other words, underdevelopment has been seen increasingly as a potential source of political instability and thus as a potential threat to international security.

For the EU, broader security aims have also been a significant driving force behind the neighbourhood policy vis-à-vis countries in Eastern Europe and in the western Balkans. Such broader security motives have also been behind the trade and association agreements with North Africa and Middle Eastern countries. The Association Agreements which include political cooperation, financial support and access to markets are seen as a means of promoting economic development and thus political stability in countries that are undergoing major change or face the threat of fundamentalism. The other side of this coin is of course that security is a precondition for development. Thus economic development in Africa, especially in regions such as Central and West Africa, has been held back by repeated political instability and wars.[3]

Normative power is derived from shared norms and values within the EU. The EU member states do share a fairly strong common position on development. The elimination of poverty is a shared common norm. But there are differences for historical reasons. The former colonial powers of France, Britain, Portugal, Belgium, the Netherlands and, to a lesser degree, Spain supported development for historical and moral reasons. Germany and the Nordic states are also very strong supporters of development, but with greater emphasis on multilateral support. The new member states in Central and Eastern Europe have no colonial links with developing countries, and with relatively low levels of GDP per capita are also more concerned about their own development. Nevertheless, eradicating poverty through sustainable social and economic development of developing countries has been incorporated as a core aim of the EU. The EU position on development is also promoted by strong developmental interests, including active development NGOs which have been fairly successful in shaping public opinion in the EU and thus the positions of the European and the national parliaments. There has also been some codification of agreed general norms in the shape of the European Consensus on Development of 2005.

When it comes to framework norms on how to best promote development, there would appear to be less common ground, and the EU norms have been less stable. For example, there have been shifts in development policy from project-based support to a greater focus on good governance and partnership with

---

[3]   If one takes a broader view of development to include the need for security and stability as well as tackling poverty, the distinction between foreign and security policy and development policy becomes less important. This is relevant to the debate on how much autonomy development policy should retain from foreign policy.

developing countries and then to a need for all policies to reflect development interests (horizontal coherence). If strong horizontal coherence can be equated to a framework norm which imparts normative power, then the EU is still some way from acquiring such normative power.

Compared to other policy areas such as trade, finance or the environment, EU development policy is not anchored in any legislative framework covering internal policy. There are of course common policy statements such as the 2005 Consensus or the aims of Policy Coordination for Development (see below). But these are policy statements rather than policies which have been implemented domestically through a series of specific, binding directives. In other policy areas, concrete internal policies have shaped the EU's external policy; this is not the case in development policy. Another distinction between development policy and trade and perhaps to a somewhat lesser degree in financial markets or environment is that there remains a national alternative. In trade it is not possible for member state governments to conduct separate trade policies. This provides an incentive to work towards a common policy in response to external drivers. In development shared competence and the lack any serious effort to merge EU and member state development policies means this is not the case.

General *member state interests* influence development policy as in all policy areas. Close links between foreign policy towards developing countries and development assistance may have made member states resistant to pragmatic cooperation in development for fear of a functional spill-over into foreign policy. The provision of ODA is also seen by some member states as an instrument of foreign policy, because it provides valuable leverage in relations with developing countries and is thus something many member states are reluctant to give up.

Member state and sector interests also converge in wishing to retain control over aid finance as this provides opportunities for national suppliers. Although there is a general trend away from tied aid, and some member states have adopted a policy of not making contracts with national suppliers a condition for the provision of aid, there remains scope for *de facto* preferences for the suppliers of countries which provide finance for a particular contract. Sector interests can also shape trade policies or other policies that have a bearing on development. Probably the most important for LDC interests are agricultural interests in the EU which have pressed for continued protection – and subsidisation – of agricultural commodities. The EU has also provided export subsidies that have undermined agricultural production and possibly food security in some LDCs. The case for coherence between development policy and agricultural support was a factor leading the EU to agree to remove export subsidies for agriculture, but sector interests have clearly been important in shaping EU policy. Domestic agricultural support could also be said to have distorted competition in markets of importance for LDCs, and here the prospects of EU reductions are most certainly tied to the fate of the DDA, as the EU is not about to end subsidies unilaterally. In terms of EU interest in LDC export markets, there has been criticism of DG Trade's emphasis on reciprocity in the EPA negotiations, but the conclusion of the EPAs has not been primarily driven by sector interests in the EU seeking access to ACP markets. The main EU export interests lie in the large emerging markets such as India, China and Brazil or perhaps a few the larger ACP markets such as Nigeria.

Sector interests have had a less direct, but no less important impact on developing country interests through their support for EU policies on fisheries (Bretherton, 2006). With dwindling fish stocks in EU waters, the fishing industry has sought access to new fishing grounds and therefore the conclusion of agreements with developing countries that offer access to the fishing grounds off, for example, West Africa, in return for payments that go to the governments concerned. This has worked against the interests of local fishing industries in some countries, which support employment and food security.

There are interest groups in the EU which press for more generous EU ODA and greater policy coherence for development. Development NGOs play an important role in promoting the case for development and sustainable development. By influencing public opinion and thus member state national parliaments and the European Parliament, development NGOs have contributed a great deal to sustainable development being elevated to a central policy objective of the EU.

In terms of the *decision-making regime* for EU development policy, competence is shared between the member states and the EU with the member states holding onto their role in development policy. Development did not really figure in EU treaties until the Treaty on European Union (Maastricht) implemented in 1992. This contrasts with trade, where EC competence was granted from the outset. Like environment, from the TEU onwards there have been provisions setting out aims for development policy in the treaties, but unlike environment these were not really acted upon with any urgency until the 2000s. In terms of the broader institutional infrastructure, development appears to have been given a relatively low priority within the EU. There has been no well-established decision-making regime at the EU level for development policy. Within the Commission, the evolution of development policy was been held back by frequent changes in the organisation of policy-making. These were with the stated aim of addressing difficulties achieving coherence or improving implementation, but there were also shaped by other issues more related to power struggles between various DGs or between EU institutions. In short EU development policy appears to have suffered more than other policy areas from changes in the decision-making procedures that have prevented the emergence of a well-established regime. With the integration of development policy into the EEAS, there is a new opportunity of strengthening policy, but it remains to be seen whether this can be achieved.

There are two key tensions present in EU development policy decision-making. First, there is the tension between foreign policy and development. As security and freedom from internal conflict or war are preconditions for development, there will always be an element of foreign/security policy in development. The concern among many development experts, however, is that EU development policy will become subservient to the dictates of foreign policy. The second tension is the more general question of coherence across EU policy areas. This concerns not just the other relevant EU external policies which influence development, such as trade and environment, but also 'internal' policies. Agriculture and fisheries have already been mentioned in this context. But there are less obvious cases where internal EU policy can have a direct bearing on developing countries' interests and exports, such as in the field of SPS measures.

Policy *coherence* has become more important for EU policy with the recognition that the provision of financial assistance cannot ensure development when other more systemic factors, such as access to markets for developing country products have adverse effects on development. The following section therefore provides a case study of Policy Coordination for Development (PCD) as an illustration of the issues facing EU decision-making in the field of development.

Policy Coordination for Development

The concept of PCD emerged during the 1990s as a central feature of development policy. It is particularly relevant for the EU given that competence is shared between the EU and the 27 member states. The concept emerged with the recognition that project funding was no longer sufficient as a policy instrument and that it was necessary to ensure that development is integrated into other areas, such as trade and environment. In other words, as the development agenda has grown, so has the need for PCD, and particularly in the EU where there are many actors spread over various policy areas that can have an impact on policies relevant for development. Indeed, as the previous section pointed out, the resources available for coordinating development policy in DG Dev have been diminished during the last decade, thus opening up a gap between expectations in terms of PCD and the capability of the DG Dev.

What Is PCD?

In the development field, PCD is simply the aim of ensuring that all relevant EU and member state policies promote development and that incoherent policies or policies that run counter to the interests of developing country economies do not frustrate progress. PCD is also important for the credibility and legitimacy of EU policy, both internally and internationally.

A deeper understanding of the challenges faced by the EU in PCD can be gained be considering the three Cs of complementarity, coherence and cooperation. Complementarity is needed because the treaties up to and including the TFEU have reaffirmed that development policy is shared between the EU and the member states. With both the EU and member states engaging directly in development policy, there is clearly a need to ensure that the two levels are complementary. Complementarity here does not mean that policy is carried out at the most suitable level (subsidiarity). Both EU and member states act on the same level. Broadly speaking, complementarity is equivalent to vertical coherence as discussed in Chapter 2.

The term *coherence* in the context of the 3Cs has been broken down into three subsidiary objectives: coherence between EU and member state policies (vertical coherence); coherence within EU development policy itself; and coherence between EU development policy and other EU level policies (horizontal coherence). As discussed in the previous section, policy-making in these different policy areas is scattered across many Working Groups, Committees, DGs of the Commission and Councils. Ensuring coherence between these diverse policy areas is likely to be extremely difficult if not impossible (Carbone, 2008). Finally, there is cooperation. For some, this refers to consultation or an exchange of information on aid programmes. For others it means more integrated, joint action in aid programmes, and for others still it means harmonisation of policies. There is also the question of the level on which policy cooperation should take place, the EU, the OECD level in the Development Assistance Committee (DAC) or the multilateral level in the World Bank or UN. Historically, the Commission has favoured efforts to harmonise member state policies and carve out a distinct EU policy and has been joined in this by France. This would lead to a stronger EU role in development policy and an EU identity. The northern member states have tended to favour greater flexibility on the level of cooperation arguing that effectiveness requires cooperation and coordination at the wider international level that includes the OECD or multilateral levels, which also bring in the US, Japan and other providers of ODA. This would clearly tend to mean that the EU role is as one level or forum in a multilevel process.

The PCD Debate in the EU

The origins of a debate on the concept of PCD go back to the mid 1980s, although there was of course a discussion on policy coordination before that. In the preparation for the SEA, the Netherlands proposed the idea of PCD, but it did not make headway in the Intergovernmental Conference (IGC) at the time. The Maastricht Treaty first established the 'three Cs'. But there seems to have been little discussion on the content of the provisions (Hoebrink, 2007). Shortly after Maastricht, the Council asked the Commission to study the Art. 130 provisions of the TEU, but at the time the Commission came forward with no concrete proposals on its application. Impetus for action came from specific member states in response to cases of incoherence in EU policy. For example, in 1993 the German Ministry for Development, supported by an active NGO campaign, pointed out that EU export subsidies for beef were damaging African producers and thus development prospects. A little later the German Ministry of Development, this time with support from the Dutch as well as NGOs, pointed out the incoherence in EU fisheries policy. These cases raised awareness of the need for greater coherence, but do not seem to have precipitated any action in the EU.

Work on PCD was advancing elsewhere, however, especially in the DAC of the OECD. With the new Prodi Commission of 2000, the Commission produce a draft position paper for the Council with a strong development focus, but this was watered down by member state opposition. The final Declaration of European Development Policy addressed the question of complementarity by proposing that the Commission focus on a number of specific objectives (sectors of policy) when it implements EU development policy. These were trade and development, support for the regulation of international trade (trade capacity building), support for macro economic policies in developing countries, support for transport, food security and rural development, institutional capacity building and good governance (Commission, 2000).

The EU policy still seems to have been strongly influenced by developments outside the EU however. The DAC again picked up work following the adoption of the Millennium Development Goals (MDGs) in 2000 by collating national experience with efforts to implement the MDGs. Led by some northern member states, there was a semi-formal coordination between successive presidencies in the 2003–2005 period aimed at carrying forward the PCD agenda. The EU also began an evaluation of PCD policies in the member state. In April 2005, the Council adopted a position on the MDGs which focused on PCD, and in May 2005 the GAERC agreed on a Council Conclusion on PCD setting out 12 specific objectives. In December 2005, the Commission, Council and European Parliament agreed on the European Consensus on development cooperation (OJ 2006/C46/01), which gave PCD a central position stating that the 'EU takes account of objectives of development cooperation in all policies that it implements that are likely to affect developing countries, and that these policies support development objectives'. The first part of the wording here is simply a restatement of the 'take account of' position that dates from the Treaty of Rome, but the latter part appears to call for other policies to contribute to development aims. The Consensus was followed by a Council request to the Commission to develop a work programme on PCD, which was taken on by DG Dev, with further work coordinated through the Presidencies in 2006–2007 that led to the adoption of a Code of Conduct on complementarity and the division of labour between the Commission and the member states. At the same time, the Nordic + group of member states (including the Netherlands and Britain) also initiated a programme aimed at harmonising their development policies.

Progress towards the development of PCD within the EU has therefore been slow and tentative. During the 1990s, member states began to introduce PCD at the national level. Up to 1996, only two member states had such policies, but by 2006, 22 had policy documents setting out at least the aims of PCD, and 15 had implemented such policies. At the EU level, progress has been made, but it has been some time coming, and efforts only really began in the mid-2000s. If one takes a closer look at specific policy areas, one can see the challenge which still remains. In the area of trade capacity building, one of the policy sectors identified for Commission leadership in 2000, member states remain active. Information on the respective programmes is shared, but this appears to be more consultation than close cooperation.

Factors Shaping EU Policy on PCD

The discussion above shows that a range of factors have influenced this particular area of EU development cooperation policy. The fact that competence is shared has clearly complicated matters. It has not only allowed member states have to retain national policies for selfish national interest reasons, but it has also frustrated the development of a common EU policy. Shared competence has also meant that member states have continued to pursue distinct national policies. Member states have clearly desired to retain the flexibility to choose between the EU level and other levels of cooperation, be they the OECD, multilateral or even sub-EU groupings such as the Nordic+ group.

Also blocking progress have been sector interests in the various specific policy areas such as agriculture, fisheries, and so on, which see PCD as a threat to their ability to defend EU interests. The 'development community', which includes for example, development ministries in the member states, development NGOs, church groups and a good number of members of the European Parliament, have made progress in making the case for PCD, but to bring about change in such a challenging area has been harder than defending the status quo.

Progress in PCD appears to have come as a result of the commitment of some member states, and within these the commitment and consistent support of ministers for development. Within the Commission, DG Dev appears to have been less successful than the development ministries in some of the leading member states in pressing the case for PCD. DG Dev's cause has also been weakened by decisions taken within the Commission that have tended to favour other policy areas over development, namely foreign policy and trade.

External factors have acted as a catalyst for greater internal EU policy coordination, such as in the case of the negotiations on the MDGs and the Monterey Conference.

Conclusions

EU development policy has been seen as ineffective in the past because of the poor performance in the distribution of development assistance. Recent years have seen something of an improvement, but as the discussion above shows, progress in PCD has been slow. In terms of the question of the role of the EU, in development policy the EU appears to assume the role of one level in a multilevel process rather than that of a leading actor. This is illustrated by the fact that the member states continue to pursue their own national development policies in parallel with those of the EU. There also appears to be little desire to move towards an extended common EU policy replacing the member state policies. The Treaty of

Lisbon retains a clear role for the member states with shared competence in this area. Even in the debate on policy coordination, there is still a view among some member state governments and development agencies that coordination should be at a broader international level rather than just at the EU level.

Institutional factors appear to be decisive in shaping the role of the EU in development policy. The first concerns the institutional set-up within the EU. Member states have retained competence and have used this to pursue distinct national policies or to pursue multilevel development strategies which encompass levels of coordination other than the EU. There are sub-groups of member states within the EU which have pressed ahead with coordination, and member state governments have also promoted cooperation in multilateral agencies such as the OECD or World Bank in parallel to any coordination within the EU. The fact that the member state governments also control most of EU official development assistance means that they are recognised as negotiating partners by recipient countries. The potential influence the EU could have as a result of the level of ODA provided is therefore not realised because the funding is divided between the EU and member states.

But the EU market power still has considerable relevance for developing countries in the sense that EU policies in a number of fields other than development affect the development prospects of many countries. When it comes to policy coherence for development, there is however no real choice between the member state and EU levels because trade and a range of other policies of importance to developing country interests, such as agriculture and fisheries, come under EU competence. If there is to be PCD, this has to include greater coherence at the EU level. Policy coherence is challenging in the national context and especially challenging in the EU context given the greater level of complexity. Progress in EU PCD has been held back by the lack of a well-established decision-making regime. Repeated changes in decision-making machinery, including splitting the development functions within the Commission, have resulted in a lack of continuity, which has in weakened EU level policy. It is striking that of the policy case studies considered in this volume development is the one most affected by the institutional changes brought about by the Treaty of Lisbon and the introduction of the EEAS. While trade and environment policies are strong enough to retain autonomy from the EEAS, development has been integrated in the EEAS. This reflects the lack of a strong, well-established regime for development policy-making in the EU, but also the fact that development falls into a somewhat different category to the other cases. Unlike the other three cases considered, there is no *acquis* or body of EU legislation for development. The object of EU development policy is entirely outside the EU, as in the case of foreign policy.

Chapter 7
Conclusions

A Greater Role for the EU in Economic Diplomacy

The first general conclusion one can draw from the preceding case studies is that the EU is assuming a progressively more important role in economic diplomacy. This shift has not happened overnight as a result of specific decisions in treaty negotiations, but as a slow and often uneven response to developments both within and outside the EU. The EU's role in external trade, which is held up as the classic example of a case of EU 'actorness', was only established over decades. It is true that the Treaty of Rome established EEC exclusive competence for the common commercial policy from the start, but as a practical issue it took many years before the EU established a role in all trade policy. In the case of international environmental policy, the role of the EU has also emerged progressively over decades rather than years, and in the case of financial regulation, the EU has yet to achieve the kind of recognition it has in trade or even environmental diplomacy.

In assessing the role of the EU in economic diplomacy, it is important to consider the *de facto* competence rather than just the *de jure* position in treaties. As discussed in the preceding chapters, *de facto* competence exists when there are well-established decision-making procedures at an EU level, and the member states elect to use that for pragmatic or functional reasons. In trade and environment, *de facto* competence has had at least as important an effect as the formal treaty texts. In the specific case of climate change discussed in this volume, member state governments (ministers and heads of state or government) have wanted to be seen to be involved in addressing the issue because of the high political profile of climate change. But in many more prosaic negotiations on international environment issues, there has been a steady shift towards a greater role for the EU.

Even if there is a general trend towards a greater role for the EU in economic diplomacy, it is important to remember that the EU is still operating in a multilevel system. The role of the EU varies across policy areas. The case of development policy shows how member states can still opt for bilateral economic diplomacy with developing countries or for development cooperation at the multilateral level rather than the EU if they believe it is more effective. In the case of financial market regulation, there remains an emphasis on the need for the EU to be in line with developments in international regulatory standards. In a sense, this is a compromise position in the EU in that some member state governments are more focused on the international level and tend to place it before the EU level. There is a desire to avoid the EU 'getting ahead' of international standards or policy. In climate change, the picture is rather different. There is a general willingness, and in some member states a desire, for the EU policies to be ahead of the rest of the world. Common positions are therefore not seen as a threat to EU policies or the EU's ability to compete internationally, but as a means of the EU to shape international outcomes and in terms of competitiveness, for the EU to be ahead of the curve in terms of adjusting to low carbon growth. In the case of trade, the EU has been seeking to shape the international agenda for some time. This has been less clearly articulated than in the case of climate change because of the diversity across areas of trade in goods and services. But in all of these policy areas, EU policy is shaped by negotiations and discourse on other levels. In many cases, the EU is adopting norms or standards that have been developed on other levels. Even in trade, EU policies have been shaped by developments and debates in the OECD and other fora.

The EU as an Actor of Forum?

The central question this book has sought to address is what determines whether the EU is an actor or merely one among a number of important fora in international economic negotiations. To be an actor, it is assumed that the EU needs to have a distinctive policy which it seeks to promote, and that it is not simply following developments at an international level and implementing the results. It also seems reasonable to differentiate between cases when the EU adopts a common position in response to or in reaction to initiatives taken elsewhere and cases when it appears as a distinctive actor with a proactive approach to economic negotiations. Finally, being an actor seems to require the EU having a strategic approach to negotiations, meaning views on how best to shape negotiations in order to obtain a result that best matches the EU interests, rather than simply entering negotiations with an EU agreed position and trusting that others can be persuaded to fall into line.

The case studies suggest the relative importance of the various factors when it comes to the EU satisfying the role of an actor in economic diplomacy. First, there needs to be a consensus on the framework norms that shape EU internal policies. As the case studies show, this consensus exists in trade in goods, somewhat less in services and not yet in investment, although the debate on the EU approach to investment policy has been engaged. It also exists in the environment and in the climate change case, but there is no such consensus in the field of financial regulation. In the case of development, there is no internal policy (legislation) on which to base EU development cooperation, so any consensus that exists must be based on policy statements rather than on concrete measures as in the case the other case studies. The argument here is that it is a consensus on framework norms rather than what have been defined as general norms, such as human rights, rule of law, and so on, or specific norms in the form of standards or specific pieces of legislation, which is an important precondition for the EU to be the actor.

The nature of the cases selected means that these conclusions are based on generalisations at the level of policy areas – in other words, trade, environment or financial regulation. In each of these policy areas, there are of course a range of more detailed policy issues. The relative importance of the different factors shaping the EU may well vary across issues at this more detailed level. For example, sector and specific member state interests linked to sector interests are likely to play a more important role at the more specific, detailed level.

Second, there is a need for *de facto* EU competence. It may not be necessary to have formal *de jure* competence for all aspects of the policy area concerned, but for the EU to appear as a distinct actor, what is required is the existence of an agreed, well-established decision-making regime governing how the EU approaches international negotiations. This exists for trade and has for some time. It exists for most environment issues most of the time, but is more recent and thus less well established. It does not really exist for financial regulation or development. In the case of financial regulation a regime was under construction when the 2008 crisis hit, but was not strong enough to cope so the EU response was *ad hoc* and based on member state coordination. In development, repeated changes to the decision-making structures within the EU have contributed to the lack of such a regime.

De jure competence is clearly a feature of any *de facto* competence, but it is not everything. In the case of trade, the scope of EU *de facto* competence exceeded that of *de jure* competence for many years before the treaty powers 'caught up'. The EU assumed responsibility for negotiating international agreements on issues which were shared or even member state competence for many years, before the Lisbon Treaty finally extended exclusive competence to all trade and foreign direct investment. To a lesser degree, the same could be said for the case of the environment. In finance, the EU has *de jure* competence for financial market regulation in a similar form to that for environmental policy, but has not acquired *de facto* competence for international negotiations on the topic, as has happened in the case of the environment.

External drivers can be important in bringing pressure on the EU to adopt a common position, which can in turn mean an extension of *de facto* competence. Prolonged pressure on the EU to negotiate in an area which is not exclusive EU competence can extend the reach of *de facto* competence beyond formal competence. The hypothesis set out in Chapter 2 does seem to find some relevance here. In trade and environment, long-term persistent pressure on the EU to reach agreed positions in negotiations seem to have been a factor in the functional shift to EU-level *de facto* competence, even if member state governments were not ready to cede formal competence. Clearly, external drivers will not always result in greater cooperation at the EU level. They must always be seen together with other factors such as the status of internal EU integration. Financial regulation is a case in point. External drivers in the form of increased competition in financial markets did not result in a common EU response, but in competition between the EU member states. It is not clear from the case studies whether crises precipitate a shift towards a more determined common EU position. In financial markets, there are clearly signs of greater efforts at the EU level in response to the 2008 crisis, but one must see if these continue once the crisis has passed. Representation in international-level bodies also has an impact. In line with the hypothesis that hierarchic representation works against EU policy coordination, there does seem to be evidence that hierarchic representation, such as in the G20, IMF or other financial institutions, does correlate with a lack of *de facto* EU competence. In trade and environment, EU member state representation in international bodies is non-hierarchic, which correlates to relatively developed *de facto* competence at the EU level.

Even if the EU appears as an actor in international negotiations, as is the case in trade and the environment, but much less so in international finance, there remains the question of its capabilities to act. Case studies of the role of EU in negotiations have suggested that the EU brings directional leadership to a negotiation (pointing the way), but not instrumental leadership (shaping outcomes in specific negotiations). Put another way, it has normative but not coercive power. In the case of political relations or foreign policy, the lack of coercive power can be explained by the absence or underdeveloped nature of any EU level military capabilities. But how does one explain the apparent lack of coercive power in economic relations? One explanation is the EU's inability or reluctance to use its market power by threatening to withdraw concessions to third countries. As discussed below in more detail, EU decision-making largely precludes the use of excessive negative linkages. There appear to be three further factors shaping the EU's role in negotiations. These are: whether the EU has a negotiating strategy as opposed to just a common position; whether the principal-agent relationship provides the right amount of agent slack; and whether the EU agent, whoever that is, has clearly defined red lines.

The cases suggest that the EU has had a long-term strategic view in trade negotiations, thanks to the existence of *de facto* competence for the EU and the lead taken by DG Trade in the Commission. The principal-agent relationship also seems to work fairly well, in that there have been fewer and fewer problems balancing EU external and internal positions in trade in goods. But the continuous engagement of member states in the supervision of the Commission agent means that negotiating aims become something of a moving target. There are therefore no clear red lines or in other words no clear 'win-set' or acceptable scope of an agreement for the EU. At all times it is possible for the member states to adjust the negotiating aims. The EU agents are therefore less able than their counterparts in other countries, such as the US, for example, to use the threat of no agreement (or walking away from negotiations) as a means of coercing their negotiating partners to make concessions. Given consensus decision-making in the EU, this tends to mean that there will always be member states favouring a continuation of negotiations. As the agent for the EU the Commission's interests are also served by continuing to negotiate as this strengthens the need to retain a common EU position. So with no hard lines, the effectiveness of the EU in negotiations may suffer.

The position in climate change is similar to that in trade. The EU has generally developed a common position in the run-up to negotiations. It has reached a position where it has clearly defined goals. What is less clear, however, is whether the EU has a negotiating strategy, or a defined 'win-set'. In the case of climate change, this may be due to the fact that there is some discontinuity in who leads the EU negotiation (at least to date) because of the rotating presidencies. The principal-agent relationship is also unclear in climate change, because the agent changes as negotiations progress. There tend to be functional 'negotiation leaders' in the early stages of the negotiation. These are followed by ministerial level representatives and – in the past rounds of climate change negotiations – by the heads of state and government joining the negotiations at a late stage. This makes the application of a negotiating strategy very difficult, especially when the heads of state all insist on participating in negotiations. The absence of a clear red line in the EU climate change negotiating brief would then explain why the EU went along with the outcome of the Copenhagen negotiation even though it delivered little.

When the EU does not possess these attributes of an actor, it will of course still have a major impact on economic diplomacy, but it will tend to follow leads taken elsewhere and be more of a forum than play an active leading role in economic negotiations as has been the case to date in international financial market regulation.

Hypotheses on Effectiveness

It is now time to revisit the hypotheses proposed at the end of Chapter 2 on what determines the effectiveness of EU economic diplomacy.

The first was that the greater the EU's *market power*, and the more able and willing the EU is to use its market as leverage in negotiations, the more effective its economic diplomacy would be. Not surprisingly, the case studies confirm this view, but provide scope for a more detailed analysis.

The trade case shows how the EU was effective in opening the US market during the 1960s thanks to the market leverage it possessed. A relatively high and common external tariff, combined with a willingness to use concessions on market access in reciprocal market access negotiations, achieved a good deal. The history of EU trade policy also shows that the deepening of the EU market in the 1980s thanks to the single-market programme gave the EU considerable leverage in the Uruguay Round negotiations. Subsequent widening of the EU to expand from 12 to 27 helped enhance EU market power somewhat. But it needs to be recalled that his went hand in hand with a stronger normative consensus (see below). EU market power may therefore correlate with the pace of internal EU reform/integration. When there is dynamic integration within the EU, the EU acquires more market power.

The relative market power of the EU in trade has however probably peaked. Growth in the US economy during the 1990s helped sustain US leverage, and since then the large emerging markets have begun to erode the EU's relative position thanks to both the growth of markets such as China and India, but equally important, the fact that these markets remain still relatively closed, both in terms of barriers to market access at the border, but also a willingness and ability to intervene to support specific industries. Governments in the emerging markets understandably follow the precedent set by the US and EC in trade negotiations and use the offer of concessions on market access as leverage in negotiations. More effective coalition politics in the shape of the G20 or the BASICs (Brazil, South Africa, India and China) has further enhanced the power of the emerging markets. In trade the multi-polarity of the trading system has been a steady process at least during the 2000s. In other areas, one of the features of recent climate change negotiations has been the greater willingness and ability of the BASICs (Brazil, South Africa, India and to a less degree China) to speak with one voice and to withhold concessions.

A good deal of economic diplomacy involves bargaining based on some broad concept of reciprocal commitments. Market power is therefore not just about market size, but also what concessions the negotiators can make during a negotiation and/or the ability and willingness/inclination to threaten to close off access to markets. There is evidence that the EU's market power in this sense is also limited. Progress in European integration has been achieved through agreement on broad framework norms (see below). Given the nature of member state preferences, these have been liberal in the sense that markets operate within a framework of agreed regulatory norms. In the trade case, the SEM led to general (partially unilateral) market opening, deregulation and privatisation, which effectively reduced the scope the EU has to offer concessions in negotiations. The only real area left in which the EU can offer concessions was agriculture, but there were limits to what could be achieved with this in the DDA because of the domestic constraints on further concessions and the limited importance of agricultural trade in the wider scheme of things. In climate change, progress at the EU level meant the EU had done most things that might be asked of it in any negotiation, so it had little more to offer in terms of concessions. One area in which the EU can gain leverage is through new EU-level regulation or standards setting which raises the bar for those wishing to sell into the EU market. In the case of financial market regulation, there also appears to be some scope for enhanced leverage in the sense that reinforced regulation following the financial crisis can have an impact on access to the EU market.

If the EU's ability to derive market power from offering concessions in value creating strategies has declined, its willingness to use threats of market closure in a more value claiming strategies appears to be even more limited. The balance of member state interests and the decision-making structures of the EU mean that there is very unlikely to be support for moves to restrict market access. The *de jure* decision-making position is qualified majority, and there appears to be a clear minority which would block aggressive use of threats or measures to restrict market access. One exception here is the continued use of a simple majority in the case of the new comitology rules for some trade instruments. In the case of capital movements, unanimity is a formal requirement for any reversal of liberalisation. In most cases, decision-making remains by consensus, and there is no consensus favouring a strict value-claiming approach based on threatening to close the EU market in order to coerce the EU's negotiating partners during a negotiation. This includes, for example, border tax adjustments in climate change or measures that restrict access to the EU market.

The EU therefore appears to be a 'soft' economic power, not because of its preference for the use of normative power, but because the broadly liberal consensus on which deeper integration is based is incompatible with policies that would make it a 'hard power' – that is, threatening or using market closure as a means of enhancing market power. A comparison could be made between the EU's position today and that of the US in the 1970s or 1980s when, having led the international trading system with liberal policies, the US faced a relative decline in its market/economic power. The US response was to resort to a more value-claiming approach, in which it threatened to close its market as a means of dealing with what it saw a free riders in the international system. The EU does not seem to have this option. The only way in which the EU can begin to increase its leverage is through the introduction of EU-level policies in the form of reregulation which might affect market access for third countries, such as in the case of the Alternative Investment Funds Directive in financial market regulation. This would then give the EU more leverage in negotiations. In negotiations with most developing countries or smaller economies, the EU still retains market power. In the case of the EPA negotiations, this derived from the fact that the EU, by agreeing to end the existing preferential agreements in order to comply with the WTO rules, was effectively threatening the ACP states with less access to the EU market. Some might argue that the European Parliament could strengthen the EU's negotiating leverage by narrowing the EU 'win-set' thanks to the enhanced powers for the EP under the TFEU and the fact that the EP may be more willing to adopt tough positions based on a more populist (less liberal) view of economic diplomacy.

Normative power in economic diplomacy derives from the EU showing how it can be done. This is clearly not a coercive power, but it has been seen as an alternative source of EU power and influence. It is one which in practice assumes a world of economic negotiations that is not based on reciprocity, but one in which other countries would be influenced or persuaded to approximate to the EU position by the success of the EU model. In terms of economic negotiations, the value of normative power therefore relies on one's assumptions about the nature of international economic negotiations. It can be safely assumed that economic diplomacy entails both value-creation (offering concessions) and value-claiming (threatening to withhold or withdraw concessions), and that reciprocity features to some degree in all *negotiations*. Ideas or norms and thus normative power may still have an influence during negotiations, especially during the earlier stages in any negotiations, such as in framing or agenda setting. But the relative importance of ideas or persuasion generally diminishes when negotiators get to the final stages in economic negotiations, which are invariably shaped by bargaining.

It has been argued here that the EU derives normative power from a consensus on what have been called framework norms. Agreement on such norms also appears to be crucial for the EU to be a distinctive actor. The case studies show that where there is no such agreement, progress on integration is delayed with the result that the EU cannot rely on sound common domestic foundations for its economic diplomacy. Agreement on framework norms is therefore a precondition for proactive EU economic diplomacy. None of the case studies provide much evidence of EU normative power having a great deal of effect on other countries. EU framework norms have not been much emulated in other countries. Specific norms in the shape of the Singapore issues in the DDA were for the most part rejected by the EU's negotiating partners. Perhaps more tellingly the EU's norms in terms of climate change have not influenced other countries. This may be due to the study not looking closely enough at how policies in the EU's negotiating partners are evolving over time. It is to be expected that normative power will only have a progressive effect in changing other countries positions. So it may be premature to conclude that EU normative power is ineffective. But the case studies have looked at the evolution of policy over a number of decades and found no strong evidence of EU norms being adopted by other countries or regions. In bilateral negotiations the EU could be more effective in 'exporting' its norms to others, such as in the free-trade agreements the EU is negotiating with a range of countries. But progress here is likely to be more as a result of the EU's asymmetric market – rather than its normative – power.

On specific norms, it is important to consider that these are seldom distinct EU norms or standards. All the case studies show that EU regulatory norms or standards are for the most part derived from broader principles or norms developed in international fora or bodies, such as the OECD, UN or international financial institutions. This does not mean that the EU cannot have normative power. Given the importance of the EU economy, its adoption of standards or norms can have a considerable impact and can determine whether the norms concerned become established international norms or not. But if there is a need for the EU to have a distinct identity in order to achieve 'actorness', then there would seem to be a need for distinctive EU norms. In this respect the crucial issue seems to be not that the EU develops entirely distinct norms or standards, but that the EU gains a kind of first mover advantage by being the first to implement norms. As international norms or standards are almost by definition open to different interpretations, if the EU is first to interpret and implement them, it will have a say in shaping them. For this to happen, however, there must be an EU consensus first. Where the EU leads in the implementation of international principles or norms, it could be said to have normative power or to have assumed directional leadership. In such cases, the EU looks more like an actor shaping outcomes. Where the EU follows in the implementation of agreed international specific norms, such as in the case of financial regulation, it probably still has normative power, but its role is as one level or forum in a multilevel/forum process.

Generalisations are difficult to make when it comes to *member state* and *sector interests*. There seems to be little doubt that the EU will tend to look less like an actor when there are heterogeneous interests among member states or sectors. In one sense however, it is possible to identify some broad conclusions from the case studies. This is that member state interests in retaining national sovereignty over key policies such as fiscal and foreign policy will tend to weaken the EU as an actor in aspects of economic diplomacy which are affected by and thus require coherence with these areas of retained member state sovereignty.

This brings us finally to the question of coherence. Theoretically, it is possible to make a case that EU economic diplomacy will be less effective if it lacks coherence. A search for greater coherence across all aspects of external policy may not, however, be a recipe for greater effectiveness. The case studies suggest that coherence becomes an issue when effectiveness in EU economic diplomacy requires common action or decisions in policy areas in which member states resist any loss of *de facto* competence. Thus EU environmental diplomacy has been hindered by the lack of agreement on fiscal measures (carbon or energy taxes) to support EU policies. Development co-operation has been hindered by the determination of the member states to retain control over assistance as an instrument of member state foreign policy vis-à-vis developing countries. EU policy in financial market regulation has been restricted by the member state determination to retain fiscal sovereignty. A search for greater coherence could therefore inhibit effectiveness if it means inclusion of such policy areas. EU development co-ordination is a rather special case in that coherence is seen as one of the main policy outputs. This bring us to the role of the European External Action Service (EEAS), which is intended to strengthen the EU's role in the world and promote greater coherence across policy areas by bringing all the major external policies under one roof. The EEAS started life in December 2010, and it will be some years before it is possible to make any judgement on how effective it will be. The contribution of this volume to the debate about the future role of the EU's external policies is in the discussion and findings of the relative importance of the various factors which shape the EU's role in economic diplomacy.

Bibliography

Allen, D. and Smith, M. (1990). 'Western Europe's Presence in the Contemporary International Areana' *Review of International Studies*, *16*(1): 19–37

Aggarwal, V. and Fogerty, E. (2004). *EU trade strategies: Between regionalism and globalization.* Basingstoke; New York: Palgrave Macmillan.

Agrawala, S. (1998). 'Context and early origins of the Intergovernmental Panel on Climate Change,' *Climate Change, 39*: 605–20.

Andresen, S. and Agrawala, S. (2002). 'Leaders, pushers and laggards in the making of the climate regime' *Global Environmental Change, 12*: 41–51.

Baldwin, D.A. (1985). *Economic statecraft.* Princeton, NJ: Princeton University Press.

Bayne, N, (2000). Hanging in there: The G7 and G8 summit in maturity and renewal. Aldershot, UK: Ashgate.

Bayne, N. and Woolcock, S. (2011). *The new economic diplomacy: Decision making and negotiation in international economic relations.* (3rd ed.). Farnham, UK: Ashgate.

Becht, M. and Correia da Silva, L. (2007). 'External financial market policy: Europe as a global regulator?' In Andre Sapir (Ed.), *Fragmented power: Europe and the global economy* (pp. 200–225). Brussels: Breugel.

Bigsten, A. (2007). 'Development policy: coordination, conditionality and coherence'. In Andre Sapir (Ed.), *Fragmented power: Europe and the global economy* (pp. 94–127). Brussels: Breugel.

Bond for International Development EU institutional reforms. Retrieved from http://www.bond.org.uk/pages/eu-reform.html (accessed October 2011).

Bourgeois. J.H.J. (1995). 'The EC in the WTO and Advisory Opinion 1/94: An Echternach procession'. *Common Market Law Review, 32*: 763–85.

Bretherton. C. and Vogler. J. (2006). *The European Union as a global actor.* (2nd ed.). London; New York: Routledge.

Bretherton, C. and Vogler, J. (2008). 'The European Union as a sustainable development actor: The case of external fisheries policy', *European Integration, 30*(3): 401–17.

Buchner, B. (2000). *What really happened in The Hague?* Report on the COP 6, Part I,m 13–25 November 2000. Fondazione Eni Enrico Mattei (FEEM). FEEM Working Paper No. 38.2001. Retrieved from http://www.feem.it/Feem/Pub/Publications/WPapers/default.htm.

Buchner, B. Carraro, C. and Cersosimo, I. (2001). *On the consequences of the US withdrawal from the Kyoto/Bonn Protocol.* Fondazione Eni Enrico Mattei Note di Lavoro, Series Index: http://www.feem.it/web/activ/_activ.html

Buzan, B. Wæver, O. and de Wilde, J. (1998). *Security: A new framework of analysis.* Boulder, CO: Lynne Ryder.

Cable, V. (1995). 'What is Economic Security?' *International Affairs*, *71*(2): 305–24.

Carbone, M. (2008, July). 'Mission Impossible: The European Union and policy coherence for development'. *Journal of European Integration*, *30*(3): 323–46.

Casey. Jean-Pierre. (2006, 20 April). 'After the Financial Services Action Plan: A repeat of the post-1992 blues?'. *ECMI Commentary*, European Capital Markets Institute. Retrieved from http://www.eurocapitalmarkets.org.

Checkel. J. (2005) 'International institutions and socialization in Europe: introduction and framework'. *International Organization*, *59*(4): 801–26.

Christensen, T. (2011). 'Governing climate change: The United Nations' negotiating process'. In N. Bayne and S. Woolcock, *The new economic diplomacy: Decision making and negotiation in international economic relations*. (3rd ed.) (pp. 303–22). Farnham: Ashgate.

Corrales-Diez, N. (2003). 'The EU representation at the International Monetary Fund'. *Austrian Federal Ministry of Finance, Working Papers* 3/2003.

Damro. C. (2006, June). 'Transatlantic competition policy: Domestic and international sources of EU–US cooperation, *European Journal of International Relations*, *12*(2): 171–96.

Daugbjerg, C and Swinbank, A. (2007). 'The politics of CAP Reform: Trade negotiations, institutional settings and blame avoidance'. *Journal of Common Market Studies*, *45*(1): 1–22.

De Larosiere, J. (2009, 25 February). 'The high-level group on financial supervision in the EU'. European Commission. Retrieved from http://ec.europa.eu/ internal_market/finances/docs/de_larosiere_report_en.pdf.

Declaration on a concerted European Action Plan of the Euro Area Countries. (12 October 2008). Summit of Euro Area Countries, Paris, France.

Delreux, T. (2006). 'The European Union in international environmental negotiations: A legal perspective on the internal decision-making process', *International Environmental Agreements*, *6*: 231–48.

Delreux, T. (2009, August). 'The EU negotiates multilateral environment agreements: Explaining the agent's discretion'. *Journal of European Public Policy*, *16* (5): 719–37.

Devereau, C., Lawrence., R and Watkins., M. (2006). *Case studies in US Trade Negotiations*. (Vol. 1.) Washington D.C.: Institute of International Economics.

Dominguez, K.M.E. (2006, October). 'The European Central Bank, the Euro, and global financial market'. *Journal of Economic Perspectives*, *20*(4): 67–88.

Duchêne, François. (1973). 'Die Rolle Europas im Weltsystem: Von der regionalen zur planetarischen Interdependenz'. In Max Kohnstamm and Wolfgang Hager (Eds), *Zivilmacht Europa: Supermacht oder Partner?* (pp. 11–35). Frankfurt am Main: Suhrkamp.

Duer, A. (2008). 'Bargaining power and trade liberalization: European external trade policies in the 1960s'. *European Journal of International Relations*, *4*: 645–71.

Duke, S. and Blockmans, S. (2010, 4 May). 'The Lisbon Treaty stipulations on development cooperation and the Council Decision of 25th March (Draft) establishing the organisation and functioning of the European External Action Service'. *CLEER Legal Brief.* Centre for the Law of the EU External Relations. Retrieved from http://www.cleer.eu.

Eeckhout. P. (2004). *External relations of the European Union: Legal and constitutional foundations.* Oxford: Oxford University Press.

Egenhofer, C. and Van Schaik, L. (2006). *Policy coherence for development in the EU Council: Strategies for the way ahead.* Brussels: Centre for European Policy Studies.

Egenhofer, C. and Georgiev, A. (2009). 'Messages from Copenhagen Assessments of the Accord and Implications for the EU'. Retrieved from http://*www.ceps. eu/ceps/download/3054.*

Elsig, M. (2002). *The EU's common commercial policy: Institutions, interests and ideas.* Ashgate, Aldershot.

Elsig, M. (2007). 'The EU's choice for regulatory venues in trade Negotiations: A tale of agency power?' *Journal of Common Market Studies, 45*(4): 927–48.

Eurodad. (2008). 'Financial regulation in the European Union: Mapping EU decision making structures on financial regulation and supervision'. Retrieved from http://somo.nl/publications-nl/.

European Commission. (1996). *Report of the group of experts on competition policy in the new trade order, strengthening international cooperation and rules.* Brussels: European Commission.

European Commission. (1998). *Financial services: Building a framework for action.* Brussels: European Commission.

European Commission. (1999, 11 May). *Financial services action plan* COM (1999) 232. Brussels Commission.

European Commission. (2000). *Joint statement of the European Council and Commission on an EU development policy.* Brussels: European Commission.

European Commission (2007) 'Communication from the Commission, Review of the Lamfalussy process: Strengthening Supervisory Convergence COM(2007) 727 final 20 Nov 2007.

European Commission. (2007). *EU code of conduct on division of labour in development policy*: Communication from the Commission to the Council and the European Parliament, COM (2007) 72 final. Brussels: European Commission.

European Commission (2009, 15 September). *Policy coherence for development – establishing the policy framework for a whole-of-the Union approach.* COM (2009) 458 final. Brussels: European Commission.

European Commission. (2009). *Towards a comprehensive climate change agreement in Copenhagen'.* Communication from the Commission to the European Parliament and the Council. COM (2009) 39 final. Brussels: European Commission.

European Commission. (2009). *Stepping up international climate finance: A European blueprint for the Copenhagen deal*. COM (2009) 1172. Brussels: European Commission.

European Commission. (2009, 27 May). Proposal on European financial supervision. Communication from the Commission {SEC(2009) 715} {SEC(2009) 716}. Brussels: European Commission.

European Commission. (2009, 4 March). *Driving European Recovery*. Communication to the spring European Council. COM (2009) 114. Brussels: European Commission.

European Commission. (2009, 23 September). Proposal for a regulation of the European Parliament and of the Council on a European Securities and Markets Authority. COM (2009) 503. Brussels: European Commission.

European Commission. (2009, 23 September). Proposal for a regulation of the European Parliament and of the Council on Community Macro Prudential Oversight of the Financial System and establishing a European Systemic Risk Board. COM (2009) 499/3. Brussels: European Commision.

European Commission. (2009, 23 September). Proposal for a regulation of the European Parliament and of the Council on establishing a European banking authority, European insurance and Occupational Pensions Authority. COM (2009) 502. Brussels: European Commision.

European Commission. (2009, 27 May). *European financial supervision*. Communication from the Commission. COM (2009) 252 final. Brussels: European Commission.

European Commission. (2009, 11 December). *Europe's financial integration report 2009*. Commission Staff Working Document. SEC (2009) 1702. Brussels: European Commission.

European Commission. (2010) *Towards a comprehensive climate change agreement at Copenhagen*. COM (2009) 39 final 28/1/2009. Brussels: European Commission.

European Commission. (2010). White Paper on Financial Services Policy 2005–2010. COM(2005) 629 final 1/12/2005. Brussels: European Commission.

European Council. (2009, 12 October). *Draft Council conclusions on strengthening EU financial stability arrangements*. 14239/09 ECOFIN 617. Brussels: European Commission.

European Parliament and Council. (2011, 16 February). *Regulation (EU) no. 182/2011 of laying down the rules and general principles concerning mechanisms for control by Member States of the Commission's exercise of implementing powers*. Brussels: European Parliament and Council.

European Think-tanks Group. (2010). New challenges, new beginnings: Next steps in European development cooperation. London: Overseas Development Institute.

Evaluation Services of the European Union. (2007). *CCC: Evaluating co-ordination, complementarity and coherence in the EU development policy: A synthesis*. The Hague: Aksant Academic Publishing, The Hague. Retrieved from http://www.aksant.nl.

Evenett, S. (2007) *'Global Europe':* An initial assessment of the European Commission's new trade policy. Unpublished.

Evenett, S. J. and Meier, M. (2007). 'An Interim Assessment of the US Trade Policy of 'Competitive Liberalisation'. (Revised February 2007.). St Gallen, Switzerland: University of St Gallen. Retrieved from http://www.evenett.com/articles.htm.

Falkner, R. (2007). 'The political economy of "normative power" Europe: EU environmental leadership in international biotechnology regulation'. *Journal of European Public Policy, 14*(4): 507–26.

Financial Services Authority. (2009). *The Turner Review: A Regulatory Response to the Global Banking Crisis.* London: Financial Services Authority.

Frieden, J. A. (2004). 'One Europe, one vote?', *European Union Politics, 5*: 261–76.

Frisch, D. (2008, April). 'The European Union's development policy'. *Policy Management Report, 15.* Maastricht, Netherlands: ECDPM. Retrieved from http://www.ecdpm.org/pmr15.

Gauttier, P. (2004, January). 'Horizontal coherence and the external competences of the European Union'. *European Law Journal, 10*(1): 23–41.

Gavas, M. and Koeb, E. (2010, April). 'Setting up the European External Action Services: Building a comprehensive approach'. *ODI Background Note.* Retrieved from http://www.ODI.org.uk.

Gavas, M. and Maxwell, S. (2009, August). 'Options for architectural reform in European Union development cooperation'. *ODI Background Note.*

Goodhart, C.A.E and Schoemaker, Dirk. (2006, March). 'Burden sharing in a banking crisis in Europe'. *Special Paper Series* no. 164. LSE Financial Markets Group. Retrieved from http://www2.lse.ac.uk/fmg/documents/specialPapers/2006/sp164.pdf.

Graziano, P. and Maarten, P.Vin. (2008). *Europeanisation, new research agendas.* Basingstoke, UK: Palgrave Macmillan.

Groenleer, M. and Van Schaik, L.G. (2007). 'United we stand? The European Union's international actorness in the cases of the International Criminal Court and the Kyoto Protocol'. *Journal of Common Market Studies, 45*(5): 969–98.

Grosche, G. and Puetter, U. (2008). 'Preparing the Economic and Financial Committee and the Economic Policy Committee for enlargement'. *European Integration, 30*(4): 527–43.

Grubb, M., Vrolijk, C., and Brack, D. (1999). *The Kyoto Protocol: A guide and assessment.* London: Royal Institute of International Affairs Energy and Environmental Programme.

Grubb, M. and Gupta, J. (Eds). (2000). *Climate change and EU leadership: A sustainable role for Europe.* Dordrecht, Netherlands: Kluwer.

Grubb, M. and Yamin, F. (2001). 'Climate collapse at The Hague: What happened, why, and where do we go from here?'. *International Affairs, 77*(2): 261–76.

Gstoehl, S. (2008, April). 'Patchwork power' Europe? The EU's representation in international institutions'. Paper for GARNET conference on The European Union in International Affairs.

Hanson, B. (1998). 'What happened to fortress Europe? External trade policy and liberalisation in the European Union'. *International Organization*, *52*(1): 55–85.

Helleiner, E. and Pagliani, S. (2008). 'The G20 Leader's Summit and the regulation of global finance: What was accomplished?'. Retrieved from http://www.cigionline/community.igloo?ro_script.

Henderson, D. (1999). *The MAI Affair*. London: Royal Institute of International Affairs.

Henning, C.R. (2004). 'The external policy of the Euro area: Organizing for Foreign Exchange intervention'. *Institute for International Economics, Working Paper* 06 – 2004.

Hettne, B. and Soederbaum, F. (2008) 'The future of regionalism'. In A.F. Cooper, and C.W. Hughes (Eds), *Regionalisation and global governance: The taming of globalisation* (pp. 61–80). Warwick: Routledge/Warwick Studies in Global Governance.

Heydon, K. and Woolcock, S. (2009). *The rise of bilateralism: Comparing American, European and aAsian approaches to preferential trade agreements*. Tokyo and New York: UN University Press.

High-Level Group on Financial Supervision. (2009, 25 February). Report, chaired by Jacques de Larosiere. Brussels: European Commission.

Hill, C. and Smith, M. (Eds). (2005). *International relations and the European Union*. Oxford: Oxford University Press.

Hodges, M. Schreiber, C. and Woolcock, S. (1991). *Britain, Germany and 1992: The limits of deregulation*.London: Royal Institute of International Affairs.

Hodges, M. and Woolcock, S. (1996). 'European trade policy the story behind the headlines'. In H.S. Wallace and W. Wallace (Eds), *Policy-making in the European Union*. Oxford: Oxford Univeristy Press.

Hoebrink, P. (2007). *Evaluating Maastricht's triple C: An introduction to the development paragraphs of the Treaty on the European Union and suggestions for its evaluation*. Retrieved from http://*www.ru.nl/cidin/research/publications_cidin/publications/*.

Holland, M. (2008). 'The EU and the global development agenda'. *European Integration*, *30*(3): 343–62.

House of Lords. (2009). Select Committee on Europe, European Financial Markets. Britain.

Jupille, J. and Caporaso, J.A. (1998). *States, agency, and rules: The European Union in global environmental politics*'. In C. Rhodes (Ed.), *The European Union in the World Community* (pp. 213–29). Boulder, CO: Lynne Ryner.

Kerremans, B. (2005). 'What went wrong in Cancun? A principal-agent view on the EU's rationale towards the DDA'. *European Foreign Affairs*, *9*: 363–93.

Keohane, R. and Nye, J. (2001). 'The club model of cooperation and the World Trade Organisation: Problems of democratic legitimacy'. *Visions*, The Kennedy School of Government, Working Paper no. 4.

Kiekens, W. (2003). 'What kind of external representation for the Euro'. Paper for Oestereiches National Bank Seminar: The European Convention on the Future of Europe – implications for Economic and Monetary Union, Vienna, Austria.

Kulessa, M. (2007, March/April). 'The Climate Policy of the European Union'. *Intereconomics*, (March/April): 64–95.

Lamfalussy Report. (2001). *Final report of the committee of wise men on the regulation of the european securities markets*. Brussels: European Commission. Retrieved from http://ec.europa.eu/internal_market/securities/docs/lamfalussy/wisemen/final-report-wise-men_en.pdf.

Lamy, Pascal. (2002, 6 May). *Europe's role in global governance: The way ahead.* Speech at the Humboldt Universitaet, Berlin, Germany.

Lamy, Pascal. (2004). *Trade policy in the Prodi Commission, 1999–2004. An Assessment*. Brussels: European Commission. Retrieved from http://trade.ec.europa.eu/doclib/docs/2006/september/tradoc_120087.pdf.

Lacasta, N.S., Dessai, S. and Powroslo, E. (2002). 'Consensus among many voices: articulating the European Union's position on climate change'. *Golden Gate University Law Review*, *32*: 1–47.

Lannoo, K. (2008, 1 December). 'Concrete steps towards more integrated financial oversight: The EU's policy response to the crisis'. *CEPS Task Force Reports*. Brussels: Centre for European Policy Studies.

Lastra, R.M. (2003). 'The governance structure for financial regulation and supervision in Europe'. LSE Financial Markets Group, *Special Papers* 149. Retrieved from http://www2.lse.ac.uk/fmg/workingPapers/specialPapers/2000s.aspx.

Manfred, E. (2009, March). 'European Union trade policy after enlargement: Does the expanded trade power have new clothes?'. *Trade Regulation Working Paper* No. 2009/22. Bern: Swiss National Competence Centre in Research (NCCR)/World Trade Institute. Retrieved from http://82.220.2.60/news-archive/index.php (accessed October 2011).

Manners, I. (2002). 'Normative power Europe: A contradiction in terms?'. *Journal of Common Market Studies*, *40*(2): 235–58.

Mathews, A. (2008). 'The European Union's common agricultural policy and developing countries: the struggle for coherence'. *Journal of European Integration*, *30*(3): 381–99.

Maxwell, S. and Engel, P. (2003). *European development cooperation until 2010*. London: Overseas Development Institute, London. Retrieved from http://www.odi.org.uk.

Maur, J-C. (2005). 'Exporting Europe's trade policy.' *The World Economy, 28*(11), 1565–90.

Meunier, S. (2000, Winter). 'What single voice? European institutions and EU–U.S. trade negotiations'. *International Organization*, *54*(1): 103–35

McEvoy, D., Lonsdale, K., and Matczak, P. (2008, January). 'Adaptation and mainstreaming of EU climate change policy: An actor-based perspective'. *CEPS Policy Brief*, no. 149.

McNamara, K.R. and Meunier, S., 'Between national sovereignty and international power: What external voice for the euro?' *International Affairs*, (*78*) 4: 849–68.

Memorandum of understanding on cooperation between the financial supervisory authorities, central banks and finance ministries of the European Union on cross border financial stability. (2008, June). ECFIN/CEFCPE (2008) Rep/53106 Rev.

Oberthuer, S. and Kelly, C.R. (2008, 3 September). 'EU leadership in international climate change policy: achievements and challenges'. *The International Spectator, 33*: 35–50. Istituto Affari Internazionali.

Odell. J. (2000). *Negotiating the world economy.* Ithaca and London: Cornell University Press.

Orbie, J and Versluys, H. (2009). 'The European Union's international development policy, leading and benevolent?' In J. Orbie, *Europe's global role* (pp. 67–91). Farnham, UK: Ashgate .

Ott, H.E. (2001). 'Climate change: an important foreign policy issue'. *International Affairs, 77*(2): 277–96.

Pauly, L.W. (2008, Summer). 'Financial crisis management in Europe and Beyond'. *Contributions to Political Economy, 27*: 1–17.

Pauly, L.W. (2009). 'The old and the new politics of international financial stability'. *Journal of Common Market Studies, 47*(5): 955–75.

Pickford, S. and Joicey, N. (2011). 'The International Monetary Fund and global economic cooperation'. In N. Bayne and S. Woolcock (Eds), *The new economic diplomacy: Decision making and negotiation in international economic relations.* (pp. 283–301).

Pisani-Ferry. J. (2005, 25 November). *The accidental player: The European Union and the global economy.* Speech at the Indian Council for Research on International Economic Relations, Dehli, India.

Pollack, M., Young, A. and Wallace, H. (2010). *Policy making in the European Union.* Oxford: Oxford University Press.

Posner, E. (2009). 'Making rules for global finance: Transatlantic regulatory cooperation at the turn of the millennium'. *International Organization, 63*(4): 665–99.

Posner, E. and Véron, N. (2010, April). 'The EU and financial regulation: Power without purpose?' *European Public Policy, 17*(3): 400–415.

Preeg, E. (1970). *Traders and diplomats: An analysis of the Kennedy Round of Negotiations under the GATT.* Washington, D.C.: Brookings.

Putnam R.D. (1988) 'Diplomacy and domestic politics: The logic of two-level games'. *International Organization, 42*(3): 427–60

Quaglia,L. (2007). 'The politics of financial services regulation and supervision reform in the European Union'. *European Journal of Political Research, 46*: 269–90.

Quaglia, L. (2008). 'Financial sector committee governance in the European Union'. *European Integration, 30*(4): 563–78.

Quaglia, L., Eastwood, R. and Holmes, P. (2009). 'The financial turmoil and EU policy co-operation in 2008'. *Journal of Common Market Studies, 47*: 63–87.

Reiter, J. (2009). 'The European Union as an actor in international relations: The role of the external environment for EU institutional design'. In O. Elgstroem and C. Joesson (Eds), *European Union negotiations: Processes, networks and institutions.* Abingdon, UK: Routledge.

Ringius, L. (1997). 'Differentiation, leaders and fairness; negotiating climate commitments in the European Community'. *CICERO Report 1997*, Report Nr. 8. Retrieved from http://www.cicero.uio.no.

Sapir, Andre (Ed.). (2007). *Fragmented power: Europe and the global economy*. Brussels: Breugel.

Simon, A. (2003). 'The new organisation of the Council of the European Union: Setback or opportunity for EU development cooperation?' *ECDPM Discussion Paper* 46, Maastricht, Netherlands: ECDPM.

Smaghi, L. B. (2004). 'A single EU seat in the IMF?' *Journal of Common Market Studies*, *42*(2): 229–48.

Smaghi, L. B. (2006). 'Powerless Europe: Why is the Euro area still a political dwarf?'. *International Finance*, *9*: 261–79.

Smith. K (2003). *European Union Foreign Policy in a Changing World*. Cambridge, UK: Polity.

Stichele, M.V. (2008). *Financial regulation in the European Union: Mapping the decision making structures on financial regulation and supervision*. Bretton Woods Project, Eurodad. The Hague: Somo Publications.

Telo, M. (Ed.). (2009). *The European Union and global governance*. Abingdon, UK: Routledge/GARNET series.

Thieme, D. (2001, August/September). 'European Community external relations in the field of the environment,' *European Environmental Law Review*, pp. 252–64.

Van Bergeijk, P. (2010). *Economic diplomacy beyond 2010: Geo-Economic Challenges of Globalization and Economic Security*. The Hague: Netherlands Institute of International Relations *Clingendael*.

Van Reisen, M. (2001). *European integration and enlargement: Is there a future for European development policy*. Unpublished paper available from author at mvreisen@xs4all.be.

Van Schaik, L. and Egenhofer,C. (2003, September). 'Reform of the EU institutions: Implications for the EU's performance in climate negotiations'. *CEPS Policy Brief*, *40*.

Van Schaik, L. and Egenhofer, C. (2005, February). 'Improving the climate: Will the new Cnstitution strengthen the EU's performance in international climate negotiations?'. *CEPS Policy Brief*, *63*.

Veron, N. (2007, August). 'Is Europe ready for a major banking crisis?' *Bruegel Policy Brief*, *3*.

De Visscher, C., Maiscocq, O., and Varone, F. (2008) 'The Lamfalussy Reform in the EU securities markets: fiduciary relationships, policy effectiveness and the balance of power'. *Journal of Public Policy*, *28*(1): 19–47.

Vitols, S., Woolcock, S. and Soskice, D. (1997) Corporate governance in large British and German companies: Comparative institutional advantage or competing for best practice. London and Bonn: Anglo-German Foundation.

Vogler, J. (1999). 'The European Union as an actor in international environmental politics'. *Environmental Politics*, *8*(3): 24–48.

Vogler, J. (2005). 'The European Contribution to global environmental governance'. *International Affairs*, *81*(4): 835–50.

Vogler, J. and Bretherton, C. (2006). 'The European Union as a protagonist to the United States on climate change'. *International Studies Perspectives*, 7: 1–22.

Vogler, J. (2009). 'Climate change and EU foreign policy: The negotiation of burden sharing'. *International Politics*, *46*(4): 469–90.

Wallace, H.S., Wallace. W., and Pollack. M.A. (2005). *Policy making in the European Union*, 5th ed. Oxford: Oxford University Press.

Wallace. H.S., Pollack. M.A, and Young. A.R. (2010). *Policy-Making in the European Union*, 6th ed., Oxford: Oxford University Press.

Wettestad, J. (2000). 'The Complicated Development of European Union Climate Policy'. In M. Grubb. and J. Gupta (Eds), *Climate change and EU leadership: A sustainable role for Europe*. (2000) Dordrecht, Netherlands: Kluwer.

Wettestad, J. (2005). 'The making of the 2003 EU Emissions Trading Directive: An ultra-quick process due to entrepreneurial proficiency?' *Global Environmental Politics*, *5*(1): 1–23.

Winham, G.R. (1986). *International trade and the Tokyo Round Negotiations*, Princeton, NJ: Princeton University Press.

Woll. C. (2007). 'Trade policy lobbying in the European Union: Who captures whom'. In D. Coen and J. Richardson, J. (Eds), *Lobbying in the European Union: Institutions, actors and issues*. (2007). Oxford: Oxford University Press.

Woolcock, S. (2000). 'European trade policy: Global pressures and domestic constraints'. In H.S. Wallace and W. Wallace (Eds), *Policy making in the European Union* (4th ed.) (pp. 377–98). Oxford: Oxford University Press.

Woolcock, S (2003) 'The Singapore issues in Cancun: A failed negotiation ploy or a litmus test for global governance.' *Intereconomics*, *38*(5): 249–55.

Woolcock, S. (Ed.) (2005). *Trade and investment rule-making: The role of regional and bilateral agreements*. Tokyo and New York: United Nations University Press.

Woolcock, S. (2007). 'The EU approach to free trade agreements'. Brussels: *ECIPE*. Retrieved from http://www.ecipe.org/publications/all-publications.

Woolcock, S. (2008, August). 'In the shadow of the eagle: The pervasive and continued influence of the US on EU trade policy'. Paper for the American Political Science Association conference in Boston, Massachusetts.

Woolcock, S. (2010). *Trade policy: A further shift towards Brussels?*. In M. Pollack, A. Young and H. Wallace (Eds), *Policy making in the European Union* (pp. 381–98), Oxford: Oxford University Press..

Woolcock, S. (2011). 'Factors shaping economic diplomacy'. In N. Bayne and S. Woolcock (Eds), *The new economic diplomacy: Decision making and negotiation in international economic relations* (3rd ed., pp. 17–41). Farnham, UK: Ashgate.

World Trade Organisation (2008). Trade Negotiations Committee Document TNC/W/52, 19 July 2008. Communication from Albania, Brazil, China,

Colombia, Ecuador, the European Communities, Iceland, India, Indonesia, the Kyrgyz Republic, Liechtenstein, the Former Yugoslav Republic of Macedonia, Pakistan, Peru, Sri Lanka, Switzerland, Thailand, Turkey, the ACP Group and the African Group.

World Trade Organisation and United Nations Environment Programme. (2009). *Trade and climate change: A report by the World Trade Organisation and the UN Environment Programme.* Retrieved from http://www.wto.org/english/res_e/booksp_e/trade_climate_change_e.pdf.

Young, A. and Peterson, J. (2006). 'The EU and the new trade politics'. *Journal of European Public Policy, 13*(6): 795–814.

Young, A. (2007). 'Trade politics ain't what it used to be: The European Union in the Doha Round'. *Journal of Common Market Studies, 45*(4): 789–811.

Index

Global Finance Series

Full series list

**The New Economic Diplomacy
Decision-Making and Negotiation in
International Economic Relations**
Edited by Nicholas Bayne and
Stephen Woolcock
ISBN: 978-1-4094-2541-0

**Financial Crisis Management and the
Pursuit of Power
American Pre-eminence and the
Credit Crunch**
Mine Aysen Doyran
ISBN: 978-1-4094-0095-0

Global Financial Crisis
Paolo Savona, John J. Kirton
and Chiara Oldani
ISBN 978-1-4094-0271-8

**Sovereign Wealth Funds and International
Political Economy**
Manda Shemirani
ISBN 978-1-4094-2207-5

**Securing the Global Economy
G8 Global Governance for a
Post-Crisis World**
Edited by Andreas Freytag, John J. Kirton,
Razeen Sally and Paolo Savona
ISBN 978-0-7546-7673-7

**Debt Relief Initiatives
Policy Design and Outcomes**
Marco Arnone and Andrea F. Presbitero
ISBN 978-0-7546-7742-0

**Making Global Economic
Governance Effective: Hard and Soft Law
Institutions in a Crowded World**
Edited by John Kirton,
Marina Larionova and Paolo Savona
ISBN 978-0-7546-7671-3

G8 against Transnational Organized Crime
Amandine Scherrer
ISBN 978-0-7546-7544-0

**Governing Global Derivatives
Challenges and Risks**
Chiara Oldani
ISBN 978-0-7546-7464-1

**Financing Development
The G8 and UN Contribution**
Edited by Michele Fratianni, John J. Kirton
and Paolo Savona
ISBN 978-0-7546-4676-1

**The New Economic Diplomacy
Decision-Making and Negotiation in
International Economic Relations
(Second Edition)**
Edited by Nicholas Bayne and
Stephen Woolcock
ISBN 978-0-7546-7047-6 (hbk)
ISBN 978-0-7546-7048-3 (pbk)

**The G8 System and the G20
Evolution, Role and Documentation**
Peter I. Hajnal
ISBN 978-0-7546-4550-4

**Corporate, Public and Global Governance
The G8 Contribution**
Edited by Michele Fratianni,
Paolo Savona and John J. Kirton
ISBN 978-0-7546-4046-2

**Elements of the Euro Area
Integrating Financial Markets**
Edited by Jesper Berg, Mauro Grande
and Francesco Paolo Mongelli
ISBN 978-0-7546-4320-3

New Perspectives on Global Governance
Why America Needs the G8
Edited by Michele Fratianni,
John J. Kirton, Alan M. Rugman
and Paolo Savona
ISBN 978-0-7546-4477-4

Global Financial Crime
Terrorism, Money Laundering
and Offshore Centres
Edited by Donato Masciandaro
ISBN 978-0-7546-3707-3

Sustaining Global Growth and
Development: G7 and IMF Governance
Edited by Michele Fratianni,
Paolo Savona and John J. Kirton
ISBN 978-0-7546-3529-1

Governing Global Finance
New Challenges, G7 and IMF Contributions
Edited by Michele Fratianni,
Paolo Savona and John J. Kirton
ISBN 978-0-7546-0880-6